THE TRIALS OF
Arthur

Christopher James Stone ('CJ') was born in Birmingham, England, in the summer of 1953, of Edward and Mary Stone, the oldest son of the oldest son of the oldest son of a long line of labour aristocrats.

A product of the egalitarian education system of the post war years, CJ went to Sheldon Heath Comprehensive School in Birmingham, and was the first person in his family ever to go to University. Not that it did him much good. Since leaving University he has done a succession of menial jobs – from machine operator in various factories, to builder's labourer, to dustman, to road sweeper, to barman, to cellarman, to cook – before, finally, becoming a full-time writer in 1993 with the publication of his Housing Benefit Hill column in the *Guardian Weekend* magazine.

He has since enjoyed a moderate success in the writing trade, with articles and columns appearing in such diverse publications as the *Independent*, the *Independent on Sunday*, the *New Statesman*, the *London Review of Books*, the *Big Issue*, the *Sunday Herald*, *Mixmag* and *Red Pepper*, to name but a few. He has also had three books published: *Fierce Dancing: Adventures In The Underground*, *The Last Of The Hippies* and *Housing Benefit Hill And Other Places*, a collection of his *Guardian* columns.

In 1996 he embarked on his legendary quest to find the modern day King Arthur. It was King Arthur's unique form of spiritual/political activism that first attracted CJ's attention and which made him want to write this book. His various strange adventures along the way are recounted in these pages, including, at one point, sleeping in a bin in mid-winter at the Countess Services on the A303, while Arthur slept by the side of the road, oblivious of the cold.

'Am I alone in thrilling to the sight of this noble throwback to the age of Celtic romance? The truth is that our Prime Minister is a grinning, charmless little twerp; our Archbishop of Canterbury has as much spiritual charisma as a raw potato; and the House of Windsor is Dullsville. I'd dump the whole pack of them tomorrow and replace them with a single Royal, Spiritual and Political Leader – King Arthur.'   A.N. Wilson, *Evening Standard*, 1997

'*The Trials of Arthur* is the amazing story of one man. But it is also the inspiring tale of an unjustly maligned British counterculture. Searching, funny, intelligent and illuminating, it is on one level a rip-roaring read, whimsical and compelling, and on another a haunting élegy to all those people who refuse to accept that they cannot make a difference in a world they know must change.'

Deborah Orr, Journalist

'This is a book about heroism, patriotism, liberty, poetry, martyrdom, history, mythology, personal self-fashioning and other unforeseen consequences of enjoying cider, cigarettes and laughs with a bunch of mates. It is an epic true story of war and religion set in Britain during the Dark Ages at the end of the twentieth century, which manages to remain at once, like its main character, passionately serious, irresistibly compelling and hilariously good-humoured.'

Professor Ronald Hutton, University of Bristol

THE TRIALS OF

Arthur

The Life and Times of a
Modern-Day King

**Arthur Pendragon
and Christopher James Stone**

Element
An Imprint of HarperCollins*Publishers*
77–85 Fulham Palace Road
Hammersmith, London W6 8JB

The website address is: www.thorsonselement.com

and *Element* are trademarks of
HarperCollins*Publishers* Limited

First published 2003

1 3 5 7 9 10 8 6 4 2

A catalogue record for this book is
available from the British Library

ISBN 0 00 712114 8

Printed and bound in Great Britain by
Creative Print and Design (Wales), Ebbw Vale

Contents

'Then Arthur smiled grimly, and Iddawg asked, "Lord what are you laughing at?" "I am laughing out of the sadness I feel at this Island's being in the care of such puny men as these, after the sort that held it before."'

From *The Dream of Rhonabwy*, *The Mabinogion* p182, (translated by Jeffrey Gantz)

I have been in the place where was killed Gwendoleu,
The son of Celdaw, the pillar of songs,
When the ravens screamed over blood.

I have been in the place where Bran was killed,
The son of Iweridd, of far extending fame,
When the ravens of the battlefield screamed.

I have been where Llacheu was slain,
The son of Arthur, extolled in songs,
When the ravens screamed over blood.

I have been where Meurig was killed,
The son of Carreian, of honourable fame,
When the ravens screamed over flesh.

I have been where Gwallawg was killed,
Son of Goholeth, the accomplished,
The resister of Lloegyr, the son of Lleynawg.

I have been where the soldiers of Britain were slain,
From the East to the North,
I am the escort of the grave.

I have been where the soldiers of Britain were slain,
From the East to the South,
I am alive, they in death!

From the *Black Book of Caermarthen*: Poem XXXIII, vol 1, p293, Skeine's *Four Ancient Books*

Plate Illustrations

Acknowledgements

To Steve and Liz for the work put in on the original project and for reading through the finished manuscript; Arthur's sister Wendy for being there, and Chesh, his brother-in-law, for his reflections; Rollo, for proofreading and giving his thoughts and suggestions; Carrie for her typing, research and endless patience with both CJ and Arthur; Cathers, the laziest person in the world for the occasional cup of tea and coffee; Professor Ronald Hutton, for allowing us to use his witness statement and, likewise, Chris Turner for his inspirational writing; Susanna for her research and cooperation; Denny for the love and chicken soup; Stewart for the lifts; Badger for the beer; Lydia Dagostino and Geoffrey Ashe for the interviews, and Carrie Kirkpatrick for the use of the film; and to the many others who have given help and encouragement along the way.

Dedication

This book is dedicated to the three Chris's, all loyal Knights, who died during the writing of it, two of whom are mentioned herein and one who is not.

King Arthur Pendragon would like to point put that this book and the tales there-in would not have been possible without the help and continued support of the Tribe and their allies, many of whom, Female aspects of the Goddess, have made many sacrifices, both personal and political, for the greater good, putting their own lives on hold to give Arthur the space to develop and the assistance he required.

For more information about Arthur and the Loyal Arthurian Warband: www.warband.org

For more information about CJ Stone: www.cjstone.co.uk

FIRST QUEST:

Imbolg

C J first heard about King Arthur – the late 20th century version – on a sunny Saturday afternoon in the late summer of 1994, on the pavement outside a pub in the café quarter of Cardiff, the administrative capital of Wales, where, maybe, the real historical Arthur – if he had ever existed – would have visited in his adventures, chasing pigs, fighting Saxons, lusting after maidens, drinking and carousing with his faithful warband.

Steve Andrews was doing his usual, telling a story about Arthur, about when he'd first met him. It was a long, convoluted story, involving a radio programme called *The Round Table* on Red Dragon Radio, and a letter from Arthur on Christmas Eve, and then Arthur turning up on Steve's doorstep one day, falling in the door, saying he hadn't slept for three days, with a Sky TV crew behind him; and then a taxi ride to a pub and someone called Bill from Barry Island, who was filmed as one of Arthur's supporters though he was just a pissed-off Nirvana fan who happened to be in the pub – but he ended up on the TV programme in any case – and a knighting ceremony at Tinkinswood, a Neolithic burial site just outside Cardiff, and Arthur drinking cider, and then, once the TV crew had gone, saying 'party till you puke,' and drinking himself into the ground.

That's how Steve talks, in a breathless rush of detail, piling detail upon detail, absurdity upon absurdity, weaving complex webs of strange verbal magic, as interested in someone called Bill from Barry Island who just happened to be in the pub, as on the central event, the meeting with Arthur himself.

And then he was onto another story, about a party in someone's back garden in Cardiff, and Arthur declaring it was Camelot and being drunk (once more), and falling asleep (once more), and someone coming up to his prostrate form, lying in the mud by the fire, and kicking Arthur and saying, 'That's not King Arthur, how could that be King Arthur, King Arthur wouldn't do that, lying drunk in the mud, pissed up like that, that's not how King Arthur would behave,' and Steve thinking, 'Yes, that's exactly how King Arthur would behave,' thinking of him as a Dark Ages battle chieftain, rather than as a knight in shining armour. And CJ got the two stories mixed up, and wrote about it, and so it went down in history that Arthur was just a crusty drunk falling asleep beside fires at knighting ceremonies with TV crews looking on.

That was when CJ decided he wanted to write a book about Arthur. He thought that it didn't matter whether he was the real King Arthur or not. The mere mention of the name, even if he was a bogus Arthur, would bring to mind the Matter of Britain, and if this Arthur was absurd, then it was only because Britain had become absurd.

That's how this book was conceived – as the story of an absurd Arthur, in an absurd Britain.

So that was 1994.

In 1995 CJ was busy with other things. He carried on visiting Steve, however, who carried on telling him stories.

There was one story about the time Arthur and Steve had gone up to knight a man called Lawrence Main, on a mountain top in mid-Wales. Arthur had had (another) motorcycle accident, and was all bandaged up. His legs were several shades of purple, and he could hardly walk. His bike was a write-off. But Lawrence Main had asked to be knighted on this specific day, in this specific place, and Arthur had hired a car, turned up on Steve's doorstep unannounced, and told him they were going on an adventure. So Steve had gone off with him, up to mid-Wales, to Carn Ingli, the Place of the Angels – of which it is said that if you sleep there you will either wake up a poet or mad – to meet Lawrence Main.

It was Halloween and pouring with rain, but later it cleared up. They got to Carn Ingli, and Arthur was having difficulty walking because his legs hurt, but he struggled up the mountain, where they met Lawrence, who was like a wild man of the mountain, wearing shorts and in bare feet despite the autumn cold, with a huge, white beard, and wild eyes like the wind-blown sky. He had a couple of tents set up on top of the mountain, and there was this young woman from Nova Scotia called Megan who was trying to hitch-hike to Ireland to find her roots. And Lawrence was doing this dream project at the time. He would get people to sleep on the mountain, and then wake them up and ask what they had been dreaming about. He had a tape recorder, and he would record everyone's dreams. So Steve slept in one tent, with Lawrence – Steve being the dream project subject this night – while Arthur had slept in the other tent with the young lass from Nova Scotia.

Actually, Steve didn't get any sleep at all that night. The ground was hard and lumpy and it was very cold, but every now and again Lawrence would say, 'So Steve, er Steve, have you been dreaming?' And Steve would say, 'No Lawrence, I still haven't got any fucking sleep.' This went on all night. And eventually it was light. But when he got up, he remembered he'd had this vision in the night. He had seen three black, hooded figures, like the Ring Wraiths from *The Lord of the Rings*, three sinister figures with cloaks like raven's wings, who had been stalking them on the mountain top. So he told Lawrence this, and it was recorded as part of the dream project. And then he climbed out of the tent and met Arthur, who was just waking up.

'Steve, you're never going to guess,' he said, 'I've been fighting psychic battles all night with Ring Wraiths ... they were coming, they were coming to get Megan, there was a psychic attack on Megan.' It had been going on all night, he said. He'd fall asleep and dream about this battle with the Ring Wraiths, firing off magical shots with his staff, and them replying with similar weaponry. They were trying to get Megan, but Arthur was defending her. And then he'd wake up and check, and Megan was fast asleep, just dreaming happily, not knowing what was going on.

So Steve told Arthur about his vision, and they agreed it must have been the same creatures.

Later, on the way home, they were in this little Welsh valley's shop down Cardigan way. And Arthur said, 'You know Steve, if I tell this woman in the shop who I am and who you are and what we've just been doing, she's never going to believe it.'

And Steve knew he was absolutely right.

There was no way a lady in this little Welsh shop was going to believe that he was King Arthur, that Steve was a Bard and Quest Knight of the

Loyal Arthurian Warband, a Druid order, that they'd just been knighting a person who was living on a mountain like a holy man, in the place where a Welsh saint used to live, and that the King had been fighting psychic battles all night with Ring Wraiths who were coming to get a young lady from Nova Scotia, who was passing through on her way to Ireland to find her roots. If they had tried to explain all of that to her there was no way she was going to believe it.

This was one of Steve's illustrations of the extraordinariness of King Arthur's life, that he did this sort of thing, that this sort of thing happened to him all the time.

CJ was getting more desperate to meet Arthur. However you saw it, he thought, whether you believed it or not, this man led an interesting life. It was a tale worth telling.

It was early in 1996 by now. He asked Steve how he might get into contact with Arthur. And Steve told him about the ceremonies at Avebury in Wiltshire eight times a year. The next one was at Imbolg, near the beginning of February, so CJ arranged to go there to meet him.

He was staying in Bristol at the time, working on a story about a man who had been shot through the neck in St Pauls, an inner city part of Bristol, on New Year's Day that year. There had been several other deaths, and the whole of St Pauls was in a state of shock, wounded and in turmoil, death piling on death, and all the drugs and the prostitution, and the closure of local facilities, and the sense of being forgotten or ignored. And, once more, this brought up the Matter of Britain. CJ was thinking, 'What's the matter with Britain?' Why had things gone so terribly wrong? Why all this hurt, this loss, this confusion?

This was what he was thinking about when he drove with a posse of people from St Pauls to Avebury to meet with King Arthur.

He was trying to imagine a better Britain, a fairer Britain, a more Arthurian Britain, perhaps, where the Arthurian ideals of Truth, Honour and Justice prevailed, instead of the lies pouring from our TV screens and in our newspapers, the dishonourable way people are treated, the injustice of it all.

He never got to meet King Arthur that time. King Arthur was at Newbury defending trees. He got to meet a lot of Druids however, and got very drunk. Which is why Avebury is one of the most popular of the stone circles, there being a pub in its midst.

Later CJ went for a walk around the monument. He looked up and there was a raven on the wing, heaving up through the mountainous air, scaling the sky in swift bursts of flight and fall, full of malevolent effort. It was like a sign, a portent, and he knew he was destined to write this book.

Not that CJ believed in signs or portents or destiny at the time.

So that was that. CJ's first unsuccessful attempt to wrestle with the Matter of Britain and to find King Arthur.

He got back home very late.

It wasn't an eventful journey.

CHAPTER TWO

What's in a Name?

Of course, King Arthur wasn't always called King Arthur. Then again, the historical King Arthur probably wasn't always called King Arthur either. Almost certainly he wasn't a king. Possibly he wasn't called Arthur. And finally, he may not even have existed, and if he never existed, how could he be called anything at all? How do legends get their names?

We'll leave it to you to work it out.

As for our current King Arthur, he was named John Timothy Rothwell, born on the 5th of April 1954 – that's the fifth of the fourth, fifty-four for all of you who like to hear patterns in numbers – of 4546273, Sgt WL Rothwell, York and Lancaster Regiment, and May Victoria (named after two queens) Rothwell née Barratt, he being a Scouser and she a Londoner.

Actually, there's some uncertainty even about these few facts. For a start WL Rothwell was not his father's real name, but an assumed name. The 'WL' stands for Wilfred Lawrence. It was the name that the young man had used on registering with the army at the beginning of the Second World War – having run away from an approved school, changed his name and lied about his age – and it was certainly the name that the distraught John Timothy (by then also known by a variety of different names) had carved upon his headstone after he died. But it was not the name he was born with.

The family myth is that his real name was Angelo Fitsgerio, and that he had changed it because, at the outbreak of war, it wouldn't have looked good to be seen with such an Italian sounding name, still less as a member of HM Forces, currently in conflict with the Italians. Of course, Arthur likes this idea and dreams of Romano-British connections, but even this turns out to be a falsehood. There was actually no such name as Angelo Fitsgerio Rothwell. Nothing on record anywhere. No Romano-British connection then – or no discernable one. Just a story, a myth, a tantalising hint of an exotic antecedence, and a brief glimpse into an era when all was in turmoil, when a boy could run away and disappear, and then reappear in a different guise – under a different name, with a falsified age, as a warrior – and prove himself a man. His given age was 14 when he joined the army. He was probably about 12.

This is the stuff of legend, of course, and does our story no harm whatsoever.

Perhaps he was called Aurelius Ambrosius, and then we would need to do very little to prove our case that King Arthur Uther Pendragon is who he says he is. Then again, perhaps not. It doesn't really matter. All we can say for certain is that Wilfred Lawrence existed, that he was a man, that he fought and risked his life for his country, that he was a hero, that he laughed a lot and drank a lot and got drunk often, that he lived and loved and fell out of love, and that his son, John Timothy as he was then called, saw the rebellious sparkle in the Old Man's eye and adopted it as his own, and that after he died, John Timothy was never the same again.

Names are very important in this story, as you begin to hear. Names are for the naming. What a person is named, by whom, and for what purpose, is part of what we are here to discover. Names given. Names cast aside. Names adopted. Names ignored. Names scrawled upon a board in the dead of night. Names as myths. Names as tools. Names fired like magical shots, forged in the flames of confrontation, to be flung screaming at the enemy, like a weapon of war, to burst like an artillery shell above the heads of the massed ranks of the infantry, to make them run in fear. Names to live for. Names to die for. Names that were never meant to be.

Even John Timothy's name was not fixed, having been named in the womb Susan Carol, and then, out of the womb and on closer inspection – this creature being too dangly by half to be a girl – Timothy John. And then, on the discovery that the commanding officer had chosen the exact same set of names for his own son, and not wanting to appear to copy, reversing them, ending up with this unsatisfactory compromise – a set of names that the young John Timothy was never happy with, and which he continued to deny or avoid or change throughout his growing life, until finally, as he asserts, he reverted to his one, true and former name, the one he bears today, and the one his parents, now long gone, call him when they visit him in his dreams.

But that was still a long way off, and John Timothy it was, whether he liked it or not. John Timothy Rothwell on his birth certificate. John Rothwell at school. Johnny at home. JT Rothwell in his run-ins with the police and the authorities and whenever he got into trouble with anyone at all – which was often: a tendency he continues to this day, but for very different reasons.

But what's in a name? It is an identity, of course. It tells you who you are. It says: this is what I am meant to be. Working Class or Middle Class, rich or poor or indifferently apportioned. It is your destiny. Some people, it is true, manage to break the constraints of their destiny. Some, by luck or by judgement, by sleight-of-hand or killer instinct, slip the net and escape into a better life. But is it really a better life, or just the other side of the same turmoil? Same name, same appetites, same fears. Same inner turmoil. Others may slide down and lose face. Some people lose fortunes too. But, generally, who you are is what you are and who you will always be. John Timothy Rothwell, king of the playground at least, idol of the bad boys, visionary exploiter of the chinks in the authorities' armour, conjurer of misdeeds, perpetrator of mischief, a misfit missing nothing, but still just plain old John Timothy Rothwell to everyone else. Nothing special. Destined to go nowhere. To be a nobody. To live and to die and then to be forgotten. Just like everyone else.

Well, no. Not like everyone else. Not in his own mind. In his own mind he was a hero. He was something. He had a destiny all right, but not to go nowhere. To go somewhere. To be somebody. To live and to die but not to be forgotten. Even as a boy he knew this.

Maybe as children we have all had thoughts like these. Maybe we have all imagined we were Somebody Else. But did we ever become who we imagined we were? Did any of us become who we were meant to be? Or did we accept the tyranny of the name, give in to it finally, accept it as destiny, and say that's who we are? I'm just an ordinary person. Why? Because that's how my father named me to be. Just like him.

Some people do change their names and some don't. Most don't, and a few do. History is littered with false names, or other names, or chosen names, with adopted identities, with altered antecedents. It is from this that myths are made. All sorts of people change their names. Mystics and spiritual people. Show business types and rock stars. Revolutionaries.

There are all sorts of reasons why a person might want to change his name. For a revolutionary the reasons are particular. Partly, perhaps, this is to avoid capture, as a precaution, as a way of hiding in the crowd, as a way of protecting family and friends, as a way of defending the innocent. Partly, also, it is because every revolutionary knows that history is written by those who seize it on a mythological level, and that the myth starts with the name.

Not that the young Johnny Rothwell was thinking like this. Johnny Rothwell now: looser, freer, partly renamed. All he knew at the time was that he wasn't who they told him he was. He was a rebel, not a revolutionary. He knew that something was wrong, but he couldn't name it. It had something to do with authority. This was something he could never accept. Someone told him he had to do something, then he didn't want to do it. Why should he do it? Just because someone told him to? Who were they to tell him what to do? What gave them the right? Because they were bigger? Because they said they had the right? But where did the right come from? Was it from some tangible source? Could you touch it and feel it? Could they even prove that it existed? Or was it assumed, like so many things, on the basis of a false identity, a false name, a false appeal to an invisible nothing that lay outside anything that really mattered? Some God who didn't exist?

Actually, his way was to laugh. He was always laughing, always running, and always causing trouble. Laughing in the face of authority. Running rings around them. Playing tricks. Getting away with it. Sometimes, maybe, not getting away with it. But always laughing.

He was getting a reputation.

And he played his parents off against each other too.

His dad was out of the army by now, having left with no discernable skills, beyond killing and survival techniques, and the ability to fight fiercely and bravely, to love unto death his fellow soldiers and be willing to die to protect them, to bark orders, to obey orders, to march up and down and to do his duty as patriotism required. None of which is in the slightest bit useful in civilian life.

So Angelo Fitsgerio, Wilfred Lawrence – Bill or Billy, as people called him – 5' 2" of compact fighting energy, a man who never backed down no matter who he faced, no matter by how much the offender towered over him, with a soldier's heart and a soldier's blood, with an urge for adventure, with an unshakable sense of comradeship, an unswerving loyalty, a man of dedication and will, with a heart of flame, who had slugged through the impossible jungles of Burma, who had burned with the insects and sweated with the snakes, with a fist full of medals – at least two of them for bravery – who had fought god knows how many battles in god knows how many countries against god knows how many enemies, who had fought the Italians, the Germans, the Japanese, the North Koreans, who had killed and watched men die, a Sergeant, used to giving orders, not to taking orders: what was he to do now?

He became a lorry driver. He drove a dustcart. He turned to drink.

And then – it was inevitable – he and May split up.

Arthur says that it was different for him – for the young Johnny Rothwell – than it was for the rest of the family. His older brother was the product of an army family, itinerant but orderly, secure in the bosom of that larger family, the British Army. And his younger brother and sister were the products of a one-parent family, brought up by their mother. Only he was the product of a broken home. And the rest of the siblings took their mother's side. But only he could see the warrior energy inside of the old fellow, that flame of fierce intensity that burned in his eyes, and that only drink could quiet occasionally. That pig-headed stubbornness, that bullish resolve. How does a man like that deal with civvy life, with the sheer mundaneness of it, the boredom, the craven waste of spirit?

So sometimes Johnny was on his mother's side and sometimes he was on his father's side, but never when they were together. Then he was on neither side. And secretly he wished they could be together again, because he knew – maybe he knew more than anyone else – that they belonged together. And he would engineer it so that they could repair their marriage, so that his dad could move back in again. Which he did – occasionally. But it would always end up the same, the old man coming in from the pub, pissed up again, and May berating him. She was a woman of spirit too, and wouldn't back down. Maybe she saw the waste of a good man and hated him for it because she loved him so much. And then the shouting and the screaming coming from downstairs while Johnny lay on his bed and listened and sobbed into his pillow. And then the shouting grew louder, became a roar and a scream. And something else would happen. Something would break. And there would be more and more breaking sounds, the crash of furniture, the splintering of wood, the thud of fists against walls, the shattering of glass, raised voices, and the police would be called, and the old man would be carted off again, lost again, dissolved into the night.

So what did Johnny do?

He set light to things.

Of course, a social worker would say that this was a cry for help. But it was not. It was not a cry – or not an ordinary cry at least. It was a battle cry, a berserker's roar! It was a volcanic eruption from the hidden depths. And it was not for help either, but for recognition. A bold declaration of his presence, here in the world. He was real. He was alive. He was … undeniable.

And fire is elemental. It is primary. It is from the source. It is life-giving and it is life-destroying. It rages as it consumes. It cracks and rips and thunders and screams. It hisses and it fumes. It whips about like flags in the wind, like an army of flags. It leaps spiralling into the air like a demon bird, as black clouds of smoke circle over the scene. It sends up sparks to light the firmament. It is ecstatic and it is alive. It breathes.

He laid his last fire before the age of 10 at a disused army barracks in Aldershot, where the family had finally settled and, of course, being so young, he got no more than a severe ticking off for it.

And everyone knew Johnny Rothwell. How could you miss him? He was always the one leading the rebellion at school, or just playing up, laughing at the teachers, ignoring their commands. Mostly, by now, he didn't go to school in any case, but spent his time bunking trains, riding around on scooters, motorbikes, canoes – any vehicle obtained by any means – occasionally getting caught and being dragged back by the police; climbing trees, stealing apples, running through fields with his faithful dog, scrambling about in a disused air raid shelter, which was one of his many secret dens. In the winter he went skittering and screaming, sliding on the frozen canal at the back of their home. He was having fun. Because – yes – that's what it was all about: fun! Fun was the antidote to the buttoned-down, wrapped, sealed, ritualised world of teachers and policemen and social workers and do-this and do-that and don't-do-the-other. Well, he was going to do it anyway. And you can imagine him, can't you, dragged back by the ear by some irate policeman after yet another mad escapade, plonked on his mother's doorstep? 'It's Johnny again, Mrs Rothwell ...'

'Yes? And?'

She was used to him. Nothing could surprise her any more.

And you can picture her too, the long-suffering dame, put upon by the world, but fiercely protective of her brood.

She was the same height as Bill – 5' 2" – but stouter and more robust. Definitely a one-man woman, she never remarried, or entertained another man in her life after her and Bill had parted. In fact, they never divorced. But she'd stand up to the old man and shout him down, take his Sunday lunch down to the pub and throw it at him if he failed to get back in time. She was nobody's fool.

Arthur remembers that she would grow her own vegetables and would take the kids out blackberrying to make jam and pies. Necessarily frugal but rich in spirit, she was forced to cut costs and make do. There's a large difference between a sergeant's wages and a dustcart driver's, especially when the old man refused to pay maintenance after they separated. But the family got by and it was down to her. One year she scrimped, scraped and saved to send Johnny on the school cruise, something he never forgot – and a favour he returned many years later as an adult, when he gave up work for six months to look after his young brother and sister while she was in hospital. Then he did the scrimping and saving to send them on their school trip.

And Arthur remembers many things. He remembers her sense of humour, and the nicknames she used. He was 'Hairy Willy', because he had long hair by now, and – as she always said – he was just like his dad. His dad was 'Shitbag' and his brother was 'Toerag'. And she would knit pullovers and crochet blankets, bake cakes and pies and do all the things mothers do; would wear a little make-up at weddings and funerals, but never otherwise; would skip through paperbacks in one sitting, and would always read herself to sleep at night. And he remembers her homilies, her folklore and her superstitions: 'Friday night's dream, Saturday told, sure to come true what ever behold.' 'Never sew on a Sunday.' 'Stir with a knife, stir up strife.' All those things that have come down to us as old wives' tales, but which might be the remnants of some long-lost,

secret wisdom. So she was respectable but wise, hard-working and independent, fierce when roused, intelligent but overlooked, deep and intui-
tive, fair-minded and even-handed, a storehouse of laughter and good
cheer, kind to everyone, simple in the most human sense, deeply concerned for all her kids. In other words, she was 'Mum'.

But Johnny would goad her when she was in a bad mood with him,
and when he'd done something exceptionally bad she'd clout him one.
Then Johnny would laugh and she'd wallop him even harder. He'd laugh
some more, she'd hit him again … and on and on until she'd worn herself out or hurt herself hitting him.

That was how Johnny dealt with the whole world. Goad it till it hit
him, and then laugh, then carry on goading and laughing till the world
gave up the fight and let him be.

It's how Arthur is still dealing with the world today, only now he has a
much clearer purpose, a mission. Still goading, still laughing, only now
he wants to change the world forever.

Back then, though, nothing was so clear. He was somebody, but no
one recognised him. Indeed, he didn't even recognise himself. He was
looking for something, but he didn't know what it was. He was the bad
boy, but he didn't know why. He was leading the world in a merry dance,
but he couldn't quite hear the music yet.

He was about 14-years old by now.

He was his father's son.

Pay day would come along and May would send Johnny off to find the
old man to get the maintenance. Or Johnny would volunteer for the task.
'Yes, Mum, 'course I'll go and get the money off Dad,' and he'd head off to
the pub. But then he'd return with little or no money and some feeble
excuses.

This went on for a long time, until May found out what had really been
happening. Johnny and the old man had been drinking the maintenance
money between them. She caught them at it one day, in the pub together.
Of course, she ranted at them both, but particularly at Bill. How could he
do this? Johnny was only 14 and he shouldn't be drinking. What was he
thinking of, letting the young boy drink? Didn't he have any feelings?
Johnny was never to go drinking with the old man again. Never, never!
And if she ever caught them at it there would be hell to pay.

So Johnny and Bill changed pubs.

By now, Johnny hardly ever went to school. Instead, he would meet his dad and work with him. He even learned to drive the dustcart. Imagine: a boy of 14 in control of this huge piece of machinery, a great, juddering tank with too many gears, smelling of diesel and rotting household waste, with a growling engine and rattling doors. And it was on one of these outings with his dad that the thing happened that would change his life forever.

He was sitting between Bill and the driver's mate. They were in the Bordon army barracks, crossing the Longmore military railway on the level crossing, when they looked out of the window. There was a munitions train screaming straight at them, horn blaring. The driver's mate leapt out of the door, but Johnny and Bill didn't have time. Bill said, 'This is it!' Johnny knew what he meant. He meant, 'We're dead, we're finished.' And he knew it too. The train hit them with a terrific crash at high speed. And then they were spinning through the air, weightless, mindless, spinning over and over, arcing crazily as this massive machine was cast aside like a child's toy. And then everything went into slow motion. Johnny could see his arms raising to his face as flecks of glass flew through the air. It was as if the glass was suspended in the air, glinting in the eerie stillness, frozen in time. He could see the splintering of wood and the wrenching of metal, as the engine forced its way into the driver's compartment. He could see it all in the eerie silence and feel it all through his own body. But it was as if he was watching it from a distance, from somewhere behind, from some distant place of safety. He remembers thinking, 'Now I'll find out what death is like.' Because even then he knew he *was* dead, or he would be dead soon. There was a kind of detached curiosity, an almost scientific sense of poised objectivity. Because he knew that death wasn't the end. He knew that there was more to come. This moment told him so, as the ancient dustcart groaned and creaked and twisted achingly through the air, and time lay in suspension.

And then it was over. The dustcart came to a shuddering halt against a telegraph pole a hundred yards down the track, as a flock of black birds rose cawing, startled into the air, and the two of them climbed out, completely unhurt. The driver's mate, who had jumped and escaped the impact, had hurt his back in the fall. But Johnny and his dad didn't have a scratch.

Later, Bill was scrambling in the cabin, trying to find his hat. He'd lost his hat and he was bloody well going to find it. The fire brigade and the ambulance arrived. The firemen were telling Bill to get out of the way, they had to rescue whoever was in there.

'Rescue? Rescue who? Who have you got to rescue? Anyway, I've got to find my hat. I've lost my hat.'

'Not in there you haven't, mate. There's been an accident. Someone needs our attention. We've got to get them out.'

'No you haven't. It was me in there. So if you don't mind, I'll just get my hat.'

But the firemen wouldn't believe him. They wouldn't believe that anyone came out of that twisted wreck of mangled metal and shattered glass alive, let alone walking, talking, scrabbling about looking for a hat. Until they looked in, that is, and there was no one there. Just an old battered trilby lying on the buckled floor.

So that was the moment that changed Johnny's life, that moment of timeless wondering, poised in mid-air on the threshold of death, knowing that it was all over. Because that moment told him something. It told him he was somebody. Not Johnny Rothwell any more. Johnny Rothwell was just a name, and who needs a name when you are dead? The dead don't have names. But he was Something. Something that wouldn't go away. Something not accountable in the mortal ledger. Something real. Something beyond. Something that was waiting. Waiting to be named.

In that moment he recognised himself as an Old Soul. He had the heart and body of a 14-year-old boy, but he knew he had been here before, that he had been here forever, that there was something in him that was eternal, eternally connected. Real. And he knew something else too. He knew that death was not the end, that it was nothing to be afraid of. There was nothing in life to be afraid of. Nothing would make him afraid any more. And if he was daring and uncontrollable before, he was to become even more so now.

He didn't tell his mum when he got home that evening. Telling her what had happened would have meant admitting that he was not at school, which would have meant a telling off. He wasn't scared of the telling off. He just didn't want the hassle. But she was telling him off about something else when Bill came round. Bill told her the whole story, while May looked at Johnny askance, glancing back and forth between the two of them, realising how close to death her two warriors had just been. The old warrior and the young warrior, both of them teasing death. And maybe a cold feeling had crept into her heart as she recognised just how precious these two were, how much alike, and for all the hell they gave her, how fine and strong and honourable. How true. And how much she would miss them if they were gone.

It didn't stop her telling them off. But it added poignancy to the words, knowing that neither of them would ever listen, that Bill and Johnny would always be the same, that they would always, in the warrior's way, test death to the hilt and push life to the limit, and that there was nothing she could do to stop them.

That was the first time Johnny made it to the front page of the *Aldershot News*. There was a picture of the mangled wreckage, and the story about their near-collision with death.

The experience set the young Johnny Reb on a new course. He began asking questions. He began reading. He wanted to find out what the old philosophers had to say. So he read books on Zen Buddhism and Witchcraft, on the Occult and on Mysticism, on Druidry, on anything and everything that could give him some understanding. He was hungry for knowledge, thirsty for the truth. But not the knowledge that school tried to teach him, which was only ever knowledge of the rules, of which rules to obey to get by in this life. The knowledge he was looking for was more fundamental than that. He was looking for a glimpse of that world he had sensed, there in that spinning dustcart: of what lay beyond death. Another set of rules – not arbitrary this time – but real, eternal. Another landscape than the one he saw around him, the landscape of council estates and canal banks and military barracks, the landscape of the present world, of named things and dreary certainty. It was the unnamed things he was interested in now. It was the uncertainty that drove him on.

When he was 15-years old he stole his old man's Bedford van so that he could go to the Isle of Wight festival. Unfortunately the brakes didn't work. He scraped a Jaguar parked in front. He had to pay a minimum of £2 fine on each of four charges, making £8 in all, and was disqualified from driving and put on probation.

That was only one of many brushes with the law.

It wasn't long before he began to get into motorbikes. Well, he'd already stolen a few, here and there, or 'borrowed' them for the ride. He'd ridden dangerously through fields and over ditches and along canal banks and back alleys, sending the mud in sprays from his back wheel; he'd raced with his mates with the wind in his hair, being chased by his dog. He'd had plenty of fun on motorbikes. But as soon as he could ride one of his own, he did.

It was a BSA 250 and he bought it from a guy he met in a biker cafe. It was sleek and beautiful, bodywork and petrol tank as black as a raven, with the BSA silver wing insignia, chrome mudguards and exhaust, and an engine that growled like an angry beast. Black and chrome, the only colours for a bike: shining like a diamond on a moonlit night.

He began hanging round with the biker gangs, getting into fights, getting into trouble, causing trouble, having a high old time of it, having fun.

Later he got involved in a fight outside a youth club. He was still on probation from the incident with the Jaguar. He was about 17 by now, and a fully-fledged biker. Leathers, cut-off denims, hair down to his shoulders, headband. In those days they called themselves greasers, or 'grebos'. The skinheads were their mortal enemy. Johnny and the rest of the bikers were on the way to the pub. A gang of skins were massing, looking for a fight. Some of his friends were inside the youth club, trying to get out. Johnny waded in as one of the skins began picking on his mate. Johnny floored him with a single punch. A hand touched his shoulder from behind, and – still seeing red from the heat of battle – Johnny turned round and landed a punch on the person behind him, who crumpled to the floor like a bag of rags. Unfortunately, it turned out to be a policeman.

So here he was, up before the magistrates again, this time for affray. Already, a few months before, he had passed the test to join the army. Not that he'd had any intention of joining at the time, it was just that he'd taken the test to help out a friend. The magistrate's verdict was Not Guilty, on condition that he joined the army.

On the steps of the court outside a policeman came up to him.

'You've got away with it this time,' he said, glowering, 'but don't you worry, Rothwell, we'll have you next time.'

'There ain't gonna be a next time,' he said, laughing as usual.

Another front-page story: 'Youth Joins Fight In Self-Defence.'

So that was it. Johnny Reb joined the army and changed his name again. Now he was Private 24341883 Rothwell, 'Sir!'

And army life suited him. He loved every second of it. He was 'Army Barmy' as Arthur describes himself now. Khaki brained. If a Sergeant told him to jump he would have replied, 'How high, Sir?' and jumped. He loved the shouting. When shouted at he would shout back in reply, always careful to add the obligatory 'Sir!' He took the piss with that 'Sir!' He was the cheeky chappie, with a joke for every occasion.

He loved the training. He loved the square bashing. He loved marching up and down. He loved the discipline, and the comradeship. He loved the uniform. He loved the mess hall. He loved the exercise. He loved puffing out his chest and pulling his shoulders back, standing to attention. He loved the firing range. He loved loading and unloading his rifle, the snap of engineered metal against metal. He loved the smell of grease. He loved the feel of the stock against his shoulder, the smoothness of the wood. He loved aiming and firing. He loved the crack of the weapon, the retort and the smell of gunpowder. He loved the spit and polish, the shining boots and burnished brass. He loved the sense of belonging.

But it was more than this. He was from an army family. His dad was a war hero. He'd been in the army for 27 years: '27 years, man and boy', as he always used to say. His mum had been in the ATS when her and Bill had met. Like his older brother, much of Johnny's early life had been on camp, in married quarters, in various parts of the country. He'd grown up with the sound of parade grounds, with the bugle calls, with the salutes, with the orderliness of army life, with the patriotism, with the Union flag snapping on the mast in the middle of the square. So, when he passed out at Exeter, with Bill and May looking on surrounded by the kids, proud of their son, of his achievements (and how handsome he looked in his uniform!) he too was proud. Proud to be fulfilling a family tradition. Proud of his position. Proud to be in that most elite of fighting forces: the British Army.

Completing his training and passing out on that Exeter parade ground in front of his parents was one of the proudest moments of his life. There was a lump in his throat. But he didn't do it for himself. It was for them: for Bill and May. He was proving himself to them, showing that he could do it, that he could make the grade, that he was a warrior too, just like his dad. And he was doubly happy to know that they were standing there, side by side, together again because of him, even if it was only for this one day.

So now he was now a fully-trained infantryman, 1st Battalion Royal Hampshire Regiment. Canon fodder, in other words. Despite the pride in having completed his training, Johnny was always a cynic and he understood the limitations of army life. The army wanted him to do officer training. This was after he was posted to Hong Kong. He was obviously the right material. It was clear that he had leadership qualities and a strategic mind, that he had brains. He would have made a good officer, but he wasn't interested. It would have meant going to Sandhurst, only a few miles from Aldershot and Farnborough where he'd been brought up. He'd joined the army to see the world, not his own home town. He wanted to continue the adventure. He wanted to be an active serviceman, one of the lads, not a superior officer. Even then he knew that this isn't the way of leadership, pushing from behind. A real leader leads from the front. He refused to go, and was rewarded by being made the Adjutant's Clerk.

He was also aware that some of their duties were questionable. He may have been paid to obey orders, but that didn't stop him questioning. He was still Johnny Reb at heart. They were being asked to work with the Hong Kong Police in the New Territories, rounding up illegal immigrants and handing them back to the Communists. So he was told that Red China was an oppressive regime, that it represented everything that Britain was fighting against. And now, here he was, sending people back into that same regime, to whatever fate awaited them, and no questions asked. Where was the justice in that? Where was that famous British sense of fair play? He thought, 'So who are the bad guys here? We're supposed to be for liberty ... the British army and all that. What's this all about? We're as bad as all the rest.' It was a wake-up call to his political conscience, the beginnings of his political awareness.

Another thing Private Rothwell didn't like about being in the army was the haircut. One day, while he was in Hong Kong, he saw a wig in a shop window, topped by a hat. The hat was for sale, but not the wig. It was a wide-brimmed, floppy hat. He tried getting the man in the shop to sell him the wig, but the man didn't understand. He didn't speak English. So Johnny put the wig on, and the hat and, gesticulating wildly, offered a price for both. The shopkeeper accepted, and Johnny walked out, with a crazy wig on and a crazy hat perched on top. And whenever he was on leave in Hong Kong he wore that wig and that hat.

But generally he was happy in the army. The British army, he says, is the best trained and disciplined in the world, and the infantry is the best of the best. So it felt good to be training with them, to be a part of them, to succeed with them, to come up to scratch. Also, he got to be around big machines. He'd always liked big machines, ever since his days driving that dustcart. He was in an air-portable battalion. They were flown around in Wessex helicopters. They would sit in the belly of these magnificent, juddering beasts, like aerial dragons, and then leap out into the bludgeoning air, before screaming down fitfully on the ends of a line. All of which would have continued to be great fun, if a tree hadn't got in the way one day, if he hadn't crashed into it and smashed his arm into fragments.

So he was down graded from A1 fit to P8 home only, UK excluding Northern Ireland, unfit for infantry service.

That's when he decided he'd had it. As the A-Clerk he cabled HQ asking for advice. He slipped a letter in with a pile of correspondence for the Adjutant to sign. A letter came back advising him of his new grading and saying that they would have no problem with him being discharged before his discharge date. He filed the letter away into his top pocket for future use. Meanwhile, orders came through to the regiment and he was transferred to a new training depot in Litchfield, as an RP, Regimental Police officer. He spent six months there, until he got bored. He turned up on parade one day in civilian clothes. You can imagine this too, can't you? Him standing there, on parade, in all his biker gear, Johnny Reb in all of his insolent glory. The Sergeant threw a fit.

'What the fuck do you think you're playing at Rothwell?' he spat. 'You can't turn up here dressed like that!'

Johnny brought out the grubby bit of paper he'd been carrying these last six months and flapped it under the Sergeant's nose. 'Read this,' he said. The Sergeant read it with increasing astonishment.

'You can't do that. You can't discharge yourself.'

'Sorry, mate, I already have,' said Johnny, grinning from ear to ear, knowing he'd just out-manoeuvred the whole of the British army. 'That's it. I'm going home.'

And he brought out a chit from the Quartermaster saying he'd handed in his kit, and another from the Armourer, saying he'd handed in his rifle. All the paperwork was in order. What could they do?

Within the hour he had a travel warrant and a leave pass to say he was on discharge leave. He was discharged with exemplary conduct.

CHAPTER THREE

SECOND QUEST:

Vernal Equinox

It was CJ's quest to find the Holy Grail. He was in Amesbury in Wiltshire for the Spring Equinox in 1996, on his way to Stonehenge to meet King Arthur. He had an hour to go to the appointment so he stopped off at a pub. The pub was called the King's Head. CJ picked it because of its name. He was reading Malory's *Le Morte d'Arthur* at the time. There was a gaggle of men at the bar, drinking lager. They looked ordinary enough. Usually CJ drinks bitter. So he looked over the line of pumps ranged along the bar and there was one local ale on offer. It was called Sign Of Spring. It had a picture of two lambs gambolling beneath a bright red heart radiating like the Sun. Well, why not, he thought? It was the Spring Equinox after all. He ordered a pint of the local brew.

There was a video jukebox in the corner, blazing out a crazed AC/DC track. CJ doesn't particularly like AC/DC, but he was watching it anyway, leaning with his back against the bar. It had been a long drive. He heard the barmaid plonk his glass down, and he turned, reaching into his pocket to pay her. And there it was, a horrible apparition. A luminous green pint, glowing like the fluorescent numbers on a clock face. He literally stood back. It looked like something which had seeped from Sellafield during some horrible nuclear accident.

'What's that?' he asked, startled.

'It's your pint.'

Everyone in the bar was looking at him. Remember, this is Wiltshire, the strangest of counties. People have sex with aliens and develop crop circles amongst their dahlias. They worship strange gods. Nothing is what it appears to be. Even the beer is radioactive.

Eventually it was explained. Apparently, they use fresh green hops instead of the usual dried ones. He took a sip nervously. It tasted green, like a pint of privet hedge. No wonder everyone else was drinking lager.

He drove over to Stonehenge. As he passed the Hele Stone he could see the faint glow of a cigarette in the darkness. King Arthur, he thought. He parked up along a track and walked back. But it wasn't King Arthur, it was Security Guards. There were two of them there, leaning against the stone out of the wind, talking in hushed voices, the light from their cigarettes illuminating their faces. They barked at him when he spoke to them.

He could see the silhouette of the monument against the night sky, hunched like roosting birds, and in the compound, moving about mysteriously, other shadowy figures. Occasionally one of them would flash on a beam, sending strange shadows scurrying and blending with the night. There seemed to be a lot of people in there performing whatever ghastly rituals their Security Guard cult compelled them to. Smoking fags mainly, and rattling keys; drinking tea out of flasks.

He waited for King Arthur. He waited and waited. Arthur didn't turn up. CJ went back to the car and fell asleep on the back seat, wrapped up in a sleeping bag. All through the night he was woken up by the sounds of cars drawing up then pulling away again. When he looked out of the window he could see figures moving around in the darkness. It all seemed very mysterious. He was thinking of King Arthur.

CJ was intrigued. He was intrigued by the idea of someone having the sheer nerve to act in that way: to go round dressing up in robes and calling himself by that name. Maybe CJ envied him in some way. Maybe CJ wished he had the nerve to be so immodest. He wondered if King Arthur ever had doubts about his identity? Was he mad? But, CJ reasoned, it didn't really matter if he was King Arthur or not. It was what he *did* that mattered. If he acted as King Arthur, then maybe he had every right to call himself King Arthur. Who knows? Maybe we are all frauds in the end. There was very little at this, the fag end of the 20th century, that CJ felt was genuinely authentic. Most people put on a face and pretended to be someone they're not. So, why not? Why not dress up in robes and go round calling yourself King Arthur? At least it was honest.

CJ woke up in the bitter light of dawn. It was very, very cold. By now, there were a number of cars lined up on the track, but no people. They must already be at the Stones. He went over to take a look. The people were there, lined up forlornly against the fence, gazing into the compound like children locked out of their playground. There were a number of Druids, with all their paraphernalia. There were a few hippies, and a few country gentleman types too, with Barbour jackets and green wellies, all shivering in the cold. But still no King Arthur. There was lots of toing and froing and stamping of feet, and a heated discussion or two. But no rituals. CJ asked what they were up to. The Archdruid hadn't arrived yet, he was told. He was on his way. Everyone wandered back to their vehicles.

The Archdruid arrived about half an hour later. CJ watched from his car as the Archdruid struggled on with his robes. They were flapping about in the wind. He had trouble pulling them on over his clothes.

Later CJ discovered that the Archdruid was Rollo Maughfling of the Glastonbury Order of Druids. He was in his 40s at the time, about the same age as CJ, with long greying hair and a full beard. He was wearing a black cape over his linen robes. He had a bucket full of daffodils with him.

And then they were having their ritual in a field opposite Stonehenge. They trooped there in a line. CJ asked how long it would last, and the Archdruid told him about 20 minutes. CJ was already cold. What looked like a concrete post sufficed for the altar. In fact, it was the stone commemorating the land as a deed of gift to the nation. They stood in a circle and held hands. They chanted 'I-A-O'. They said, 'All hail to the Sun', and 'All hail to the Earth'. They I-A-O'd the Sun and they I-A-O'd the Earth. Someone handed daffodils about. They I-A-O'd the daffodils. There were prayers about peace and love and living in harmony with the Earth. It was freezing, freezing cold. CJ was stamping his feet with the bitterness of it. They raised their arms and dropped them again. They held hands and then let go again. They all-hailed this and they all-hailed that, while CJ's fingers became numb. It went on and on. CJ had stopped caring. He couldn't all-hail another thing.

He left. He literally ran from the scene, leapt into his car, and drove furiously to Amesbury, a few miles down the road. He was praying that there would be a café. There was. He all-hailed his cup of tea, drinking it down quickly. He bought another one, and all-hailed that too, clasping the mug in his hands with a holy feeling of relief and joy. It was a religious experience, in an overpriced, plastic café in Amesbury. Maybe he'd not found King Arthur, but he'd discovered the Holy Grail. The Holy Grail is a cup of tea.

CHAPTER FOUR

Arthur

So here he was again, Johnny Something-Or-Other, young, free, single, out on the razz again, still looking for his elusive name.

He was in Farnborough for a while, working with his cousin as a self-employed paint sprayer, then as a roofer and fence erector. Any old job, just to make a living. But something was still calling him, like the sounds of a distant party carried on the night air, drifting in and out of earshot, floating on the wind. Something he needed to see or hear or find out about. Something indefinable but real. Just wanting to move, to go places, to see things, to experience. The old nomadic urge.

Actually, it probably involved an argument with his mum, over drink and girls or some such other matter, and ending with the usual accusation, 'You're just like your dad, you are.'

So, if he didn't know where he was going in life, he at least knew where he was going geographically.

He was going up to Liverpool to find his dad.

Bill had moved back there some time ago, while Johnny was still in the army. He'd left Aldershot and all associations with army life, left his home, his wife and his family, gone off to seek his roots. Left without a forwarding address or a by-your-leave. Just gone, disappeared.

Johnny knew he had to find the old fellow. And once he was in Liverpool, it wasn't hard.

One thing we haven't yet said about Bill was that he was very musical. He'd joined the army as a drummer, and later learned to play the bugle. He had played in an army band, a variety of instruments. His favourite item of musical equipment was the mouth organ. It was light and easy to carry, ideal for entertaining in the pub. He could play it like a virtuoso, bending the notes and stretching them, adding vibrato with his hand, or depth and colour with a glass, howling with it, wailing with it, wheeling about like a bird in flight, playing all the old tunes, stamping his feet to the rhythm, making a party wherever he went.

All Johnny had to do was to go round the pubs in Liverpool and say, 'Where's the old fellow who plays the mouth organ? You know, mouthy little git, always getting into trouble. Wears a trilby.' Everyone knew who he was.

So he went into a pub one Liverpool night, and there he was, Bill, that trilby on his head, pint in hand, laughing as usual, sharing a crack with his mates. And Johnny joined them and they all got laughing drunk together.

Bill had a bedsit, and Johnny moved into another bedsit down the hall. Later they got a flat together. Johnny got a job as a dog handler and security guard. Back in uniform again. And he and Bill were a team. They'd go down the pub and Bill would play the mouth organ or the spoons, and Johnny would do Cossack dancing, and then Johnny would go round with a hat. It was how they got their beer every night.

The old man was a joker. In the army, so legend had it, he'd painted a skeleton on the body of a real live horse in fluorescent yellow paint, and so started a rumour that the camp was haunted. Another time he and his friends had dragged the pub piano into the busy road outside and started playing it. And once he'd stopped the traffic by measuring the road with a six-inch ruler while a friend had stood by with a clipboard taking notes. Down on his hands and knees in the middle of the road, carefully marking off these six-inch measures. He was taking the piss out of the measured world out there. And now they were both at it, Johnny and Bill, getting arrested for planting light bulbs in the middle of a traffic island while drunk. They were as mad as each other. If either of them came up with an idea, the other would have to follow, no matter how insane it was. Everything was possible. Nothing out of bounds.

And Johnny loved to hear tales of the old man's war exploits, and knew well that – despite his cheerful disposition – this old fellow had seen hell. His mum had told him that she had been informed that Bill's entire unit had been wiped out in Burma, and that Bill was dead. Until she saw him on *Pathe News*, that is, wearing an Australian bush hat, now fighting along side the Americans, the only survivor. He was wearing a beard and the only way she recognised him was by one of his tattoos. And Johnny knew that one of his medals was a United Nations Oak Leaf – mentioned in dispatches for bravery in Korea – and another was the Military Medal. As an ex-British soldier himself, Johnny knew the significance of that. His dad was the real thing, a war hero, mentioned in dispatches. So when Bill regaled the pub with his tales, laughingly, humorously, stretching them out for comic effect or poignancy, Johnny knew the diffidence of unstated things, knew the hero under the hat, the man behind the pint, the hell behind the laughter, and could feel proud to say, 'This old feller is my dad.'

But Johnny was getting restless again. Those old itchy feet. He just couldn't keep still for a moment. Always moving, moving on, drawn by the relentless call of the horizon, always wondering what lay beyond the limits. Army family children are often like this. They simply can't stay still. Arthur's older brother is the same, while the younger siblings, brought up by May after Bill had left the army, are quite settled and content.

So he got a job in Lancashire, as a supervisor on a country park project. That was after working as a bouncer, a bingo caller and a stand-up comic by night. Another of his names: Roy North, stand-up comedian. He wasn't very good at it.

All the time he was still on his mystical quest. He was initiated into the Lancashire Witches and later joined the Universal Free Church where he became the Reverend JT Rothwell UVFC, psychic investigator.

It was around this time that he met Liz. Liz's parents settled in Lancashire after being forced to elope to England from Northern Ireland, one a Protestant, the other a Catholic. She was a hippy chick and he was a biker dude. Two free spirits, chasing the dream. She'd just come back from working in a kibbutz in Israel. She got a job on the country park where Johnny was supervising. He was her boss. They fell in love immediately. She was slim and gorgeous, with a wild nest of red curls, a head of flames. He was burning with desire for her. They made love with a fiery passion. So here he was again, setting light to things, watching the conflagration in her eyes, the flames that seared and leapt and consumed them both.

One day at work, Johnny was playing clock patience in the office. She was just hanging round, waiting for him to finish. He said, 'Tell you what, if I complete this we'll get married.'

She said, 'OK, then.'

They were trusting their future to fate, to the turning of the cards. The last card has to be the King. And it was.

They were married on St Valentine's Day, as a romantic gesture. The problem came when she tried to sign on and was told that she wasn't allowed to any more. He was her husband now and he had to keep her. They had never intended living together but society insisted.

They moved back to Farnborough and Johnny got a job as the senior supervisor on the Basingstoke Canal Restoration project, then as fore-man, Parks and Gardens, including grave digger and sexton for Ash Parish Council. Then he returned to the building and civil engineering trades where he had worked as a labourer before joining the army. Only now he was the general foreman of six and nine million pound contracts working for Laing Management Contracting. Always an extremist – Johnny could never do things by halves – he became a workaholic, two years solid with-out a day off including bank holidays. Not only the foreman, but also the first aid officer and key holder.

That's how it was. Not Johnny Reb any more, but one half of Mr and Mrs Joe Public, with a house, and a mortgage, TV, car, fitted kitchen and wall-to-wall carpets, with matching bedspreads and curtains, washing machine and fridge, dining table and cutlery, and brown paper envelopes landing on the mat – the telephone bills, the rates, the gas and electricity bills – and work, work, work.

One day they woke up and looked at each other. They were lying there, looking into each other's eyes. Things had changed, without them even noticing. They had kind of drifted into this life without even planning it. What had happened to the free spirits they once had been? What had happened to the dream? Weighed down by work and possessions, eaten up by care, they hardly saw each other any more.

They looked and looked, saying nothing, and then they both knew. This was it. They'd done everything they were supposed to do, but it would never be enough. It was life they thirsted for, not things. It was the spirit they cared for, not the latest washing machine. It was breath and adventure and fierce, wild dreams, not a mortgage, a television and a down payment on death.

They were soul mates, but they'd lost their souls.

And so they decided. They talked it over and decided. They walked out of the house, just like that. They left it there, fully furnished, the key in the

door, with the car still in the drive, keys in the ignition, the TV on, chattering away to itself like some lunatic on a street corner, no longer making
any sense. They even left their half-eaten breakfast things on the table.
Casting off the past, searching for a future. Liz disappeared to manage
a riding stables in Tintagel in Cornwall, while Johnny slipped on his
leathers, got on his bike, kicked it off with a roar and rode off into the
sunset, breathing the free air once again.

Later, he acquired a caravanette and a bike trailer. He called the caravanette his Battlecruiser. And that's how he lived, wandering around the
country, a nomadic biker chieftain, drinking, fighting, travelling, getting
laid. He was doing the free festivals – Windsor, Stonehenge. Mixing with
the travellers and the hippies. Observing the mad Druid types at their
rituals. Getting high on his own brand of barbarian wisdom.

He had many names. He was Mad Dog in Windsor. This was because,
when things kicked off, when the violence erupted, his eyes would flame,
and people knew not to cross him. There was nothing he wouldn't do. He
was Bacardi in Liverpool, this being his choice of tipple at the time. He
was Geronimo to his dad, because of his hair. He was Viet to some people
because he had slanting eyes and looked like a Vietnamese. He was Terry
Solo in his imagination after Napoleon Solo in *The Man From Uncle*. He
was Ace in Lancashire. And Wolfdog, and Maldore, his witch and wizard's
names. And Johnny Reb of course. Always Johnny Reb. It didn't matter
what people called him, he would always answer. He was none of these
people, but he was more.

When he was ready, he returned to Farnborough. He had remade himself yet again. He was parked up under an oak tree near his sister's flat. He
wore a wide-brimmed leather hat, like a cowboy hat, and another name
was born. Now he was John the Hat, the baddest outlaw biker in the
county, with hefty leather armbands and an uncompromising stance.
With a long police coat like some crazy cowboy outrider of the badlands
of the soul. Righteous. Wild. Dangerously alive.

He gathered some friends about him and they formed a biker club.
At one time they were the Gravediggers, at another they were the
Saddletramps. He was John the Hat, the Pres, on a custom built Triumph
Thunderbird. Then there was Custer, so called because he had long fair
hair and a little Vandyke beard. He rode a Triumph Trophy and spoke
with a plum in his throat. Chesh the Bard on his Harley, a little fat geezer

with broken glasses with only one lens, tied together with string, and a ponytail right down his back: called Chesh because of his Cheshire Cat grin. Bob, or College Boy, or the Manic Mechanic or Manic, who studied mechanics at college and then worked in a garage. He rode a BSA and kept the others' machines on the road. Simple Simon, who looked like a pop star, who always wore red leather and rode a Norton Commando. Tank, the wheel man, who drove a number of, usually, fast cars. And there was John's sister, Wendy, with her mother's fighting build and her father's fighting spirit. And Lynda, Tracy, Maria, and Marnie, as the girlfriends, riding pillion in proper biker style. These were the Inner Circle.

John's role was to look menacing, get stoned, get drunk, get laid, and laugh a lot about nothing. It was good to be the Pres.

Finally, there was Kris Kirkham, the Whippet.

Chesh, John and Custer were out on their bikes one day, just burning up the road. They stopped off at a café. And there he was, in tatty denims and leathers, this little, wiry, wired-up character, playing pinball.

The advantage of being a biker is that you always have something to talk about. You talk about your bikes. The Whippet's bike was a non-discernable little bits of this and little bits of that called Boom-Boom. So they had a conversation about the Whippet's bike, laughing at it, and then about the other bikes, and then about everything in general and nothing in particular, and within 10 minutes they were all fast friends. Brothers, as they put it.

According to Chesh, the Whippet was as loud, obnoxious, funny, in your face, as anyone on earth. As mad and as dangerous. He had a bike to laugh at and a heart of steel. So, of course, John had to match him. Stunt for stunt, speed for speed, danger for danger. There was nothing these two wouldn't do to outmatch the other. Like white lining the wrong way up a duel carriageway. Like screaming round roundabouts at full throttle. Like swerving through gaps hardly wider than their bikes, or leaning ever closer to the ground on a fateful bend. Burning up tyres and miles, racing with Beelzebub on blind nights of danger, stealing life from the road.

One of the others would take them to the side. 'You'll get yourselves killed,' he'd say.

'OK,' they'd say.

So, for a day or two John and the Whippet would stop their crazy brinkmanship. Until one of them pulled off another stunt and the other would have to follow.

They had this game called the Three Counties' Chase. They'd pick up a motorcycle cop in Farnborough, say, and allow him to chase them through Hampshire, Surrey, and Berkshire, before losing him back in Farnborough. They were on the borderline between the three counties. So they'd be screaming through the lanes at speed, giving the copper something to think about, racing with their hearts, mad as drunkards with the speed, taking shortcuts and back streets and alleys, before screeching into the clubhouse garden, hiding the bikes under a tarp, and then laughing like demons as they entered the flat, arms around each other's back. 'We had 'im there, mate, didn't we. We really had 'im. Should have seen his face when we shot past 'im. Should have seen his fuckin' face.'

The clubhouse was first Wendy's flat, later a series of squats. They'd sit around, drinking, and playing mad games. Like Squeal the Bard, stabbing at Chesh with their daggers and knives until he squealed, usually after one of his particularly bad impromptu recitals of his own brand of gibberish poetry.

Arthur has since evolved another version of this game, called Burn the Journalist, where he sets light to CJ's trousers in an attempt to make him flinch. No poetry from CJ, however. He has a prosaic sort of soul.

But they were good days. Good people. Wild, mad, spirited, free. Full of danger and bravado, the breath of life. They were like 10-year-olds, but with the confidence of adults. And like children they knew how to play, how to test the limits, and how to really laugh.

That's what any of them would have said, if asked to describe their lifestyle. 'It's a laugh, isn't it? It's a laugh.'

John was the hard man of the gang. He used to carry a three-barrel zip gun in the inside pocket of his police coat, and a double-headed fire axe in a specially made leather holder. A zip gun is a kind of home-made gun. The pre-loaded barrel would lock on to a sort of spring trigger mechanism. But they were real bullets.

One time they were at war with another outlaw gang. John was round at his sister's, stoned. He was in that moronic state you can get in after too much dope. Brains like boiled pig's intestines. Suddenly he heard the roar of a bike, and the door opened. He thought, 'Fuck, it's them!' and let off a blast from the zip gun, pulverising his sister's door.

Then Wendy popped her head around the door.

'What the fuck are you doing?' she asked.

The roar of the bike was the opening sound effect from 'Leader of the Pack'. All Wendy was doing was coming in to find out if he wanted a cup of tea.

It was a good job she had a sense of humour.

The only other time he brought it out was during a meeting with the Pres of the enemy club. They were facing each other across the table. Except that the other guy had his mates with him. There were about half a dozen of them, milling about looking threatening. John's hand strayed into his inside pocket as he loaded the zip. He was being very casual and unobtrusive about it. He was on his own, surrounded by the bad guys. He slipped the gun out and held it under the table, like a poker player with the winning hand, he says. No one saw this. He just had this gun pointing directly at the other guy's most sacred organ while they talked.

Allegedly.

Biker culture had been going since the 50s. In those days bikers called themselves 'rockers', and based their style on their own interpretation of the current American rockabilly style, with quiffs and shirts rolled high up the arm. Only where American kids mostly drove cars, the British kids rode bikes. They were cheap and easy to maintain, and the British bike industry was the best in the world. Rockers were the first post-war British tribe. Working class and proud, they were forging an identity in the shifting uncertainty of the post-war world. Later they developed an enemy in the 'mods', stylised working-class dandies who wore Italian clothes and rode Italian scooters. The rocker style was more practical, based entirely around the bike. Leather jackets and denim jeans, motorcycle boots and silk scarf. Even the obligatory handkerchief dangling out of the back pocket had a practical purpose. It was to wipe your hands on after working on your bike. Their drugs were sweet tea and cigarettes, chips and danger. They hung around in cafes and raced each other around the city streets and country lanes, and became known as 'café racers' or 'ton-up kids'. They rode fast – 'doing the ton' – and often ended up killing themselves. Like James Dean, they were Rebels Without A Cause.

Later, a new style emerged. This was after the film *Easy Rider*. Once again, it was American-based, but more free and easy, more laid back. The Americans rode custom-built Harley Davidsons, 'chops', with extended front forks and high handlebars. The riding style was more like sitting on a sofa, than the chin-down, arse-up style of the old rockers. The new bikers called themselves 'greasers', an adopted insult, and their enemy were the skinheads, an evolution of the mods.

That was John's style at the time. Greaser. Not a chopped Harley though – he was proud of his British heritage – but a chopped Triumph.

They thought of themselves as 1%-ers, the outlaw biker elite. They would wear a badge with 1% on it on their cut-down denim jackets. This referred to a statement made by the American Motorcycle Association in 1964, that 99% of motorcycle enthusiasts were good citizens. The outlaw clubs were declaring their allegiance to the 1% of the biker population that the AMA refused to acknowledge. Or as one Californian Hell's Angel once famously said, 'We're 1%-ers, man – the 1% that don't fit in, and don't care.'

There was a sort of creed to go with the lifestyle, a code of honour. Like: never grass to the cops; never bring out a knife unless you intend to use it; stand by your mates; never back down; and know that whatever you do has to be justified, not only to yourself, but to your mates too. These were unwritten laws, not stated, but understood. The measure of a man was that he stood by these things. Those that broke the laws would be punished, depending on the seriousness of the crime. At the very least, they would be ostracised from the group. One of their words was 'righteous'. Righteousness meant adherence to the unwritten codes.

The greasers made a sort of pact with the hippies. They didn't necessarily like each other: it was a class difference, greasers being, like their rocker predecessors, mainly working class. But they liked the free festivals and the parties. They liked the drugs and the free love. They liked just hanging around.

Often they became hippie enforcers. At the Rolling Stones concert in Hyde Park in 1969, they acted as stage bouncers, keeping fans away from their idols, while later greasers policed the free festivals. John, too, had been involved with this. One year at Stonehenge, he and a bunch of bikers had torched the heroin dealers' cars and thrown them all off site. Even then he was a fighter for justice. He didn't like what heroin was doing, and true to his creed of action, he simply did something about it.

But we have to be clear. We've named a lot of tribes and young people always form themselves into exclusive tribes, defining themselves by style. Mainly they are urban in character. But something happened to the bikers when they started going to Stonehenge. It was like they picked up something from the site itself, something more fundamental. As if they grew psychic roots that buried down into the earth, into the remote past, to draw up a kind of spiritual water, to refresh and revive a dried-up part of their souls. After a while they stopped being cowboys on mechanised horses. They became something else. They became Warriors. Knights of the Road.

There was something about sitting around a camp fire at night, weaving tales, with the silhouette of the stones nearby – those remote stones, so mysterious, so implacably ancient – that called upon the spirits of the ancestors to join them at the party, to commune with them. A party that had been going on at the time of the Summer Solstice for thousands of years. And hadn't the mysterious builders partied just like this? And weren't the modern day revellers, just like their ancient counter parts, starlight inspired, moonlight inspired, sages of the campfire soul?

The style shifted again. It became more self-consciously Celtic. Celtic geometric patterns as tattoos. Celtic knot-pattern jewellery. Wrist bands and necklaces. Earrings. Celtic designs on the tee shirts. And the leathers were like armour, and the bikes like iron steeds. They were the barbarian hordes come back to claim their own.

The energy is profound. To see a mass pack of bikers on their growling steeds come roaring down the highway. The sound is incredible. Indescribable. As if the devil and all his engines were being unleashed upon the world.

That was the energy that John and the rest were all hooked onto. That righteous spirit.

The Saddletramps began to recreate the energy of Stonehenge at a monument near Farnborough. It was a ruined castle at Odiham called King John's Castle, built in 1207, where King John the Plantagenet had spent the night before sealing the Magna Carta. John the Hat began organising parties there. Full Moon parties, not for any mystical or spiritual reason, but because on full moon nights they could get their bikes down the towpath by the canal without being seen. The parties became justifiably famous. Infamous. Other biker gangs would be invited. Anyone who would enjoy it. And they'd drink and party, and dance and fall about and fuck and fight and have fun by the brightness of the moon, by the light of the fire. Under the moon. Under the stars. In the infinite vastness of the Universe.

And John acquired yet another name: King John, after the castle where his parties were held. He would always make a point of bringing his fire axe out at some point in the proceedings. To chop wood, or some such practical use. And to let people know it was there. The zip gun remained a secret shared by the Saddletramps alone.

Sometimes rival gangs would turn up to trash the party, and they would have to defend themselves. Sometimes they just did stupid things, like throwing the bonfire into the canal, for no apparent reason. Once they threw a Robin Reliant, a three-wheeler car, into the canal, because it was an insult to their biker sensibilities. Bikes are good, cars are all right, but three-wheelers? It just wasn't on.

So they picked the car up and threw it in the canal.

The guy who owned it was looking for it. 'Have you seen my car? It was here a minute ago. I'm sure I parked it here.'

'It's over there, mate. Look. In the canal.' And there it was, dark against the moonlit glint of the canal, looking like a shopping trolley. Which is what it was, really.

'Oh no,' he whined, almost crying. 'My car!'

On one occasion, John was taking the Whippet down to Somerset on the back of a borrowed Yamaha. The Whippet had had his van impounded by the Somerset Police, having been caught driving while disqualified. It had all his worldly possessions in it. They got to Somerset and picked up the van, stashing the 'Yam' in the back and setting out to make the return journey. It was a foggy night, like driving under sea. John was having to peer into the swirling greyness ahead to see, leaning close over the steering wheel. On the motorway the electrics went. They had no lights and no power. They were stuck on a busy motorway, obscured by the fog and the darkness, with no lights. The Whippet dove out and tried pushing the van onto the hard shoulder, while John steered, when an articulated lorry loomed out of the fog and smashed into the van at speed. John just had time to leap out before the lorry hit. It shattered the van. Three lanes of motorway strewn with debris from the crash. Bits of this and bits of that. All of the Whippet's stuff, pots, pans, clothes, books, all his cherished possessions, including his guitar. The Yamaha came bounding out, making sparks up the road. It was like a scene from a Hollywood disaster movie, and strongly reminiscent of John's previous confrontation with the munitions train at Bordon barracks as a boy. John waved at the traffic through the fog, trying to prevent a pile up, while the lorry pulled in, its hazard lights flashing. When the police arrived they were looking for the dead, including the imaginary rider of the Yamaha. They couldn't believe that anyone could come out of such an accident alive. The lorry driver was unhurt but shaking, while John and the Whippet just looked at each other and laughed. They were perfectly nonchalant about the whole thing.

They led charmed lives. They were warriors, trusting to the Fates. Death wasn't something to be concerned about. You lived, and then you died. That's all there was to it. And death comes to all of us in the end. That was how they lived. That was what they believed. Not that they welcomed death, but they didn't fear it either. Death was just the final culmination, the finale, of a life well lived.

We are coming to the end of this part of the story. John's biker days lasted for many years. In many ways they were the most important years of his life, before the name change, that is. They were his apprenticeship for what was coming next. Being a biker was more than just a lifestyle. It was an identity. And it provided you with most things.

By now, Chesh was running a business and was married to Wendy. He was a workaholic. So there was always work for the gang. And there was comradeship and good times. Company when you were lonely. Help when you were in need. Back-up when you were threatened. Women to chase. Drink and dope and high times. Conversation. Speculation. Dreams.

John was down at Liz's place in Tintagel, and there was a phone call from his sister. He didn't want to answer it. Something told him it was not good news.

'John?' she said.

'Yes.'

'It's dad …'

'Don't say anything.'

He knew.

He rode back in turmoil, thinking about Bill. So the old man had finally kicked it. His heart had given out. That soldier's heart, so full of courage: it had let him down at last.

John rode fast, watching the road as it skimmed by beneath him. It was as if his thoughts were unravelling with that road: indistinct, a blur of flecks and lines, too fast to catch detail.

Bill was buried with full military honours. A bugler in full dress uniform played the Last Post under an oak tree about 50 yards distant. The
coffin was draped in the Union Jack, and John, the two brothers, and
their cousin Bob, who had lived with them as a child (so he was almost
like a brother) carried the coffin.

And then, two weeks later, May was gone too.

She died of a brain haemorrhage. It was almost as if their strongest
parts had given up at the same time: Bill's heart, May's brain. But it was
like she couldn't stand to live without him, even if she couldn't live with
him either: as if life would be too empty, too meaningless, without Bill
somewhere in the world.

May was cremated, because that was her wish, but her ashes were
interred with Bill. John was late, and had to ride through the graveyard on
his bike, before casting off his leathers to reveal the suit beneath. Some
people were offended and said, 'What would she think, him turning up
on his bike and wearing leathers like that?' Those that knew her knew
exactly what she would have thought. 'Typical John.'

He left a wreath he knew she would like, and with the wreath was a red
silk rose, with the card saying, simply, 'For May, Love Wilf.' That rose
stayed on the grave for a whole year, and Arthur still possesses it.

And now the people who had named him were gone, and Johnny
Whoever-He-Was was on his own in the world.

The next two years are a blur. Outwardly he was the same old Johnny
Reb, the same old John the Hat, the same old Mad Dog, the same old
King John. He spent all the time stoned, off his block. He revelled harder,
he partied harder. He laughed a lot and got drunk a lot, and screwed
around as usual. He was bigger, badder, bolder. He took even more risks.
He was even more dangerous. It was buckets, bongs and booze. It was
madness and mayhem. With his parents gone, he didn't have to worry
any more. There were more close calls. More feats of ecstatic brinkmanship. More dices with death. He lost one whole year somewhere. Simply
expunged from his memory, drained down the plughole of his mind.

Something was going on inside him. Something was stirring. Something he still had no name for. A kind of destiny. Like an ancient force
rising from the depths, without form. Without identity.

It was Christmas. It could have been any Christmas. He had lost track of everything. He was sitting round someone's squat with a spliff in his hand. He looked at the spliff and thought, 'What was I doing last year? I was sitting here with a spliff in my hand.' It might as well have been the same spliff. Time seemed not to have moved.

He threw away the spliff and that was the last time he smoked dope.

He got himself a job. Well, he'd always worked, but he got himself a better job. Which is where he met Angela.

She was dark-haired and attractive, and had hidden depths. They were decorating old people's homes and doing gardening jobs. John was her boss. She was married at the time but soon walked out on her old man and moved into the Battlecruiser with him. Her husband made a complaint to the police, claiming that she'd been kidnapped by 'Hell's Angels'. The police paid a prompt visit, only to find out, of course, that she hadn't been kidnapped at all, but had simply left him for another man. Later, her husband was warned that he would be arrested for breach of the peace if he continued pestering them. This is because the police knew that John was likely to – in his own terms – 'twat him one.' He was likely to break the husband's nose.

Angela was the opposite of Liz in some ways, having been one half of Mr and Mrs Joe Public, and then run away with the bikers.

And then, in June that year, they were round at the Whippet's squat. It was a dank, dismal place. The Whippet had only just moved in, so there was no furniture. They were sitting on boxes. The Whippet was there, and Marnie, the Whippet's girlfriend, and Angela.

The year was 1986.

Earlier in the evening, John had rung up Liz in Tintagel. He'd said, 'This is stupid Liz. We're not really married. Why don't you go for a divorce?' And she agreed.

Angela must have thought it had something to do with her, the fact that she was his woman now. But it hadn't. He was clearing the decks. Getting rid of all the old baggage. Making room for something new to come into his life.

And then he began writing on a board. It was a shelf from an MFI cupboard unit, white laminated chipboard. And he had a marker pen. And he started writing all his names down.

He put 'King John' in the middle, that being his current nickname. He always wrote 'King John' with a three-pointed crown above the K. And then around it he put all of his other names: Johnny Reb, Bacardi, Mad Dog, Ace, John the Hat, Terry Solo, Rev JT Rothwell; and his social security number, his army number. All of the names. Every name he had ever been known by. Everything he had ever been. It was like he was searching for something in this welter of identity, as if, perhaps, this dumb white board could explain it to him.

He passed the board over to the Whippet.

'I'm bored,' he said. He meant, 'My whole life is on this board and I'm bored of it.' He knew the Whippet would get the pun. They were like psychic brothers, connected on a fundamental level. It was as if they could read each other's minds.

'You're not King John,' said the Whippet, after a significant pause.

'No, I know I'm not King John. But I'm not any of the other names either,' he said. He thought the Whippet meant, 'You're not King John, you're just John, my mate.'

'No, what I mean is,' the Whippet said, catching his eye with a raven's piercing glance, 'you're not King John, you're King Arthur, the Once and Future King.'

His first reaction was, 'No, I don't want to be King Arthur. I want to be Merlin or I'm not playing.'

He'd been involved in the occult for years, and had adopted the wizard's role with a certain panache. But the Whippet was having none of it. He threw over a book. It was a book about King Arthur by Gareth Knight. 'Here, read this,' he said.

It was one of those moments of high tension. Of magic. Like that moment when he was poised, spinning in a dustcart awaiting death, with the shards of glass coming at him, frozen into a slow dance. Or when he had turned the cards, waiting for the King to appear, which would mean he would marry Liz. A moment resonant with strange echoes, as if a ghost was moving between them.

He was looking at the index in the book and picking bits out.

He read, 'Arthur in his triumph,' and he thought, 'No, it's Arthur *on* his Triumph, and it's there, parked up outside the flat.'

He read, 'His wife in Tintagel,' and he thought, 'I know, I've just been speaking to her.'

He kept opening the book at random, and always there would be a line describing his life. His life, not somebody else's.

Arthur's life.

He suddenly saw that it wasn't a matter of choice, whether he be Arthur or Merlin, or any one of a thousand other names. It wasn't a matter of playing. This was reality.

For the first time in his life, something made sense. For years now he'd felt wrong. Out of place. Empty. It was as if his life had become a dream lived by someone else. And now here was the Whippet telling him he was someone else.

He was filled with a peculiar sensation, as if all the questions he had ever asked were being answered at once. It was a kind of click. Or rather, a multiple click. Like the click of greased metal against metal, slotting in sequentially, as if everything was fitting into place at last. As if his soul had been engineered for this task, and this task alone.

As satisfying as kick-starting a bike to hear its nomadic roar.

As real as a party on a starlit night.

As true as the moon.

He thought, 'Oh fuck, this is real shit.'

He looked up at the Whippet. He said, 'You know, if I go for this, I go for it all the way? There's no turning back?'

'I know,' the Whippet said.

Not many words were said, but there was a volume of thoughts.

The Whippet was offering a magical challenge. There was a strange light in his eyes, firelight reflected in a lake. Something was passing directly between them. As if their brains were locked together, positive to positive, negative to negative, jump leads between bikes. The Whippet was looking at the being in front of him and saying, 'Go for it! Go for it. You are Arthur.'

That was the biker way. Go for it!

And all the time, in Arthur's head, the rational voice was offering him warnings. 'They'll say you're mad,' it said. 'You'll be cut off from everyone. Everyone is gonna think you're a nutter.' That was Johnny's voice, slowly fading away.

And the mad warrior King Arthur would answer, 'Who gives a fuck? I'm Arthur, and that's it.'

And he was.

Arthur.

CHAPTER FIVE

Excalibur

So Arthur left the Whippet's flat, first thing the following morning, the day after his naming, and went straight to see a solicitor. He was going to change his name. He was going to change his name officially, by Change of Name Deed. No half measures here. If he really was Arthur he wanted the world to know. He wanted that name on his passport and on his driving licence. He wanted it to be made official.

He made an appointment for the following week.

It was later the same day that the doubts began to set in.

Remember: the man we called John was brave. Fearless, you could say. Fearless to the point of foolhardiness. There was no enemy he wouldn't face down. No odds he wouldn't accept. No danger too great.

But what he was about to embark upon – if he dared to do it – was far more frightening, far more dangerous, far more foolhardy than anything he had undertaken before. He was facing something more daunting than death itself. He was facing the world's derision.

He was no fool. He knew what people would say. They would say that he was mad. How many people would understand? How many people could understand? He was going to break up the bike club, give everything up, for what?

For a fantasy?

What would his friends think? What would anybody think? How would the authorities react?

He had stood his ground in endless battles against rival bikers, against the police and the establishment. He had given the world a run for its money. He had stood upon his dignity, upon his biker code and his loyalty. But how would the world look upon him now?

It would laugh at him, of course. It would call him a nutter.

So, although his heart was firm, his head was in turmoil. Doubts buzzed around it like a plague of flies around a shit pit. They were the What-If flies. What if this and what if that. What if this wasn't his destiny? Could he really be so vain as to make such a claim? What if his friends rejected him? What if they tried to section him under the Mental Health Act, have him put away in an institution? What if it was all a horrible misunderstanding? What if the Whippet had meant something else entirely? Questions, questions, questions.

Actually, it is these very questions that show that Arthur was never what you would call clinically paranoid. The true paranoiac doesn't ask such questions. The true paranoiac feels certain about his identity, but at the same time persecuted because the rest of the world fails to acknowledge it. From the beginning, Arthur was in no doubt that very few people, if any, would accept what he was saying. He didn't feel persecuted. Just naturally – and sanely – worried what other people might think.

He needed confirmation.

There was an obvious place to go.

The last time he'd been to Stonehenge there had been a tragic accident. This was in 1984, two years previously, before the Stonehenge Festival had been suppressed by the Establishment. He'd gone there with a number of friends, dropping them off at the festival before going on himself to Tintagel to see Liz. They'd set up camp, and John had lent them his portable camping gas ring and refill.

On his return to the festival, at first he couldn't find his friends. Then he learnt why. One of them, Martin, was in hospital with serious burns while the other, Wendy (not his sister), was dead.

The camping gas burner had ignited and set light to the tent.

He had made statements to the police about the offending burner, and not been back to Stonehenge since.

Actually, there is some significance in the dates here, and a little bit of history is required. 1984 was the last of the Stonehenge Free Festivals. The festival had been going since 1974, by some people's reckoning. It was a yearly celebration of anarchist, hippie, biker and punk culture, a festival of madness in the heart of the yearly cycle. Some said it was older than this, since photographs existed showing that gatherings had been taking place at the solstice at least since the 50s. And even longer than that, if you count the traditional Druid ceremonies, going back to the 18th century. And since time immemorial, according to the more romantic notions. Since the dawn of time. What else was this place built for, but to mark off the seasons and to hold parties by?

But by 1985 the powers-that-be had decided that enough was enough. The festival was getting out of hand.

It had started off as a little hippie festival – just a few hundred people sitting about and talking. But by the mid-80s it was growing exponentially. Up to a quarter of a million people were turning up, several stages, hundreds of bands, and the festival went on for the whole of June. More than this: it was encouraging people not only to attend the festival, but to take up the traveller lifestyle. Every year more and more people were buying buses and trucks, painting them up in bright colours, fitting them out with all the luxuries of home, and going out on the road in them.

People were discovering new ways to live. Some built tepees, emulating the Native Americans. Others built benders, emulating the skills of Britain's own traditional travelling communities. People learnt how to make earth ovens for cooking bread. They learned how to cook on an open fire. New skills were being acquired. People thought, 'Well, if we're going to live in the open air, we can at least be comfortable.' They made sweat lodges as ritual and cleansing spaces. They practised long-forgotten arts of healing and divination. And, as each person learned each new skill, so the word was spread. It wasn't only possible, it was real. It was happening.

It was as if the stones themselves were imparting new meanings into people's lives, as if, in being there, they were resonating to some lost or hidden truth: the monument itself acting as a receiving station for information broadcast at some remote time in history.

So the festival had to be stopped. The powers-that-be said so.

We have yet to find out exactly who 'the powers-that-be' were. Certainly, English Heritage and the National Trust, along with the Wiltshire Constabulary. But probably also unaccountable members of the Wiltshire establishment simply angered that such a laugh-in-your-face act of collective anarchy was taking place regularly under their very noses. Something had to be done.

What was done amounted to a police riot.

On 1 June 1985, the festival convoy was ambushed on the A338 near Shipton Billinger, on their way to the A303 and Stonehenge. The road was blocked, front and rear. Festival goers were attacked in their buses. Later they broke into a nearby field and an uneasy truce ensued. Later still, they were attacked again. People were dragged out of their buses and beaten to the ground. Mothers with children alongside the men. Pregnant women. The police were totally out of control. Homes were set on fire, lives and livelihoods destroyed. A day that has gone down in history as the Battle of the Beanfield, though it was less a battle, more a rout. The festival people had no way of defending themselves.

All of this is on the record. This story has been told many times.

These were crazy, dangerous years in the life of the British Nation. Margaret Thatcher had come to power in 1979. By the time of the Battle of the Beanfield, she was in her second term of office and full of a maniacal self-confidence. She'd just defeated the miners in their yearlong strike. The whole of the British Labour movement was on the run. Police tactics had been deliberately changed. No longer expected to fight crime, the police force was being used more and more as a weapon of social control. After the miners she'd taken on and defeated the anarchist and traveller's movement: a much easier target. The whole country was polarised. Some people adored Thatcher, others loathed her. There was no halfway house. For some it was a wealthy time: the wealthiest time they had ever had. Council house sales and spiralling wages kept the working class in check. People were busy buying shares in the newly privatised national industries. They felt like they were joining the propertied classes at last. It was a smug, comfortable time for many. And they watched in careless indifference as trade union, human and civil rights were eroded in front of their eyes. What did it matter?

For others, for those who had rejected the constraints of 'normal' life, for travellers in particular, and for those who had lost their jobs in the rapidly declining heavy industrial sector, these were much more difficult times. For a miner or a steelworker – for many other workers – whose sense of self worth and identity were bound up in the epic scale of the industrial landscapes they inhabited, loss of job meant loss of dignity. Loss of manhood. Loss of pride. The miners had taken their defeat very hard. More than just a trade union, the National Union of Miners was the very backbone of a way of life, a relationship not an organisation, an act of love.

Britain was at war with itself.

This period corresponded approximately to John the Hat's lost years, to his inner search and his turmoil. His rebirth as Arthur came when – as it were – the war was already lost.

It is important to remember this time. It is important to remember the faces of the miners – so full of quiet, sad dignity – as they trudged their defeated way back to work, to watch their industry finally decimated and their communities destroyed. It is important to remember the squalid sites the travellers ended up on – no longer able to travel – while they licked their wounds and festered, turned to drugs and alcohol as their only compensation.

And it is worth asking, if there were winners and losers in these battles for the soul of Britain, whether the outcome could be called 'just' or not?

The significance here is that it was almost exactly a year after the Beanfield that the Whippet named Arthur. Almost exactly a year when Arthur and a few friends travelled down in a bright yellow work's van – called the banana van, for obvious reasons – to seek guidance. The significance is that Arthur's great battle begins with Stonehenge.

But that was still some years down the line. What he was looking for now was a sign.

It was dark when they pulled in to the car park. He and the Halfling, his chargehand at work, scrambled over the newly-raised fence, put up to keep the festival goers out and the fee-paying public in. Stonehenge was being turned into its own opposite. It was being turned into a theme park.

Security guards were in abundance, this being the first year since the effective banning of the festival. Nevertheless, Arthur and the Halfling managed to make it to the centre of the stones.

And that's when it happened.

The sign.

He was standing there in the midst of these ancient stones, in the heart of this sacred temple, his mind concentrated upon the question in hand, when something came at him out of the darkness. It seemed to come from nowhere, or from one of the stones. It was as if it had emerged from the stone, this great, black rustling thing. It came out of the stone in a rush of wind and something touched his forehead. He was so startled he didn't know what it was at first. It was there, upon him, and then it was gone, ghost-like into the night.

It was a bird, a huge, black bird, one of the ravens that nest under the lintels, and its wing had brushed his face. It was like an act of consecration. As if something from nature had, priest-like, laid a hand upon his forehead to offer blessings for his chosen course.

This is what he had been waiting for.

The security guards quickly rounded on the Halfling and ejected him from the Stones, leaving Arthur to wander around by himself, absorbing the significance of this encounter.

The question was, what if he really was Arthur and did nothing about it?

'What if?'

The question was there in the darkness with him. It was like the play of lights from the security guards' torches, flashing this way and that over the stones, trying to find him.

In other words, it was a false question, and it didn't belong here. It was a question that the stones themselves would not have countenanced.

'What if?'

To have had the hand of destiny touch him, and to have rejected it.

'"If" is the middle word in life,' as King John would often say. 'Why "Y"? Because it's a bent letter and you can't straighten it,' as the Whippet would retort.

The only epitaph Arthur could accept was: 'No Regrets.' It was his biker code. Now it would be Arthur's code too.

And for that reason alone he was left with no choice. 'Go for it!' And if it turned out that he wasn't King Arthur, at least he'd given it his best shot; and on the million-to-one chance that he was, well, history would never have forgiven him for failing to live up to it. History would have forgotten him. Worse than this, he could never have forgiven himself, because he, at least, could not have forgotten. He would have gone round for the rest of his life saying, 'What if?'

So now he knew. The weird had spoken. It was written in the wind, in the darkness and the stars, in an omen, in a portent, in a ghostly encounter with a raven in the dead of night. His destiny.

The ghosts of the stones themselves seemed to comfort him, to guide him. Their stolid presence, squat, shadowy giants in centuries-held poses, observing the passing world, seemed to link him back to some heroic age.

He thought, 'Well, if the world wants to laugh at me, if it wants to call me a nutter, then that's what I'll be. I'll be the nutter who thinks he's King Arthur.' And he laughed.

It was at this moment that the security guards seized him, and escorted him from the Stones. The police were waiting outside. They wanted to impound the van. 'You can't do that!' Arthur said. 'No, no, it's the works van,' added the Halfling. Both of them were breathalysed, being the keepers of the vehicle. But – despite the fact that they had been drinking – they both passed the test.

They drove back to Farnborough.

It was only in the morning that Arthur realised that there was a raven roosting in the oak tree where the Battlecruiser was parked. He'd never noticed it before. It seemed like yet another omen.

The following week he went to collect his Change of Name Deed from the solicitor. Unfortunately, they'd made a typling error. They'd spelled his name as 'Arthur Utter Pendragon'. This was 10 June. Arthur had wanted to change the Deed by hand and have them sign the correction, but the secretary insisted that it had to be done properly. Thus it was that his new official name was finally confirmed as Arthur Uther Pendragon on 11 June 1986. St Barnabas's Day.

Arthur says that prior to 1986, Britain was a Christian nation, therefore it was not possible to change your Christian name. In '86 it became a multi-cultural nation and you didn't have Christian names any more but first or forenames instead. Prior to 1986 be would not have been able to change his forename, and would have had to call himself John Pendragon.

So he was Arthur.

But not quite.

He was Arthur, but he had no idea what being Arthur meant.

He hadn't even read any Arthurian books. It wasn't as if he'd been intrigued by the legend as a child and then set out to emulate his hero in adulthood. He was going to have to learn on his feet.

And other people were uncertain about the name. They'd start off saying 'John' before suddenly remembering what his new name was. So they'd call him J'Arthur: John and Arthur combined. Part biker, part … well something else entirely.

Changes came strangely, often unexpectedly, and from surprising sources.

One day he was working on his Triumph. He had the air filter off and, as he kicked it over, the bike backfired through the carburettor and set the fuel pipes on fire. He was sitting astride it dabbing frantically at the fire with his gloved hand, trying to put it out. But it wasn't going to go out, and as the fire began to melt the plastic petrol tap on the full fuel tank, he decided that discretion was the better part of valour and dismounted, standing back to watch, guarding his eyes, as the fuel tank erupted in a 20-foot column of flame. It was parked up outside the clubhouse and, not wanting to miss any of the action, he sent one of the girls off to get him a bottle of Bacardi from the off-licence and sat back to watch the show. So that was that. His pride and joy. The love of his life. The very heart of his biker identity. Gone.

Well, at least it was a spectacular end to the beast. And he couldn't help laughing at the absurdity of it all. What else could he do? He was roaring with laughter as each new spurt and splutter came out of that once magnificent machine, as it cracked and sizzled and popped about on its stand like some crazy jumping jack at a circus of fire.

Afterwards he set about rebuilding it.

He designed and had a frame built, raked to an angle to suit the new extender springer forks. He completely rebuilt the engine and built the chop around it, all custom made one-off parts. It was his phoenix, reborn from the fire.

It was as if in rebuilding the bike he was rebuilding his life.

He got rid of the Battlecruiser and replaced it with a long wheelbase Transit van to house the new chop. He called the Transit his Iron Horse Box to denote its status as home to his Iron Steed. Then he bought a caravan to live in and life continued as normal. Or as normal as either John or Arthur's life had ever been. Which is to say: not very normal at all.

Meanwhile the council were trying to evict him. His sister passed a petition around the estate, calling for 'The Man In The Van' to be allowed to stay. They had to call him 'The Man In The Van' because, although he was strictly Arthur to himself and, occasionally, J'Arthur to his friends, he was still John to everyone else.

The hilarious thing about this was that most of the estate agreed to sign the petition. This despite the fact that the Whippet had been slipping out late at night and siphoning their petrol for years, and that everybody knew it. And despite the fact that they'd been holding raucous, no-holds-barred parties, and roaring about on their bikes being chased by infuriated coppers, firing off zip guns at imaginary enemies in the dead of night and being generally anti-social and weird. And – as if the wild biker lifestyle wasn't enough – now here he was telling everybody that he wasn't called John any more, but Arthur. And not just any old Arthur – as in Arthur Rothwell, say, some mad biker fanatic who simply fancied a name change – but Arthur Pendragon, the Once and Future King of All Britain.

It takes all sorts to make a world.

And people are surprisingly adaptable.

Perhaps it is time to take a pause and to reflect upon the meaning of all this. So far this has been the story of one dysfunctional child becoming a dysfunctional adult in a dysfunctional world: a squaddie, then a biker, causing mayhem and having fun. A product of his times, no doubt. A product of this society. But with this one essential difference: that latterly, he had begun to make claims that to some might seem spurious, and to others might seem mad, but that – whichever way you look at it – certainly separated him from the crowd.

So where does truth come from? Where does knowledge? Where does identity come from? Where does being?

What makes us what we are?

Nothing is proven or disproved.

We can measure the stars and name them, but do they tell us anything about ourselves?

We can watch the fidgeting fingers of a brain scanner flicking back and forth across the screen, but does it tell us what our purpose is?

Some people would like to tell us that we have no purpose. We are flecks of matter in an unredeemable Universe, scattering about according to vague chemical whims.

Others talk of God, without ever having met him.

We know that the past exists, but do we know how to understand it? We may think we have a future, but can anyone build hope for it?

Maybe the Arthur of legend was a man, who existed once, who fought the Saxons and defeated them, bringing peace to these Isles after years of bloody conflict.

People suggest that he may have been a Roman-trained cavalryman turned mercenary. There are all sorts of theories. Maybe he was Scottish, maybe he was Welsh, maybe he was Cornish. Maybe he fought specific battles in a specific area, maybe he sallied forth over all of the Isles. Maybe he just chased pigs. Maybe he was no more than a pig rustler with a bad reputation.

The Dark Ages were full of strife: called 'the Dark Ages' not because they were without light or civilisation, or honour, or valiant endeavour, but because we really know very little about them. Maybe there was banditry and murder. But there was most likely poetry also, and art, and fine work, and intelligence. There was something to defend.

So a man could have arisen at this time and he may have been called Arthur. It makes a certain kind of sense. And if contemporary records miss him out of the picture, later writers were not unaware of his fame.

What is certain is that something happened in that period: something worthy of note, something adequate, at the very least, to blazon the name of Arthur across the centuries, to keep that name alive, and that out of this legend arose a mystery and a philosophy that lives to this day.

If it could ever be said that there is magic in a name, then it must be true of the name of Arthur.

So maybe there was a man, and thereafter there was a legend, and after that again a vast and complex literature full of resonance and strange mystery, and forever and a day the name of Arthur will be synonymous with the Islands of Britain, with the idea of Britain. So – and it depends on your philosophy, of course – there's another way of looking at Arthur. Maybe Arthur is a spirit or like a spirit, the personification of the land of Britain.

And who is to say – assuming this to be true – what kind of man that spirit might choose to inhabit.

If Geoffrey of Monmouth can reinvent the myth to give glory to the new Norman elite; if Chrétien de Troyes can picture Arthur's doings in the courtly atmosphere of his own 12th century Europe – if he can give him the face and the dress sense of Henry II, and reflect his own world and his own concerns in a story about a mythical King; if Malory can rewrite Arthur to fulfil a chivalric ideal; if Spencer can use Arthur to glorify the court of Elizabeth, and Tennyson the court of Victoria, then we can do the same.

We can write our Arthur to glorify the lives of the dispossessed of the land of late 20th/early 21st-century Britain. We can make our Arthur a

British soldier, the son of a soldier, brought up in army camps and council estates, a truant, a persistent offender, a jack-of-all-trades, a traveller, a
mad biker chieftain wielding an axe who, in a moment of revelation, in a
20th century squat, accepts the mantle of Arthur and who heads out into
the world to seek Truth, Honour and Justice.

We can make him what we like.

And if you think back to the Dark Ages, past the plate armour and the
golden crown of medieval depictions – past the courtly love quests and
the mannered poetry of unrequited love – to a ruder, ruddier, randier
time, when Arthur might not have appeared quite as constrained as later
images suggest, then what do we get?

If you picture him, then, as a Dark Ages battle chieftain, a soldier,
trained in the Roman army, leading a wild band of nomadic horsemen in
defence of Britain against the barbarian invasion; if you picture him fighting, berserker style, on horseback, charging into the fray, sword flailing
and flashing red in the sun; a leader not a follower, laughing in the face
of death; if you imagine him carousing after battle, getting gloriously,
unadulteratedly, insanely drunk before falling into a ditch to sleep: if
you can see him like this, then you have some picture of our own Arthur.
Trained in the British, not the Roman, army. With a wild bunch of
nomadic bikers behind him. Valiantly berserk. On a chopped Triumph,
rather than a horse. Fighting with fist and fury. President of an outlaw
biker club, and then, latterly, a head of a massive Druid order. A leader
with a large number of followers who follow, not because they are in awe
or deranged or deluded by the force of his personality, or weak willed or
stupid or out of their depth, but because he's always first off the mark to
do what they were going to do anyway. With a vast tendency to overdo it
on the cider, before falling into a ditch – any old ditch – to fall asleep.

As 24341883 Private Rothwell he carried a L1A1 7.62 self-loading rifle
and a bayonet. As John the Hat, a double-headed fire axe and a three barrel .22 zip gun. And now as Arthur a 4-foot broadsword and dagger; the
difference being, as he has on many occasions demonstrated, both in the
field and before the courts, that his current weaponry, powerful though it
is, is for magical purposes only.

In other words, if you wanted to train up a 20th-century Arthur, you
could have done no better than to have given him Johnny Rothwell's life.
Or, as Arthur himself says in one of his well-known aphorisms, 'There's a

pre-Roman Arthur and a post-Roman Arthur, and a post-Thatcher Arthur, and that's me.'

As to whether you believe it or not: well it's entirely up to you.

So, enough of the history. Let's get on with the life.

Arthur spent the first year as Arthur keeping pretty low. He didn't dress like Arthur. He dressed like a biker. He didn't necessarily act like Arthur – even assuming he had any idea how Arthur might act – he acted as he always had done. He had his passport and driving licence changed to reflect the name change, and if anyone asked him his name, he'd tell them. But he wouldn't put any weight or significance upon the fact. His name was Arthur Pendragon. He came from Aldershot and Farnborough, and he was a biker, getting up to all the old tricks.

So it was a sort of interim time for him, a kind of limbo. He broke up the bike club (some people never forgave him for that) and started hanging out with another group of friends. He remained close to the Whippet, though, and to Wendy, his sister, and to Chesh, his brother-in-law.

As part of his research, CJ had interviewed Chesh and Wendy. It was an obvious question: what did they think when John suddenly announced he wasn't John anymore, but Arthur? Did they think he had gone mad?

Chesh was quite succinct about it. He said that, as bikers, they had always accepted people for what were. He said, 'If he'd said, "I want to be the most famous milkman in the world," we'd have said, "Well go for it. You can be the most famous milkman in the world."' As it was he said he was Arthur.

So, although there was a certain amount of resentment from some quarters, the close biker fraternity were quite supportive of him.

And – thinking about it – what other group could have accepted this startling revelation with such equanimity? If they'd been a gang of skinheads, say, or a yard of yuppies, a field of farmers or a forest of tree surgeons – any group you can name – what would they have said?

They would have laughed at him, of course. They would have ribbed him and ripped him apart, and never given him the space to develop. The yuppies would have rung up social services to have him committed, while the skinheads would have kicked his face in.

But, as bikers, Chesh and Wendy said, 'Well, if you want to be Arthur, you can be Arthur. We'll support you no matter what you say you are.'

As for Arthur, he was just being himself.

And there were the usual adventures.

Since the break up of the bike club, Chesh had set up a rally club. This was an ordinary biker outfit. They weren't outlaws. They were invited up to a bike rally in Scotland, being run by Pegasus MCC. They asked Arthur and the Whippet along for company.

This was a mistake.

Pegasus were straight, front-patch wearing bikers, as opposed to back-patch outlaws. In other words, they were motorcycle enthusiasts who liked to get together for the occasional outing on a weekend. They were nice, polite, inoffensive people who liked to ride – and talk about – motorbikes.

What they weren't expecting was this bunch of fazed-out crazies, steaming for the crack.

No one from Pegasus (the classical reference makes it clear where they were coming from) had planned for such mayhem. Madness wasn't meant to be on the agenda. But then, they hadn't bargained on Arthur.

The Whippet's girlfriend, Marnie, was there, along with Angela. Arthur had done his usual, and slipped off with one of the other girls. When he got back, he'd turned a corner to hear screaming. He recognised Angela's voice. There was a fight going on, a gaggle of people snagged up in some struggle. Arthur saw red. He simply waded in, fists flying, thinking that Angela was in trouble and needed his help. It was dark and he wasn't thinking too clearly, or looking too hard, and landed a hulking fist in the face of the first person who got in his way. It was the Pegasus President's wife. Not a good idea. She simply crumpled to the floor and fainted. He knocked out another couple of blokes trying to hold him off before the Whippet waded in to calm him down. The Whippet knew what was really happening. The fight in the middle was the two women going tooth and claw at each other because Marnie had caught Angela snogging the Whippet. The people around were trying to separate them. So the Whippet knew the whole thing was actually their fault. Two blokes were holding onto Arthur from behind and the Whippet tried talking to him. Only now the Whippet was in the way and Arthur wasn't listening. He could see the Whippet's mouth moving – blah, blah, blah – but none of the words had any sense. Arthur was still in full berserker mode. He freed his arm and: Bang! Across goes the fist, and virtually wipes the Whippet's nose off his face.

Another day at the office for a couple of outlaw bikers. Except that one of them was now supposed to be a legendary figure from the mythical past.

And – you have to ask – would the historical Arthur have acted like this?

The answer is: who knows? Probably. Possibly. Maybe.

Before he became King.

But Arthur and the Whippet were always doing this: always getting into fights, always trying to knock each other's block off, always trying to wind each other up, and then landing a blow. And in this case they had their excuse. 'Women, huh? Trouble, with a capital T.' And that was that.

Needless to say they were never invited back to a Pegasus MCC rally.

We could go on. A lot more happened in this intervening year. The usual absurdity, stock craziness of the biker elite. Of course, Arthur might be embarrassed by it all now: now that he has attained a certain amount of recognition and status, that is, now that his views are taken seriously by members of the establishment – by English Heritage, for example, and the Wiltshire Constabulary. But the truth is, he wasn't complete yet. He wasn't quite Arthur. An essential component was missing.

What was it?

Excalibur, of course.

How could he really be Arthur without Excalibur?

It was obviously a question he had asked himself.

By now he'd met Guy Acton, known as Guy the Rant because he never stopped talking, 6' 1", and built like an oversized flat iron, who worked with Chesh. He'd also met Fraggle.

Both of them were peripheral to the biker scene. John had known them, though not all that well. Now, as Arthur, having given up the old crew, he was hanging round with them more and more.

Fraggle was this tall, blond, Aryan looking chap – very right wing, having been in the Royal Navy – who rode an 800cc Japanese bike, and who kept down a proper job in an office. He would start up his bike in the morning and let it run before he set off to work, going back in to drink a last cup of tea. Of course, Arthur knew of this habit. One day he went round there on the back of someone else's bike and, dismounting quickly and remounting the flashy Japanese machine, roared off down the road on it. Just for the crack – as usual. Fraggle had come running out frantically screaming. But it wouldn't have taken him long to work out who it was who would have done this to him. Who else could it be? There was only one person.

Later, Fraggle had wanted to lose his job, but his bosses wouldn't let him go. He was indispensable. But he wanted to get the sack. He kept trying to get the sack. In the end he asked Arthur to help him out. So Arthur did. He rode up the steps of the office building one day, after Fraggle had finished work, in through the swing glass doors and into the lobby, roaring to a screeching halt in front of the enquiry desk where Fraggle was waiting. It was all prearranged. Fraggle jumped on the back, stuck on a lid, and they roared back out again, kicking open the doors on the way. Mission accomplished. Fraggle was asked never to come back.

So it was Fraggle and Guy Acton and Angela, exactly a year to the day after Arthur's official renaming at the solicitor's: 11 June 1987. It was also, coincidentally, the Queen's official birthday, and a general election at the same time. Margaret Thatcher was going for her third successive election victory. Arthur had decided that he wanted Excalibur.

They drove over to Glastonbury.

The full moon was shining like a polished engine part as they climbed the Tor, the mists swirling across the Somerset levels, a gleaming lake of silver. A perfect night.

Angela – who was by this time calling herself the Lady Angela – was fascinated by Marion Zimmer Bradley's interpretation of the Arthurian myths, *The Mists of Avalon*. It was probably she who had suggested they go to the ancient West Country pilgrimage town, knowing its historical association with the legendary Arthur.

She had written a spell, or a poem in the appropriate style, and she read it out in a loud, clear voice.

And then they waited.

They waited.

The mists swirled about the Tor, the glow of the streetlights of the town over Chalice Hill an orange fire in the sky, the tower of St Michael's chapel casting a grim shadow over their huddled, expectant forms. A swift wind blew up, seeming to augur the coming revelation.

And they waited.

They waited and they waited.

What were they waiting for?

They were waiting for Excalibur, of course. They were waiting for the mists to rise and for a ghostly form to emerge. An ethereal boat, with the Lady of the Lake in it, complete with white, drifty, medieval clothing, like some Pre-Raphaelite goddess. A thin veil would cover her face and they would catch a brief, blinding glimpse of her magical beauty. She would climb out, while strange music drifted through the translucent air, as she raised the sword. Arthur would, of course, fall to his knees, praising her loveliness, while she knighted him, before finally passing the sword on to him. Excalibur. Which he would take to his heart in triumph as it shone like a jewel in the night.

Something like that.

CJ considers that they had probably been reading too many cheap paperback novels.

So they waited.

No rising mist.

They waited.

No ghostly form.

They waited.

No boat. No Lady of the Lake. No ethereal music. No Excalibur.

Nothing.

Just the wind and the shadows and the orange glow of the streetlamps down below.

And while Guy and Fraggle were getting restless, fidgeting about, sighing under their breath, stamping their feet and cursing quietly, Arthur was lighting up a cigarette. They waited some more.

Meanwhile, the rest of the nation was watching the election results on the TV.

Did they read out the poem again, in the hope that it would activate the magic?

Well if they did, it didn't work. Arthur didn't get Excalibur, and Margaret Thatcher won the election.

They drove back home, Arthur feeling lost and dejected. No one dared say anything to him in the car. He just looked out of the window and glowered.

It was 28 days later. Arthur and Angela were driving through Farnborough and Aldershot in Arthur's van. This was Johnny Rothwell's patch and Arthur knew it like he knew his own motorbike. Every intricate part. Every nook and cranny, every nut and bolt, every highway and byway, every pipe and funnel of it. He'd kicked cans as footballs down these streets as a kid to hear the ringing clatter. He'd ridden his bike while his dog had chased his heels. He'd set fire to large parts of it. Later he'd been chased by the police through it, had fights here, defended his honour here, snogged girls as a teenager and fucked them as an adult, lived, loved, but never regretted on these dull, grey, prosaic streets of home.

It's not Glastonbury. Marion Zimmer Bradley never set a mystical Arthurian novel here, full of magic and secret charms. There's no such thing as *The Farnborough Romance* or the *Aldershot Zodiac*. There's no mysterious signs etched into the landscape. No legends, no mystery, no mythic presences. It's an army town, full of soldiers.

Nevertheless, Arthur knew his way around.

He took a wrong turning.

'Shit!' he said, preparing to do a quick swerve or a three-point turn. And then the lights turned red and they were stuck.

If the lights hadn't turned red, Angela would not have looked.

If Angela hadn't have looked, she would never have seen.

If she hadn't seen, they would have driven on oblivious.

But the lights did turn red, she did look, and she did see.

'Wait a minute,' she said, pointing back up the road. 'They sell swords in there. Why don't we take a look?'

It was a shop called 'The Casque and Gauntlet', a model armourers. They made arms and the like for historical re-enactment societies.

Arthur knew it was all rubbish. He didn't want a sword made for some poxy re-enactment society. He wanted Excalibur. Nevertheless he parked the van and reluctantly went back with Angela to take a look.

And there it was, in the window, as part of a display. Excalibur. Wow!

There was no mistaking it, a hand and a half Celtic Broadsword with a full fighting blade, with a gilded gold pommel and hilt, with Excalibur embellished in gold lettering upon the hilt, and King Arthur and a dragon on one side, and a Celtic Rampant Dragon on the other, double-edged with a gold leaf Celtic design on the tang.

Arthur just looked at it and it was instant recognition. He thought, 'I am Arthur and you are Excalibur. You are Excalibur and I am Arthur.'

Unfortunately, it wasn't for sale.

He went into the shop and asked about it.

The owner of the shop had made it for the film *Excalibur*. You can see it if you get out the film, rising from the water at the beginning, exactly as Arthur had dreamed. Mists and lakes and boats. Everything. This sword had done all of that.

'I want to buy it,' Arthur said.

But the man wasn't interested. He had another version of it, a lightweight version he'd made for the actor to handle in the battle scenes. He got that out and showed it to him, let him handle it. It was an exact copy in everything but weight, but it wasn't Excalibur. It wasn't a fighting sword.

'No, I don't want that one, I want the real thing,' said Arthur.

The man looked at him. 'Why do you want that?' he said. 'Anyway,' he added, 'I promised I'd only sell it to the real King Arthur, if he ever returned.'

So Arthur threw his passport over the counter.

'I'm the real King Arthur,' he said, 'and I've got to have that sword.'

The man opened the passport, and looked at it. Then he looked up at Arthur. You could see the gears shifting in his brain, the cogs whirring. He looked back at the passport and let out a little soft laugh of resignation.

'I can't argue with that. How much you got?' said the man.

'I've got a hundred quid.'

Even Arthur knew this was silly. The man had charged the film company £5,000 for it. He'd already told him that. It had gold on the pommel and the hilt, and gold inlay on the tang. It was sprung steel, a real fighting blade. Aside from that, it was a film artefact, and worth even more because of that.

The man looked at him again and laughed bitterly. You can't refuse fate. 'Go on then. A hundred quid and it's yours,' he said.

And Arthur got out the money and slung it across the counter and the man got out the sword from the window display, laying it lengthways along the counter, and then Arthur took the handle, gripping it and lifting it, and then the sword was in his hand, a living extension of his arm, a living thing. Perfect weight, perfect balance, perfect form. Charged up with its own electrical energy. Sizzling with light.

Excalibur.

It was only on re-reading Angela's spell that they realised it had asked for him to be re-united with Excalibur by the next Full Moon. This very day.

CHAPTER SIX

Merlin

S o he had the sword. And not any old sword. Excalibur, the sword of Britain, made for the film *Excalibur*, having appeared at the beginning of the film emerging from a lake being held aloft by a woman's hand, and thus – in a peculiarly technological and 20th-century sort of way – having fulfilled all the prophesies.

It had adventured, this sword, in the hands of actors, through a myriad of stage-lit scenes. It had flashed its sparkling brilliance into the minds of a million viewers. It had lived a crazed existence as a film star – the only star in the film – being shunted from scene to scene by bodyguards, perhaps to be brought out ceremoniously whenever it was needed, wherever the action was.

And holding it in his hand outside the shop, Arthur knew. This was no ordinary sword. This was no ordinary time. He was no ordinary man. He was standing on the crux of a time, at a spiritual crossroads, on the pavement where legends are born.

He took the sword home to examine it. As an object it was perfect. Beautifully crafted, honed with all the skill and intelligence of a master craftsman. The swordsmith had put a part of his own life into its creation, had plied it with his patience, had poured into it his dreams, had entered it with his thoughts, had beaten it and shaped it, had shared his secret musings with it and offered total surrender. He had taken time over it, put effort into it, and invested it with love. It moved with simple grace and magic, weaving through the sunlit air with sparkling laughter. It seemed to have a life of its own, dancing as Arthur swung it about. He was playing with it, of course, wielding it, getting a feel of its weight and balance, gripping it to know its sturdy precision, holding it up ceremoniously to catch the sunlight.

And it sang.

If you hit the tang – the inlaid part of the blade near the hilt – with the heel of your hand, it gave out a long slow note, deep and serene, like a bird in flight.

Sprung steel. Woven with artistry. Magically endowed.

It was like a dream. More than he ever could have hoped for. And justification for the strange course his life had now taken.

He was Arthur. He was Arthur because he had Excalibur. Arthur and the sword were united.

Having Excalibur was the institution of his political office, he says now. Before this moment he was Arthur Pendragon, biker chieftain, rabble-rouser without a cause. Now he was King Arthur Pendragon, the people's king.

Not that he wasn't still without the occasional twinge of doubt. Here in the West we have no imagination for such things: no structures of thought to explain the strange events that were, it seemed, continually unfolding. As a citizen of Tibet or India, the explanation would have been simple. People would have said that he had been re-incarnated. And it's odd how, as Westerners, we can allow the Dalai Lama this explanation of himself, can support him, of course, and sometimes even believe him, but when a Westerner makes a similar claim, well, the prevailing culture calls him mad. We are so ground down with our materialist interpretations that we can't allow for any other ways of looking. We see the past as full of superstition, while the present knows all there is to know. And if the early Greeks believed in reincarnation, along with the early Britons, then that was just a more primitive way of guessing at the world's mysteries.

The world has no mysteries any more. So there's no re-incarnation, no life after death, no god, no goddess, no genius of spring and field and lake and mountain, no presence in this world that's not our own, no beauty that's not made in a factory, no story that's not on TV, no life that can't be found in a supermarket, no wisdom to be acquired, no ancient knowledge, no heroes that can't be bought and sold, no dreams, no visions, no magic, no journeys of the soul.

And didn't Arthur agree? Didn't he too sometimes think that he might

be half-crazy? Crazy to be on this road? Crazy, deranged or just plain stupid? He wasn't sure which was worse.

But, just as Stonehenge had spoken, quietly and firmly, from its moonlit stillness at a previous time of questioning, so now the sword spoke. It
spoke of deeds yet to be done. It spoke of a hundred unrealised adventures. It spoke of quests, of shields, of knights, of a fellowship of the
sword. It sparked a fire in his brain and set his imagination alight.

So he and Angela decided to move. They decided to move to the heart
of the Arthurian landscape. They decided to move to Glastonbury.

Just before they left they went to a Spiritualist Church meeting. They
were with Bob – the Manic Mechanic, from the Saddletramps days – and
Maria. They sat at the back. There were the usual introductions, singing
hymns and the rest, and then the medium began her routine. 'The gentleman at the back,' she said, 'with the headband.'

'Oh yeah,' thought Arthur, sceptical as usual. 'It's because she hasn't
seen me before. She's trying to draw me in.'

'Does the name Arthur mean anything to you?'

'Ye-ah?' he said, sitting up, suddenly intrigued.

'Spirit tells me you write poetry. Trust it, even if those around you
doubt it.' And then she added, 'And when you go on your quest, Spirit
tells me, trust him that you shall find,' and she moved on to the next
punter.

And that was an odd thing. She was right, and not only about the
name. The poetry was a new thing, an Arthurian thing. It was not something he had ever been interested in before. He'd begun writing poetry
almost as soon as he became Arthur.

So Glastonbury it was.

They hitched the caravan up to the back of the Iron Horse Box the following day, stuck the chop in the back, and set out for Glastonbury and
the healing lands of Summer.

Ah, Glastonbury. Thy sweet springs. Thy sacred mounds. Thy ancient
mystery. Thy strange New Age indulgences.

Actually, as we've said before, Arthur knew very little of the legendary
figure whose name he now bore. He didn't read books, or not all that
often. He probably had a vague idea of what it was about. He'd have
known some of the names. He'd have heard of the Holy Grail, of course,
(who hasn't heard about the Holy Grail?) and of Camelot. Perhaps he'd

even learnt, by a form of cultural osmosis, of the ancient connections between Glastonbury and the name of Arthur. If so, it was fairly unconscious. We can say this about Arthur: that he was working on an instinctive rather than a learned level. He was not setting out to re-enact how he thought Arthur might have been. He was Arthur, therefore how he was, that was how Arthur was.

His reason for coming to Glastonbury was that it had worked before. He'd cast a spell on the Tor, asking for Excalibur, and Excalibur had come into his hands. So now he had one more favour to ask of his favoured magic place.

He wanted to find Merlin.

All he had to do was wait.

But Glastonbury does, indeed, carry a powerful Arthurian resonance, as many visitors to the town will know.

There is a story that Guinevere was abducted here by the tyrant Melwas, King of Somerset, who had a stronghold on the Tor, and that Arthur laid siege to it but failed to capture it, and that it was only through the intervention of the monk Gildas that he managed to get her back. Later, it is said, Arthur again attacked the stronghold, capturing it this time, so that it became an Arthurian position.

This story is consistent with the archaeological evidence, which does, in fact, place a fortification on top of the Tor at the appropriate time.

Another story says that the young Arthur was a visitor to the Underworld beneath the Tor, and that there he was given the sword of power and the cauldron of rebirth.

Local tales have always insisted that the nearby Iron Age hill fort at Cadbury was, in fact, Camelot. Again this is consistent with archaeological findings, there being evidence of resettlement there in the Dark Ages.

And stories abound in the area about the ghosts of Arthur and Guinevere wandering solemnly through bleak and windswept places in the dead of night.

The most powerful of the Arthurian connections, however, is the one that places the site of his burial in the Abbey, discovered by monks in the latter years of the 12th century, between two pyramids. He was said to be buried 16-feet down in a hollowed oaken log, alongside Guinevere. He was buried beneath a lead cross-pinned upside down under a stone slab so that the inscription could not at first be read. Once they'd released the cross, the inscription was plain. It said, 'Here lies the famous King Arthur, buried in the Isle of Avalon.' Which would be pretty compelling evidence if there weren't any number of variations on the wording and inconsistencies in the story.

The cross was still in existence as late as the early 18th century when it was held by a man named William Hughes, an official of Wells Cathedral. It was seen by John Leland around 1540 and illustrated for the 1607 edition of *Britannia* by William Camden, copies of which are still in existence. Unfortunately, the lettering, though not 12th century, is not 6th century either.

Which is not to say that it wasn't, in fact, a marker for Arthur's grave, just that the cross couldn't have been made at the same time that Arthur was buried.

But it's more than this. It's more than the apocryphal and historical connections that link the name of Arthur with the town of Glastonbury (or that link the name of Glastonbury with the mystical Isle of Avalon): there's something in the town itself, or in the countryside around and about. An atmosphere.

Even the cynical CJ has felt it, whenever he's been compelled to visit the town. Something about the Tor, with its three-dimensional maze, like the opening of a uterus, or the twin springs that rise there (one white, one red) from the lower slopes. And standing atop the Tor it can seem that you're looking out over the reclining form of a woman: the Tor itself a proud, jutting breast, the rounded slopes of Chalice Hill like soft buttocks, and the bent line of Wearyall Hill a stretched-out limb. It's as if you are embracing the body of the goddess herself, the very landscape being evidence of her existence.

'Glastonbury', the word, is an Anglo-Saxon translation of the Celtic name for the town: Ynys Witrin, the Isle of Glass. And Avalon – a name with which Glastonbury has long been associated – means the Isle of Apples.

Glass citadels or castles are a recurring theme in fairy tales, and apple orchards are said to be places of prophesy and divination.

Before the Somerset levels were drained, the sea may have washed these shores. Even now, on damp days when the mist rises across the levels, it can seem to be an island in a sea of furling cloud. Perhaps it is the resting place of the dead, a last stop on the soul's journey to the

Otherworld, where Gwyn ap Nudd, Lord of Ghosts, sets forth on the Wild Hunt, hair and eyes blazing, accompanied by his grisly hounds across the mountains of the sky. Sometimes too, it is said, Arthur will accompany him on these wild jousts, raging through the heavens on his trusty charger, at the head of his band of knights.

The Isle of Glass, the Shining Isle, palace of the senses, where Cerridwen the enchantress, possessor of the cauldron of rebirth, lies hidden, awaiting those who seek her.

So Arthur and Angela were dotting around and about the town in the Iron Horse Box with the caravan, parking up in car parks and lay-bys and under trees, and beside bridleways and green lanes, here and there and everywhere until, eventually, they found a more secure spot. It was in an apple orchard in Langport, about 12 miles from Glastonbury, just outside Wagg, where Arthur quickly found a welcoming hostelry. Langport and Wagg are said by some to be incorporated as parts of a great earthwork, known as the Great Dog of Langport, celebrated in an old Somerset Wassail song:

> *The Girt Dog of Langport has burnt his long tail,*
> *And this is the night we go singing wassail.*

Wagg, of course, is where the tail lies.

And Arthur did indeed possess a dog at this time: called Cabal, after the mythical Arthur's famous dog, a male Alsatian cross (a mixture of everything) that he'd picked up from near Aldershot before he left.

Cabal was devoted to Arthur and hated everyone else. Arthur had found him in a dog's home. He'd seemed a nice enough creature. So Arthur had put him in the van and driven home, only stopping off at a café for a cup of tea. So he was sitting in the caff, when a mate turned up.

'That's a fucking vicious dog you've got there Arthur,' this friend had commented.

And Arthur had gone out to look. Cabal was going mental in the van, trying to attack anyone who came close by.

'Oh no,' Arthur thought, 'what have I landed myself with?'

He realised he was going to have to get into the van with this dog, even now slavering insanely, baring it's yellow teeth and growling with vicious intent. He looked like he was ready to kill.

Only when Arthur got in the van, Cabal licked him.

'You're my mate, Arthur. I'll protect you,' said Cabal in simple dog lan-guage, using his tail and his tongue, looking at him with friendly eyes.

And, indeed, Cabal did protect Arthur, not allowing anyone to come near the caravan without Arthur's permission. Sometimes not even then.

Even Angela wasn't safe from that crazed dog's angry loyalty. Arthur had to keep Cabal tied up outside the van. Angela was always scared that she might be bitten.

The man who owned the orchard – a yuppie, down from London – was doing up the old farmhouse. It was an ancient building, constructed of local stone, with a thatched roof. It was mentioned in the Domesday Book: that's how ancient it was. And Arthur had free parking in the orchard, plus cash in hand, for helping with the work. They were taking it down, a wall at a time, and rebuilding it, stone by stone. Arthur was helping out, mixing up, doing the labouring to start with, but as the work progressed and the builder discovered that Arthur had had experi-ence in the building trade, he was given more complex tasks to perform. The builder taught him how to lay stones, and a variety of other arcane building matters.

It was a perfect situation. Arthur could choose when he worked and when he didn't. He could work every day of the week or he could work none. It was entirely down to him. If he needed money for something specific – to do something on his bike, say, or to travel – he would work more. If he was in contemplative mode, working on himself and his plans – then he didn't have to do any.

But it is a nice irony that King Arthur should begin his reign as a labourer on a building site.

It was early in his time in the orchard that Arthur, still worried about his sanity, took the Mensa test and passed it. Mensa is an organisation that caters for people with the highest IQs – the top 2%. Which makes Arthur, if not a certifiable nutter, then a certified genius at least.

But it was now time to start being Arthur. His first task, he decided, was to 'out' himself.

Up till now he had been a biker with a peculiar name. He still remained a biker in that he wore leathers (although he began to refer to his jacket as his 'leather armour'), but he decided that he should begin to look more like Arthur too. So he designed and made a robe out of sackcloth to wear over his leathers, with a rampant red dragon – symbol of the Celtic Nation – emblazoned across the front. Meanwhile Angela made a scabbard out of a cardboard poster case covered in felt, and inscribed it with various hexes, amulets and charms for protection.

In fact, there's an early photograph of Arthur dressed like this, which CJ has seen. Arthur is standing beside the caravan, a Union Jack flapping nearby, with the sackcloth robe and a headband, holding Excalibur up at a jaunty, ceremonious angle. Arthur looks slightly uncertain and his handling of the sword lacks his later confidence. It looks like he is practicing.

Arthur, of course denies this. He may have been uncertain what his role was at this time, but, he says, he never lacked confidence.

Nevertheless, the photograph shows him putting on a brave face.

So Excalibur was housed, and Arthur was dressed. The next pressing requirement was to form the Warband.

This was the vision that possession of the sword had given him. A vision of a circle of comrades all fighting for the same cause. He saw a gathering of the warband at council in a darkened space, lit only by firelight. There were 150 of them, he decided (a figure taken from Malory): 30 kings, 100 knights, 13 Druids and 7 mystics. The round table, as he saw it, consisted of the 150 shields locked together in a circle, their heraldic devices thus appearing 'magically' before each of them as the round table was formed.

The Warband would consist of three categories of knights. Firstly, there would be the Shield Knights, people who came to him remembering, as he did, their once true and former names, and who would therefore be entitled to carry their heraldic shield, ready to begin the formation of the table. Next, there would be the Quest Knights, people who, though convinced of their past, were still on a quest to remember their former names and to claim their heraldic identity. Finally, there would be the Brother Knights, people whose feet were set firmly in the 20th century but who were drawn to the Arthurian values of Truth, Honour and Justice. It was the Brother Knight's quest for a truer, more just, more honourable world, that the ancient knights had awoken to help deliver. The Shield Knights and the Quest Knights – as Arthur himself – had returned, not to press for the reinstitution of their own heroic values, but to be of service to the Brothers in their battle to make a better world.

Actually, you can see Arthur's tidy mind at work here: forging structures out of his imagination, planning, conceiving, struggling to create form. Arthur always did think in threes.

Not that this structure arose over night. It was an organic process, a plan that Arthur conceived almost in retrospect, once he'd begun meeting people and talking to them.

Part of his vision was that bikers were latter-day warriors. It was how he had always felt about himself. Being a biker meant winding up figures of authority just for the sake of it. Being big, bad, wild and outrageous. That was his training, as it were, for his new role, whatever that turned out to be. But it seemed natural to him to want to seek allies in the biker community and it was with this in mind that he put an advert in *Back Street Heroes*, a popular biker's mag.

It read, something like:

> *King Arthur, a biker on a Triumph Chop, living in Somerset, has returned to reunite and reform the table round. He is seeking Knights worthy of the Sword, who feel part of this destiny to fight for Truth, for Honour and for Justice.*

The surprising thing is that anyone answered it. But they did.

The first one to come along was Parcival, known as Parsley.

It began with an exchange of letters. Parsley wrote, and Arthur replied. After that Parsley visited him in the orchard. So there he was, roaring through the rusty iron five-bar gate towards the caravan on his bike. He parked up and dismounted, as Arthur stood on the step, slipping the bike onto its stand. He was wearing shades with a silk scarf about his face. All in leather, trim and muscular, about the same height as Arthur (maybe 5' 8" or 9"). Pulling off his gloves he laid them on the petrol tank. Unwrapping the scarf. Unclipping his helmet, and lifting it off his head with both hands, shaking his head as 3' of neatly tended dreadlocks cascaded about his face.

Well, what had Arthur been expecting? Parsley hadn't mentioned that he was black. Why should he? He also hadn't mentioned that he was a handsome dude, slim built and athletic like a dancer, laid back and stylish, but with a fiery, intense belief system. Or that he was from the East End of London. Or that he was the son of a Seventh Day Adventist minister and a proselytising Christian.

The only thing Arthur knew about him was that he was a biker.

So there you have it. The first of the Shield Knights. Black. Working Class. Christian. An East Ender. A biker. A warrior. A knight.

All of which is self-evidently self-contradictory, and all the more real for that.

They shook hands and went indoors.

Arthur's first meetings with the knights always went like this. Angela would cook a meal. They'd eat. Later they'd go to the pub. There would be a period of scrutiny as the men weighed each other up. Arthur was always scrupulously welcoming. He's a welcoming sort of a person. He'd drink with the drinkers, smoke with the smokers, philosophise with the philosophers. They'd talk about this and that, warming to the various subjects. Mostly the conversations were about what was wrong with the world, and what they would do to change it. As the first evening wore on, whoever it was would start to see the vision. One man's dream is but a dream. But 150 of them sharing the same dream, then it becomes a reality. Something would begin to be forged between them. Something substantial, despite the fact it was only made of mind-stuff. It was palpable. It was real. A bond of brotherhood. In the end there would be an acknowledgement. Yes, you are Arthur. You say I am Arthur? If you say I am Arthur, you must be Parcival. Arthur would never name them himself. They would always name themselves. And then they would go beneath the sword to swear to Truth, Honour and Justice.

Which is how, basically, it happened with Parsley that first time, but with one or two particularities.

Firstly, that Parsley was evangelical the whole time, weaving biblical quotes and references into the conversation, being apocalyptically intense. Secondly, that Parsley was a vegetarian.

'So tell me,' asked Arthur, 'if you are vegetarian, how come you eat fish?'

'Jesus was a fisherman,' replied Parsley in a matter of fact voice. What can you say to that?

Arthur chose not to comment.

So Parsley spent the weekend in the orchard. They talked, they drank, they smoked together. They philosophised. They made plans. They compared notes. They looked into the future. They compared their pasts. They weighed their dreams and named them. They planted seeds of hope for the future. They divined the springs of intellect and took long, refreshing draughts. They made numerous calculations based on tried and tested formulas. They broke wind. They laughed. They visited far-away and exotic places as travellers of the mind. They came back again having learned something new. They became rivals. They became friends.

And when the weekend was over, Arthur gave Parsley his first quest.

He wrote a note and sealed it in red wax, using the Rampant Dragon design on the hilt of the sword, and gave it to Parsley. He told Parsley to go to Farnborough on the way home and to call on Bob, the Manic Mechanic, and Maria. He was to stand on the doorstep and say nothing, then hand them the note.

So that's what he did.

He rode over to Farnborough, and pulled up outside of Bob and Maria's place.

Maria heard the bike and went to the door. She expected it to be someone she knew, one of the Farnborough posse. Only it wasn't. It was Parsley, this handsome black dude. Which only added to the surprise. There aren't that many black bikers. Certainly none at all in Farnborough. And he just stood there silently while he handed her the note. This is what the note said:

> **Arthurian Seal of Authority.**
>
> *This Document introduces Sir Parcival of the Grail, Quest Knight of the Arthurian Warband.*
>
> *Let all Brother Knights, Quest Knights, Fellow Shield Knights and other Knights, Friends of the Warband show this Knight such honour and courtesy, brotherhood and friendship as they would show myself.*
>
> *And let all Ladies show such hospitality to this Knight as they might show me.*
>
> *Let him be fed if he be hungry, given drink if he be thirsty and rested if he be weary.*
>
> *Signed and sealed on this day,*
>
> KING ARTHUR PENDRAGON
REBORN 5.4.54
REX QUANDAM REXQUE FUTURUS.

And Parsley spent the next three days there being seriously entertained.

After Parsley there was Cai, then Balin, then Rex de Winter and after that a whole host more. They were writing to him. He was writing to them. They were coming to visit him. He was going to visit them. He was making contact. He was being acknowledged. And this, of course, was the confirmation of the reality of his office. He wasn't a king in the hereditary sense. He was a king because he was being acknowledged as such. King in the ancient sense, meaning Chief, or Big Man: an office bestowed upon him by the people, by those who gave him credit, an office held by him by force of will, by his willingness to put himself at people's service, by his qualities as a leader. A leader who led, not one who pushed from behind – by his extra large personality, his large laugh and his large spirit, his large sense of his own absurdity. Arthur had all that. The people who came to him were never greeted by pompous ceremonial, but by a man who laughed at himself and who remained all the more convincing because of that.

The process is called triangulation. In order to find an unknown point on the map you need two other points of reference. Three points in all. In terms of his own internal map, Arthur's three points were these. Firstly, that the Whippet had named him. Secondly, that he had found Excalibur. Finally, that he was being acknowledged by others, by people who came to him of their own accord, without prejudice or favour, who identified with what he said and believed from their own points of reference.

Rex de Winter, for example, was a technical author and the editor of a number of books on aeroplane design. In his 50s, with a polished accent, and smartly dressed in a sport's jacket and tie, he was not the sort of person who Arthur had, in the past, associated with. He came through a letter written to the 'Entre Nous' column of the Mensa magazine. It appeared in the following form:

> *With apologies to Arthur Rex*
> *Entre Nous item as received:*
>
> *Can you help? King Arthur has returned reborn 5.4.54. A nomadic biker chieftain and fellow Mensan. He is seeking reincarnated knights and land on which to rebuild Castle Camelot and reform the fellow-ship of the Table Round, ready to sally forth and save the nation when required. Any help appreciated. Arthur Rex.*
>
> ARTHUR PENDRAGON, SOMERSET, ENGLAND.

> **Editor's letter:**
> *Dear Arthur Rex*
> *We have your submission for the 'Entre Nous' column of the*

International Journal *but cannot print it until we also have your correct name. Of course, we are willing to withhold your name from publication if you desire, but we MUST have it on file nevertheless.*

Please let me hear from you again.

Sincerely Mary Jane Stevens.

And from Arthur:

Re: your letter of 28 August, photocopy overleaf, please find enclosed photocopies of my driving licence, UK passport, and Mensa membership card. Please find also for your information a copy of The Latter Day Book of Arthurian Bards.

So you see, I really am whom I claim to be and not some John Doe (to use the American vernacular) and I feel an apology would not go amiss, don't you?

Yours, Arthur Rex

REBORN 5.4.54

REX QUANUM REXQUE FUTURUS

(The documents of Arthur Uther Pendragon's identity are certainly persuasive. And the delightful book has a picture (unreproducible, alas!) of the author on the cover. MJS).

This went out in the international edition of the magazine, and elicited replies from a number of Americans as well as British nationals, many of whom became knights.

The Latter Day Book of Arthurian Bards was a collection of poetry Arthur had begun putting together. It contained poems written by various members of the Warband, including Arthur himself, and was a continually evolving piece of work. Arthur always carried it around with him and as each new member joined, so they would normally submit a poem for inclusion.

The book was their Bible, if you will, their spell book, their CV, their witness, their testament, chapter and verse. Only it was not transcribed by some great and holy prophet or penned by an arcane Druid philosopher. These were their thoughts, their philosophies and their heartfelt dreams in the here and now, and, as with any Round Table activity, it was a joint venture. Everyone contributed to it. It became the focal centre around which the Warband revolved.

Meanwhile Arthur was getting a reputation.

He was also, by now, a Glastonbury fixture.

He would appear in Glastonbury, with the sword, robed up. He would be meeting people atop the Tor. He would be meeting people in the town. He would be meeting people on walks around the luscious Somerset countryside. In pubs. In cafes. People were obviously interested in him. Who wouldn't be? This figure out of the Dark Ages strutting about looking weirdly menacing. He was bound to attract attention.

But, as anyone who knows the town will confirm, Glastonbury is a most peculiar place. If he was Arthur, there was almost certainly at least a half a dozen Arthurs in the town at the same time. And if he was waiting for his Merlin, there were probably quite a few of those about as well. And there were Archangels and Angels and Buddhas and Maitreyas. Maybe a Jesus or two. A multitude of reincarnated witches, warlocks and wizards. And fakirs and fakers and fabulous dreamers, and people in serious need of medical attention. And harmless lunatics and not-so harmless lunatics, and people who just wanted to tend their garden, but who had an obsession with a certain kind of illegal plant. All sorts. That's Glastonbury. A place where strangeness is the norm.

So, on the one hand, Arthur was just another of the Glastonbury crazies, making strange claims about the future of the world. On the other, it was surprising just how many would meet him and go away convinced.

He was making connections all over the country. People would talk to him in Glastonbury and then return home, and a few days later there would be letters from people in whichever town it was, making enquiries. Often they would end up joining the Warband.

One day he was sitting in a café in Glastonbury, drinking coffee. A couple of men came up to him.

'So you think you're Arthur Pendragon, is that right? You're King Arthur?'

'Well, I think so.'

'We've heard that there's another King Arthur in town, claiming to be the real King Arthur.'

'Tell you what,' said Arthur, 'why don't we meet, and then we'll find out who the real King Arthur is.'

So they made the arrangement. It was to be noon the following day, on top of the Tor.

'I've heard that high noon's a good time for a confrontation,' Arthur said.

The following day he was on top of the Tor, with Excalibur, when the other Arthur arrived. He was a hulking American, wearing a poncho, cowboy boots and sunglasses.

'You Arthur Pendragon?' he said, huffily.

'That's right. You King Arthur?'

'That's right. So what makes you think you're Arthur then?'

'Well there's this for a start,' Arthur said, showing him Excalibur.

It was like the Gunfight at the OK Coral. They were staring each other down, waiting for the draw. And then Arthur passed over the *Latter Day Book Of Arthurian Bards*. 'Read this,' he said.

The other Arthur went and sat in the tower of St Michael's Chapel on top of the Tor, and read the book. When he came back he handed it back to Arthur.

'OK, you're right. You're King Arthur,' he said. And he got on his knees and was knighted for Truth, Honour and Justice. As a Quest Knight, as he had yet to find his real name.

And if this story sounds fanciful, let CJ confirm it. He too has witnessed a scene where someone claiming to be King Arthur has met Arthur and not only backed down, but actively embraced the man as the real thing.

It happens all the time. Usually they only have to see the sword to be convinced.

So, that was how he spent his time in the apple orchard in Langport. Meeting people. Making contact. Writing letters. Compiling and getting published a book of poetry. Travelling to all parts of the country to meet interested people. Gathering the Warband about him.

Knights were coming to him from all over the place. From Back Street Heroes and the biker community. (Indeed, he became a news item in the biker press for a while, after the appearance of the advert.) From Mensa. From Farnborough and Aldershot, where some of the old Saddletramps, both inner and outer circle, were being converted. From around and about Glastonbury and, by word of mouth, from all over the country. He had also, by now, contacted the Worshipful Arthurian Society and the Pendragon Society, two groups interested in Arthurian lore.

So weeks turned into months and months turned into years. The apple trees blossomed, grew fruit, were harvested and shed their leaves, once, twice, three times in all. The seasons shifted through their cycle. In the summer months he could sit outside the caravan – when he wasn't doing his labouring work on the farmhouse – and compose letters. There were many letters. At night, sometimes, he would build a bonfire and look into the embers to see what it told him about the future. In the winter, when the rains came and the earth turned to sludge, he would sit indoors with the Calor Gas fire burning while Angela read him passages from Malory, and from other books of Arthurian legend.

It was from one of these books that he learned the significance of St Barnabas' day in the Arthurian myth: 11 June, the day of his name change. Near the site of Arthur's burial in Glastonbury Abbey, he read, 'harde by', as a visitor commented around 1500, there grew a marvel, a walnut tree protected by a wall, which did not come into leaf until St Barnabas' day each year. King Arthur's day.

And so it continued. Moments of magic, portents, signs, mysteries on mysteries, as men and women of all walks of life came to him and bowed beneath the sword, as he laid his plans, and thought his thoughts and dreamed and conspired with the elements; as rains fell, as winds swept clean, as fires burned, as hills and valleys heaved. The world turned. Light became dark became light. Owls hooted like spectral visitors in the trees at night. Bats flitted eerily through the twilight evenings.

Nelson Mandela came out of prison while Arthur was in that apple orchard. The Berlin Wall fell. Mrs Thatcher invented the Poll Tax, much to the disquiet of the British People. There were more attacks upon civil liberties and the trade unions. More public assets were being sold off, at a snip, to any old private bidder. The gap between rich and poor became a gulf, an ocean. Riots flared. Dreams died. The Underclass was invented, as a category, to explain the social divisions. The vision of Old Britain as a sanctuary of kindly virtue, was fading fast. It was a hard-nosed world now, in which the only important thing was money. Society didn't exist. Ideals didn't exist. Arthur didn't exist. There Was No Alternative.

So, while all this was going on, the non-existent Arthur continued, unaware of his non-existence, smoking cigarettes, drinking cider, thinking and dreaming, inventing himself as he went along.

At night he would let Cabal off the lead to roam free, and several of the local working bitches became pregnant by him. One or two of the farmers threatened to shoot him. The only reason they didn't was out of respect for Arthur.

For a while, late at night, he would be awoken by a peculiar shuffling noise beneath the caravan. He had no idea what it was until, late one evening, coming home from the pub, he caught a black-and-white, snuffling form in the headlights of his bike and discovered the source of the sound. His caravan was situated across a badger track and, oblivious to the human presence above them, the badgers were keeping to their customary routes.

Towards the end of their time together, Angela got a job as a checkout girl in a nearby supermarket and would come home exhausted and ratty in the evenings. Is this what being the wife of a king amounted to? They were on the point of splitting up.

And then they did split up. Angela went back to live in Farnborough while Arthur stayed on by himself in the caravan.

It was approaching Beltane 1990. He'd been Arthur for nearly four years now and what had he achieved? He was in possession of Excalibur, of course, and had started raising the Warband. He'd managed to get *The Latter Day Book of Arthurian Bards* privately published, and he'd made contact with all sorts of people, not only in Britain, but in other parts of the world too. He was beginning to make a name for himself. But was it enough? In his private moments, Arthur was always hard on himself. He thought, 'Either I'm for real, or I'm the biggest con going.' Surely there had to be more? Surely there was some greater purpose in all this? Weren't there quests to fulfil and battles to be fought? Was it simply enough to just go around calling himself King Arthur – even if many people were acknowledging him as such – wasn't King Arthur actually supposed to *do* something?

The trouble was, he still had no idea what it was.

Angela was gone and he was on his own.

And then the magic kicked in.

Someone gave him a telephone number. This was on the very same day that Angela left. It was for a man named Rollo Maughfling. That's his real name. He was the head of the Glastonbury Order of Druids. Well, Arthur had heard of the Druids, naturally. He'd attended the Stonehenge festival for years and seen them in their white robes and regalia, doing their sunrise ceremony amidst the stones. And he considered himself something of a wizard, of course, having studied occult matters for years. He knew, too, that the contemporary Druids based their beliefs on what they understood of the ancient Celtic philosophy of wisdom, and that the historical Merlin was renowned as a Druid. Perhaps it was time for the modern-day Arthur to meet the modern-day Druids?

He rang the number and Rollo answered. Arthur introduced himself and Rollo invited him along to the sunrise ceremony on top of the Tor the following morning. It was May Eve. Tomorrow was the first of May, Beltane.

'And bring your sword along,' added Rollo, mysteriously.

So that night Arthur went up to the Tor with Excalibur. It was a typical festival night. Lots of people milling around. A few beers. Travellers turning up in their vans and parking on the road below. People drumming and chanting. Sharing spliffs. Chatting to each other, enjoying each other's company. Some of them were in strange costumes, robes and headdresses and ponchos and gowns. The usual Glastonbury crowd. Arthur was wandering up and down the Tor all night, getting invited into people's vans, being passed beers, taking a swig or two of whatever was on offer. He kept asking people if they were Druids. The answer was always the same. 'No, we're not Druids, but the Druids will be up in the morning.'

So he was waiting for the Druids.

After a while it began to get light. The shadows of night were scurrying towards the far horizon. The sky was painted in magical colour, peach and purple and bright, translucent pink. And then Arthur saw them processing up the Tor, all dressed in white: the Druids. It was a moment of instant recognition. Yes, he knew these people. Not personally. But he recognised their provenance, their mystery.

It was obvious which one was Rollo as he was at the head of the procession. Bearded and slightly balding, with long, dark hair, dressed in the Druid white, but with a black, velvet cloak about his shoulders, a Glastonbury horse brass about his neck, he led the procession to the shoulder of the Tor beyond the tower of St Michael's chapel.

They formed a circle and Arthur joined.

The sun was rising.

A hush descended and Rollo began the proceedings.

Druid ceremonies can take a variety of forms depending on the Order conducting them, but the formula is always fairly similar. First of all there is a call to the four quarters – 'All hail and welcome!' – to the East, to air and to the spirits of the air; to the South, to fire and to the spirits of fire; to the West, to water and to the spirits of water; to the North, to earth and to the spirits of the earth.

Rollo has a resounding, theatrical tone, full of pomp and fire, perfectly suited to this kind of dramatic performance, giving voice to the elemental, seasonal and spiritual nature of the celebration. This was the time of the Beltane fires when people would gather through the night to give welcome to the coming of spring, the season of sexuality and abundance, of the May Dance and the lover's bower, of the secret tryst and the lover's embrace, when lovers meet beneath a May Moon, when young men and their maidens may venture to the woods to collect the May Flower, to meet in secret and to make love. The season of the May, of May hopes, and May dreams, and May loves and May reckonings. Of all this Rollo spoke.

He intoned the Druid Oath, solidly and resonantly, which the circle then echoed.

We swear by peace and love to stand,
Heart to heart and hand in hand.
Mark, oh Spirit, and hear us now,
Confirming this, our sacred vow.

Three times they said it.

He talked about the *I-A-O*, the sacred mantra of the West. He said:

'The "I" represents the sun at spring and autumn equinox, rising due East. The "A" represents the sun rising north-east at summer solstice and south-east at winter solstice. The "O" represents the Earth's passage around the sun, which the ancients knew about. And as this is a nature religion, the "I" also represents the phallus of the solar god, the "A" represents the lovely open legs of the Earth Goddess, and the "O" represents the sound of their cosmic lovemaking, from whence all creatures and all life are born.'

And then he led the circle in the mantic chant, 'I-A-O', the stretched letters blending together in a single syllable which rose and fell about the circle in a vortex of rounded sound.

Arthur was caught up in the proceedings, enjoying the evolved ceremonial in all its high-flown splendour.

He did notice, however, that something was missing. He noticed they were missing a sword.

Rollo was continuing with the ritual. He said, 'At this point we would normally draw the sacred Sword of Albion and declare it Excalibur for a year. Unfortunately, the Sword of Albion is not available, being away on a quest at the moment. However, we are honoured to welcome King Arthur Pendragon into our circle ...'

Arthur suddenly noticed they were looking at him. He was standing there amongst the Druids in their white frocks and regalia, feeling tatty in his leathers and sackcloth – slightly tattier than usual after a night of fierce celebration – and they were all looking at him in silent expectation. What was it they wanted?

Oh yes, the sword. There was no other sword in the circle.

So he drew it instinctively and raised it high, feeling its magic power once again in his hands.

He wasn't quite sure what they were expecting of him.

At that moment the sun came out from behind a cloud and a shaft of sunlight hit the sword like a brand of fire. The sword shattered the sunlight sending prismatic sprays of dazzling colour into the air. It was an explosion of light. Everyone gasped at the sight of it, of this shimmering, intense, brilliant, electric sword burning in the morning sunlight. A shiver went round the circle, as Arthur slipped the sword into its scabbard again.

Rollo continued the rite. They intoned the *I-A-O*. They gave blessing to the May branches they had brought into the circle. They sprinkled water from the Chalice Well. They passed around the circle offerings of bread and mead. They called an Eisteddfod and people read out their poetry or sang. Rollo performed hand-fastings and did blessings. Finally, they closed the circle by calling hail and farewell to the spirits of the four direction and the four elements, and Rollo concluded with three cheers for the festival of Beltane and Glastonbury Tor: 'Hip, hip: hooray! Hip, hip: hooray! Hip, hip: hooray!'

And it was over.

The Druids were gathering about Arthur, chattering wildly. Everyone wanted to talk to him.

'You are Arthur, aren't you? And that's Excalibur.' That was the gist of what everyone was saying.

The significance of that fierce explosion of sunlight was not lost on anyone. Everyone wanted to look at the sword.

When they saw it – when they looked at the inlaid tang, and the pom-mel, and the blade, at the heraldic emblems embossed along the hilt – they were even more convinced. This was Excalibur. This man – with his straggly locks, and his tattered robe, and his crumpled leather, and his full, fighting beard, looking like an unruly tramp on a mad bender – he was a king. He was King Arthur.

'Yes. Looks like a tramp, says he is a king.' That's how Rollo saw it.

The Druids had been calling for Arthur to return for centuries. And now he had.

They were going to have to handle it.

CHAPTER SEVEN

Stonehenge

Every human being carries a myth. It is more than a story, it is more than a fiction, it is the sense of self-identity. It is who we are. It is culture. Without the myth we cannot live. We cannot explain ourselves. The myth is the living culture within us.

In the old times, the myth centred on place: on specific places. The myth made up stories about those places. The places drew people to them. The people were entranced by those places. They gathered. They told each other stories. They span webs of enchantment to explain themselves to each other. It was the places that told the stories. They were the enchanted places, the holy places. The people were made holy by them.

Arthur's story, of course, is that he is Arthur. It is a good story. It is a story of high adventure, connected to certain places, like the old stories. It was told to him in a squat in Farnborough, and then again at Stonehenge, and near Glastonbury in an apple orchard, and on top of Glastonbury Tor. Meeting the Druids helped the story to grow stronger.

The old stories told of gods, but the gods were in the places, not separate from the places. They were the voices of the dead talking. They were the voices of the night. The voices of the mists and the rain. The lonely calling of the raven, riding the air. The whispered voices of the forest wind, the willowing laughter of the forest stream. The roar of the waterfall, the tinkling of the spring. The voices spoke to the people where the stories were strong. In the mountains and the high places the voices raged like angry gales. In the vales of peace the voices were the voices of the plants and the animals. The plants and the animals were like the people.

They also liked to gather. The people loved them and listened to their stories. The stories told of deeds once achieved and deeds yet to be achieved, of the people's birth and rebirth, of the people's place in the fellowship of being.

The Druids, too, tell themselves stories. They tell themselves stories of the old times. They believe themselves to be the representatives of the old philosophers returned. This is also a good story. It is a story of magic, of science and the arts, of learning and of Nature. The Druids have evolved systems of ritual to express their understanding. The Druid ritual is a way of focusing their belief in the old philosophies, in the old truths, and of their place in the modern world.

The people were resourceful. They were builders. They knew the work of the hands. They could carve, they could paint. They built shelter from the coming winds. They knew when the winds would come from the position of the sun in the heavens, from the position of the stars. The knowledge they had gained was greater than the sum of their individual wisdom. They were listening to the Universe and understanding its workings. It was complex and strange. It was hard to remember all of these things. They devised calendars to remind them of the intricate circling of the heavens, and then built them in stone in the places of legend where the stories began. The buildings were circles. The buildings were temples. They were the temples of the heavens. The buildings contained the myth. The buildings were outside and inside. They were inside the circles of the circling heavens, but outside, in the rain.

Rollo Maughfling, the head of the Glastonbury Order of Druids, who Arthur met for the first time that fateful Beltane morning, has a story too. It is a story about the area where he was brought up, on the peninsular of Land's End, a place known locally as West Penwith, associated in legend with the lost lands of Lyonnesse.

Rollo's story is the story of how he became a Druid. How as a child he was taken to Trencrom, how his father carried him on his shoulders through the bracken and the gorse to where the Cornish Druids would meet, every May Eve, to celebrate Beltane. And how in his wild youth he had met John Michell, literary interpreter of the visionary kingdom, and later Alex Sanders, the famous witch, and became his pupil. And how, later again, he was initiated into the 21 years of training required to become a Druid.

This is a metaphorical statement, of course. There are no Druid colleges anymore. His training was self-administered, and like Arthur, like CJ, he was learning on his feet.

Finally, it is the story of his name. It is a very peculiar name. It is derived, says Rollo, from the Maughlin mountain on the west coast of Ireland, and is the Saxon corruption of the old Irish name, which in the Welsh became 'Myrddin', Norman French 'Merlin'. So Rollo's story and Arthur's story correspond. Rollo is Arthur's Merlin.

Arthur's story grew stronger still, as his and Rollo's story combined.

What Arthur didn't know at the time was that, just as he had been waiting for his Merlin, so Rollo too had been waiting for his Arthur. He'd gone to bed the night before that fateful May Eve actually thinking about the matter. Thinking, in fact, that the whole movement to restore access to Stonehenge needed an Arthur as well as a Merlin. And then, the following day, there was a phone call and a cheery voice said, 'Hello, my name's King Arthur!'

Meeting the Druids had a catalytic effect on Arthur. It wasn't only the fact of Rollo's history or his name. It was being accepted by members of an alternative establishment. It was having backing from some source other than his own. The Druids had established themselves over more than two centuries. They had become something of a tourist attraction at Stonehenge, until the banning of the festival, and then the suppression of their own ceremonies in succeeding years. They too were incensed by the lack of access. They were well-known and had at least a degree of official backing. There was an organisation with its own rules, its own procedures. Arthur knew instinctively that he could work with them; or, if not with them exactly, at least around them.

Historically, for the most part they were dilettante antiquarians looking for an alternative to the customs and mores of the Christian Church. Their roots were in the 18th century. They were quaint and eccentric and decidedly from the upper crust – Rollo himself has a distinguished lineage. But they shared Arthur's concerns about the state of the Islands. Their fervent patriotism – like Arthur's – was inclusive, not exclusive. It was welcoming of other cultures and other stories. They too were searching for another kind of Britain than the one that was currently on offer, another kind of myth.

Later, a new Druid type emerged. They were veterans of the old

Stonehenge festival who, much like the bikers, had become entranced by presence of the stones and influenced by them. They were recreating the Druid myth in a new form as an extension of the pagan and traveller movement. They saw themselves as revivalists of the ancient Nature religion of these islands, as Pagan Priests, with a pagan congregation, in the biker and traveller movements.

This was where Rollo came in. Rollo is one of the rock'n'roll Druids, influenced by the festivals.

And isn't there a mystery here, that these old piles of stones can have such an effect? That their message – whatever it is – has carried down the ages, inspiring new generations to join the chorus? They speak of something that went before, before the time of ignorance and stupidity, when the people were like holy scientists, observing the immeasurable Universe with diligence and care, while feeling its immense love for them, as a Mother loves her children. The stones speak of a time, long before history, when the people knew their place in the Universe, not as the centre, but as parts of a greater whole, circling in the circles of the heavens like the eternal stars.

And the people looked to the heavens from beneath the encircling moon. They read the stars and knew them. They understood the heavens by their motion. They devised systems. They knew measure and they knew number. They watched the stars in their eternal course and measured their regulatory flow. They saw the ebb and flow of the Universe. They heard the music of the spheres.

All of this knowledge is writ in stone in the ancient monument we know as Stonehenge.

Arthur was still living in the caravan in the apple orchard in Langport at this time and, true to his restless nature, he began a new round of recruitment in another pub. It was called the Rose and Crown, more popularly known as 'Eli's' after a former landlord. The new band were the regulars at the pub, mainly artisans in the local community. It was there he met a jeweller who made his iron circlet (for strength) and a saddler who made him a new leather scabbard, replete with a copy of the cross supposedly found above Arthur's grave in Glastonbury. The old scabbard was burned and, with due ceremony, its ashes placed inside the new one.

Meanwhile, Rollo had been negotiating with English Heritage (a government organisation charged with the preservation of heritage buildings) about access to Stonehenge for all members of the public for the autumn equinox ceremony in September that year. He invited Arthur and the Warband along to act as stewards. English Heritage (or 'English Heretics', as Arthur liked to call them) were being evasive. They wouldn't give a straight, 'yes' to the prospect, but they wouldn't give a simple 'no' either. They were dangling the Druids on a string. It was always 'maybe next time …' But it never was. Consequently, Arthur and the Druids arrived at Stonehenge for the equinox, only to find that everyone was being denied admittance.

This was also to be the first official gathering of the entire Warband, Arthur having called them together for the occasion.

The rituals are always carried out at dawn. People arrive the night before, or during the night, and park up in the droves near the monument, where they while the time away, drinking and chatting or warming themselves by their wood-burning stoves, much as the Old People would have done. It was the same this night. Arthur arrived and Rollo introduced him to another Druid, Tim Sebastian, Archdruid of the Secular Order of Druids. Tim was an old rock and roller, who had been in a 70s concept band called Gryphon and who had also, like Arthur, attended many of the festivals. In fact, Tim remembered Arthur from his pre-Arthur days as John the Hat, roaring out of one particular festival at the head of a huge V-formation of bikes. It was at Stonehenge-in-exile at Westbury, near the Westbury White Horse, the same year as the Battle of the Beanfield. It was a memorable sight. They were like the barbarian hordes, Tim thought. Arthur told him that, in fact, they had been arrested and that John was leading them off site in a dignified retreat.

It was a misty, damp, cold September dawn when they tried to get access to the stones. Of course, they were denied. Some of them leapt the fence, using the Hele Stone as cover, and gathered inside the stones. Later, some of those inside the fence joined hands with those outside. They formed a circle around the Hele Stone, over which the sun rises on Summer Solstice, holding hands through the fence and chanting and, according to Arthur, the fence disappeared. Not metaphorically: actually. By collective will they made the fence disappear. After that they were evicted from the site and everyone went their separate ways. It was a minor symbolic victory.

But to Arthur it wasn't enough. Not nearly enough. There was a new fire burning within him. He was incensed at their treatment by English Heritage. Incensed at the lack of access. Incensed by their summary dismissal, as if they were nothing, as if their views didn't count. This was their monument, their temple. It belonged to the people of Britain – to the stars, to the Earth – not to some unaccountable government body whose only motivation was to fleece the tourists and make money. And what else was it for if not to remind us of our heritage, to remind us of our past, to give shape to our thoughts, as a focal point in history? What other purpose could it possibly serve, if not as a gathering point at these sacred times of the year, to mark off the seasons in their turning, to remind us of who we are?

Who made these stones? Who put them here? Whose art put them together? Whose observations of the stars laid them out in this exact formation? Whose labour brought them across such immense distances? Whose skill, whose knowledge, whose intelligence? Whose mind was it that could conceive and execute such a task?

Was it English Heritage? Or the British Government?

Who were we back then, when Stonehenge was built? How did we dress? What were our customs and our laws? To which gods and goddesses did we pray? What were our industries? Did we make art? Did we sing? Did we dance? Did we celebrate our lives in poetry and prayer? Were we generous to our neighbours? Did we wake at dawn to the thrilling of the lark? Did our hearts thrill too and rise singing into the air? Did we embrace our friends when we saw them? Did we drink a toast to those we had lost and invite them to our memories? Did we call upon the ancestors to commune with us? Did we share our thoughts? Did we share our dreams? Did we share our food? Did we share our lives with the whole of creation? Did we laugh loudly at our own jokes? Did we love our folk with fierce intensity? Did we call down the stars in our ecstasy? Did we stand firm in the heat of battle? Did we love our children and teach them? Did we love the chase and the hunt? Did we train the hawk and the dog? Did our hearts too chase laughing after them across the wild, restless plain? And in the forest and the glade, would we momentarily stop in our travels to give thanks to the Earth that made us, for our lives, for our souls, for our bones and for our blood? Were we rich then or were we poor? Were we free people or slaves? Did we read the stars and name them? Did we explore the alchemy of thought in the temple of the sky?

Did we align the monuments in the sacred landscape to give substance to our dreams?

How many days have gone by since this monument was raised? How many nights has it stood here, on this dark plain, contemplating our ways? The stones are our grandfathers. They belong to no one or they belong to everyone. No one has the right to claim them as their own.

So, King Arthur had his cause at last. He had a battle worthy of his name. He was going to free the stones for the Druids and the free people of the Earth. He was going to gain complete public access for the quarterly festivals for which these stones had been laid. He was going to institute public ceremony here again for everyone to enjoy.

He had a cat-in-hell's chance. He was taking on the full might of the British Establishment, the Law, the Police, the Judiciary, the Government, the wealthy landowners of Wiltshire.

He decided to put his trust in the goddess and come out fighting.

He set up what has since become called 'the Stonehenge Picket'.

He moved out of the caravan, giving up his job and all hope of an income, and with his brother-in-law Chesh's help, set up a camp about two miles from Stonehenge in a small wood. The camp consisted of a tarpaulin draped over a hollow formed by a fallen tree, with a hammock slung between the roots of the tree and the trunk of a living one. That was it. His new home.

When we say that he was putting his trust in the goddess, it is meant to be taken literally. He'd left the caravan in the same way he'd left his home and his mortgage in a previous existence: just as it was, with cups and saucers and plates and books, a radio and a TV, with food in the cupboard and milk in the fridge, with the remains of his last night's washing up in the sink, with a dustpan full of dust, a half-empty sugar bowl and a half-full ashtray. He had no money, no cigarettes, no food. He refused to take any money from the State. And every day he would walk over to Stonehenge and stand outside the entrance to the tunnel with a picture frame in which was written, 'Don't Pay, Walk Away'. He was encouraging people to view the monument from the road rather than pay English Heritage for the privilege of being allowed entry and then being herded around like a flock of sheep, with the monument roped-off at a respectable distance. He was doing this on behalf of the Council of British Druid Orders, the Arthurian Warband and the Free Peoples of

Britain. And he stood there, day after day, week-in week-out, through rains, through mists, through the lonely, cold winter, stubborn as a rock, like one of the stones in the monument, impenetrable, inert, his mind solidly fixed upon the goal. That was his life. Rising damp and cold in the morning mist, and falling from his hammock. Wrapping his cloak around him. Strapping on Excalibur. Placing the heavy iron circlet like a cold weight upon his brow. Breakfasting on stale bread left over from the day before, and rainwater from the roof. Walking to Stonehenge and just standing there. He asked nothing. He refused nothing. People would offer him sandwiches or the occasional cup of coffee and he would accept them. People would ask to be photographed beside him and he would allow it. He would answer questions when asked. But he didn't impose himself, nor shout slogans. He just stood. And then, in the evening, once the monument had been closed, he would trudge his way back to his lit-tle camp and light a fire in the spluttering fire bucket in an attempt to dry out his clothes, dodging the swirls of abrasive smoke which eddied and plumed in the heavy air, listening to the patter of rain on the tarpaulin, before falling into his hammock, exhausted, to sleep.

It was a dismal, wet winter that year. It rained and it rained. And Arthur stood his stubborn ground, a carved sentinel, proud and immobile, full of concentrated effort, spurning the elements. The lady in the English Heritage café took a shine to him and would bring him cups of hot, sweet coffee to keep his embattled spirits alive. Until English Heritage warned her off, that is, and told her to stop giving him sustenance. She ignored them, of course, and Arthur always got his cup of coffee, no matter what English Heritage thought. And occasionally people would visit him from Farnborough or Glastonbury and bring him presents of candles and ciga-rettes, and while away an hour or two with him, bringing him the news or the latest gossip before leaving him for the comfort of their own fireside. And he stood, like a guard, to attention, through the blistering winds, bringing stinging sprays of rain like hard sharp darts across the bitter plain. And he stood, this foolish man, with a heart so fierce it raged against the elements and all that they could throw at him.

What chance did English Heritage have against such resolve? Those cosseted people in their central-heated offices, with their paper work and their plans, with their tidy minds and their tidy lifestyles, who thought that when Stonehenge had been given to the Nation, it meant that it had been given to them.

They threatened to take out an injunction against him, to remove him from their property.

In order to deliver the message, they sent someone down from head office in London. It was Brian K Davidson, Chief Archaeologist West Country. He told Arthur that he'd earned the nickname Mordred for his role. He had a deal to offer Arthur. He told him that English Heritage would let him use one of their castles – Tintagel was mentioned – if Arthur would only leave Stonehenge, but that if he refused they were going to take out an injunction against him. Arthur didn't have to think. He rejected their offer.

Afterwards, he blagged a lift as far as Farnborough on Brian's journey back to London and on the way they had an interesting discussion. In later years, after his retirement, Brian was seen at an Avebury ritual, and in 1999 his immediate supervisor at the time was also seen being dragged out of Stonehenge by the police. Arthur says it illustrates how grey battle lines are when they're drawn, and it goes to show what he always says: there's no them and us, they are only us who don't know it yet.

Arthur told Brian to pass the message on: that if he were moved he would merely continue his vigil by the roadside.

They dropped the injunction.

And so it went. Days, weeks, months. Rains, mists, hail and snow. Damp mornings and cold evenings. The sizzling of the fire, the spluttering of the candle. The moon in the trees. The raven's caw. The icy winds blowing. The branches of the trees creaking like aching bones in the night.

Occasionally, friends would arrive and 'Kingnap' him, taking him to Farnborough or Glastonbury for the evening, for a meal and a bath and the stinging taste of cider.

Once, an American ticket tout for the Grateful Dead drove him 50 miles to Farnborough for a good night's sleep, and then the 50 miles back again in the morning so he could continue with his picket.

And then there was Arthur's first appearance in the press during this time, in the *Salisbury Journal*, 1990:

ARTHUR MAKES A POINTED PROTEST

ran the headline. Followed by:

A colourful protester claiming to be a reincarnated knight of King Arthur's Round Table has mounted a one man picket at Stonehenge.

Arthur Pendragon left his job as a builder to start his peaceful protest outside the entrance to the ancient monument on Friday.

'I will stay here for ever and ever until they open the Stones for the Equinoxes and Solstices,' he declared.

Dressed in robes and standing beside his own version of the Sword of Excalibur he passes the time shouting, 'Don't pay, go away', at bemused tourists.

'They shouldn't pay because the Stones should be free. Their money just lines the coffers of English Heritage,' he told the Journal.

Arthur is one of 150 biker Knights from the Arthurian Warband, who believe they once served the legendary King Arthur.

'It is not just my protest. I am also representing the Grand Council of British Druid Orders and the common people who want free access to the Stones for worship', he said.

Archdruid from Glastonbury Abbey, Rollo Maughfling, helped Arthur on his first day by talking to tourists and collecting signatures for a petition.

On one occasion, someone gave him a five-pound note saying, 'Get yourself a drink.' He resolved to do just that. So bedraggled, sworded, robed and wet, he walked into Amesbury, the nearest town, and entered the first drinking establishment en route. It was a British Legion Club.

The doorman looked at him slightly puzzled, wondering who on earth this wild creature could be. 'Sorry mate: members only,' he said.

'I thought the British Legion was set up for ex-service men?' said Arthur.

'That's right,' the doorman said.

'Private 24341883 Rothwell, 1st Battalion Royal Hampshire Regiment!' he barked in reply, standing to attention and giving a sharp salute. He was asked to wait there.

The doorman returned with the Chairman, who looked Arthur over, laughing, and said, 'Well, as one infantryman to another, I'll sign you in as my guest.'

So, Arthur entered the British Legion Club and went to the bar for a drink. There was already a drink waiting for him. He poured that down his throat in greedy gulps (how long was it since his last drink?) while people gathered around, asking questions. He was already a celebrity after the *Salisbury Journal* article and other articles in the local press. Everyone wanted to know him.

'So you're King Arthur are you?'

'Well, I think so.'

'So what makes you think you're King Arthur?'

And he'd tell them the story.

Someone took his cloak and hung it over the radiator to dry and, before he'd finished his first pint, there was another waiting for him.

Someone came up to him. 'Are you hungry?' he said.

'Er ... Just a little bit,' said Arthur, understating his case by at least three miles.

And they sent out for fish and chips.

It was his first hot meal in more than a month.

And they kept plying him with drinks and questions, with ribald commentary and laughs, with comments on his dress and support for his stance, with observations about Stonehenge and about the Druids (who, they said, they'd been welcoming to this town for many years), with memories of the festival, both good and bad (the off-license did very well, they said, while the supermarket suffered some losses), and of the police presence in the town (it was in a state of siege over the solstice period, they said, people could hardly get in and out of their own homes), with complaints about civvy life and fond reminiscences about army life, and it was all that Arthur could do to spend his five pounds. He made his way, zigzagging through the night at closing time, back to his little camp, where he flopped into his hammock, weary, drunk, but proud.

Even in the midst of battle there are times of great joy. Indeed, in the midst of battle the joy is seen for what it is – sheer normality, the ordinariness of everyday existence – and is all the more poignant, more special, more memorable for that.

But this was a strange kind of battle: one befitting the superficiality of 20th-century life. There he was, day after day, positioned before the turnstiles at English Heritage's entrance to the site, and his main activity, aside from stamping his feet to keep out the cold, was to pose for photographs. He must have had a thousand photographs taken while he was there, either of just himself or posed with the family of the Japanese tourists –

who had absolutely no idea of who he was or why he was there. Most of them thought he'd been provided by English Heritage for this precise purpose: to be photographed. He was like one of the guardsmen in front of Buckingham Palace: a little bit of quaint English colour in the midst of the grey English landscape. And all over the world there are photographs of King Arthur in family albums. King Arthur leaning on his staff. King Arthur smiling broadly surrounded by diminutive Japanese teenagers. King Arthur with the head of the household, looking suitably heroic. King Arthur holding up his placard saying, 'Don't Pay, Walk Away.' King Arthur brandishing Excalibur. King Arthur, the legend. King Arthur, the man. King Arthur, the myth made real.

And in every photograph there was a raven too, as there was always one perched on the fence behind him, giving the photographer the evil eye.

In this time, Arthur came down from his running weight to under 10 stone. He remained at his vigil from September 1990 till the middle of January 1991. While he was there, Margaret Thatcher fled from office in a welter of tears to be replaced by John Major, Saddam Hussein invaded Kuwait, and Britain fought a war. In the end, a friend of his sister decided that he had had enough and that he should come home with her to Farnborough and commute the distance to the picket. In order to do this he had to ask permission of the Hampshire Constabulary to carry Excalibur to and fro between Stonehenge and Farnborough. Permission was duly granted in the form of a letter which Arthur carries to this day (as he does a number of letters from other Constabularies, obtained in succeeding years, also giving him specific permission to travel with Excalibur across specific counties to specific destinations).

So it was that the Stonehenge picket ground to an unsteady halt. There were other more pressing matters to command his attention.

However, this was not the end of the battle for Stonehenge. Only another 10 years to go to complete that quest.

CHAPTER EIGHT

THIRD QUEST:

Summer Solstice

T he third time CJ tried to meet with King Arthur he came within three doors of him, but they were still unable to speak. He was three doors down in the cells at Salisbury police station. Both of them had been arrested.

CJ had a specific arrangement to meet Arthur at 9.00pm on the evening before the Mid-Summer Solstice 1996, near the Hele Stone at Stonehenge. Unfortunately, the Home Secretary, Michael Howard had placed a four-and-a-half mile exclusion zone around the monument. CJ asked one of the policemen on the cordon why he wasn't allowed entry. 'It's the Solstice,' the policeman said, 'very important. Tomorrow the sun rises over the Hele Stone. If you go in there you will automatically be arrested.' It seemed as if the police were buying all the hippie rhetoric about Stonehenge and the Solstice. That policeman was doing a propaganda job for them.

CJ drove into Amesbury and found the pub where all the hippies were. There were several girls with bare midriffs dancing enthusiastically to Bob Marley's 'Stand Up For Your Rights'. Other people were lounging around on the floor, leaning against their sleeping bags. It was like a scene from the early 70s. There was a minor amount of drug dealing going on. CJ was in the toilets and someone was rolling a joint. A straight-looking, beefy man in shorts entered. The guy rolling the joint said, 'I hope you don't mind.' The man in shorts laughed. 'Not if you give me a smoke,' he said. He was a lorry driver. They spent the next ten minutes sharing the spliff and comparing notes.

Later, they were all preparing to march to Stonehenge. CJ was ranting by now. He had this clear picture in his head, of Stonehenge as a kind of cosmic switch. It had been laid down by the Ancients, he thought, to denote the moment when left-brain consciousness gave way to right-brain consciousness. He was absolutely clear on this point. The human brain is a consciousness-receiver and Stonehenge is the transmitter. He had to be there. This was the kind of thing he was saying to the policemen on the cordon when he arrived. So, it's no wonder he was arrested really. He was arrested for talking New Age gobbledegook.

To be fair to the coppers, they gave him ample opportunity to turn round and go back. It was when he tried to march through that they arrested him. They wrenched his hands behind his back and clamped on the handcuffs. This was extremely painful. They have these new plastic handcuffs, not so much instruments of restraint as weapons of torture. Once they were on, CJ was unable to move. Every time he moved, they got tighter. After that, every policeman who gave him a hand was his best friend, rather than an oppressor as he'd seen them as before.

He was taken to Salisbury police station where the handcuffs were removed. He shook his hands in relief. One of his thumbs had gone numb. He started arguing with the Desk Sergeant. There was a piece of recording equipment, obviously used for doing interviews, behind the Desk Sergeant's desk. It had the letters CJS and some numbers written on it, as some form of code. This seemed highly relevant. It was all part of his quest. Even the random numbers on a piece of police equipment contained a special meaning. Eventually he was put into a cell. There was a young man with blond hair and an older guy who told CJ his name was Henghist McStone. It was an alias. Obviously a reference to the monument itself. CJ said, 'Henghist, that's a Saxon name, isn't it?' It seemed amusing that a man with a Saxon name should be going along with all this Celtic Knight stuff. CJ was told that Arthur was in the building, but that he couldn't see him. But there was someone in the next-door cell calling himself Galahad. He had large, soft brown eyes. He made a good Galahad. CJ and Galahad chatted through the iron grating. Galahad said that Arthur and the others had been arrested for loitering by the roadside.

Later, a number of them were taken back to Amesbury police station. CJ spoke to one of the coppers accompanying them. He said, 'Isn't this a waste of money? Wouldn't you be better looking for paedophiles?'

The policeman admitted that, yes, the money being spent on this would be better off spent on catching paedophiles. But he was under orders, he said. He was only doing his job.

Finally, they were thrown out of the police station at dawn the following day. 'We no longer consider that there is any risk of a breach of the peace,' they were told. CJ came out to find Galahad and another man, clasping their staves and looking vulnerable in the early grey light. He offered them a lift. 'We're waiting for our mates,' they said. CJ was feeling too frazzled and hungover to wait around. He said his goodbyes and left.

But it struck him once again the symbolic resonance of this monument. Why else would the police go to all this trouble to stop a few hippies from going there? Stonehenge is like a magnet for all the weird and wonderful cults on the planet. But it has another meaning too. It was built by nomadic tribes, and it was always a place of celebration. There are people who claim that the monument is the Heart of Britain. Maybe that's just rhetoric. But the sight of Stonehenge on that solstice morning, still guarded by policemen with helmets and shields, wreathed about with fences and strangled with barbed wire, strung up like a wild animal in a trap. If it is the heart, CJ thought, then it is a sorry symbol for the state of Britain today.

CHAPTER NINE

Druid Law

I t was after the Stonehenge picket that Arthur decided that he was a Druid.

He didn't decide to become a Druid. He decided he already was one.

Not a learned Druid. Not an academic Druid. Not an antiquarian Druid. A natural one. A biker Druid.

It was after a conversation with one of Tim Sebastian's friends from the Secular Order of Druids that it came to him. He was talking about the Stonehenge picket, how he'd slept in that hollow between the live tree and the dead tree, when this person had said, 'You're more of a Druid than I am.'

'Yes, I am,' agreed Arthur. Of course he was a Druid. It was perfectly clear. But he wasn't just talking Druidry. It wasn't an academic exercise for him. He was living it, every day of his life. This was a new kind of Druidry. Warrior Druidry. Druidry with energy and verve. Druidry with a mission, not to pontificate about the meaning of Stonehenge, but to fight for it. So he set about turning the Warband into a Druid Order.

Now, what to call it?

Rollo's order was called the Glastonbury Order of Druids. The GODs. Tim's order (with tongue planted firmly in cheek) was called the Secular Order of Druids. The SODs. So it was a question of God's Law or Sod's Law. Either would do. And Arthur simply added an L to make the point clear. He changed the name from the Arthurian Warband to the Loyal Arthurian Warband. The LAW.

Later he would put the name to good use, using the LAW to challenge the Law. And if anyone asked why he was doing what he was doing, he had a stock reply, 'I'm doing it in the name of the LAW.'

And there was a serious point in all this, too, because Arthur felt – now more than ever before – that he was subject to a higher law than the law of the land. Even when he was making these changes, the British Government were instituting laws of their own. The so-called 'Community Charge' was one of these. Better known as the Poll Tax, it was a tax on being poor or on being itinerant. The Government knew well that the overall effect – aside from being a regressive tax, burdening those less well off and rewarding the better off – would be to disenfranchise whole groups of people. The tax was based on the poll register. If you registered to vote, you got a Poll Tax bill. So people refrained from putting themselves on the register for fear of being landed with a bill they could ill-afford to pay. The people who fell off the register were generally the poor people or people who had opted out of the consumer society. The people Margaret Thatcher (or one of her tribe) had called 'medieval brigands'. The traveller community. The people Arthur considered were, if not his congregation, then his constituency at least.

So Arthur decided: firstly to register to vote, then to refuse to pay.

His argument would be that he was an impecunious mendicant: a renunciate. Which was perfectly true, of course. He no longer worked in the ordinary sense, but was now a full-time Arthur, dedicated to the cause. He took no money from the state or from traditional labour, but relied on the goodwill of others. In other words, if he was an effective Arthur, an Arthur that other people could believe in – if he acted as Arthur should act, if he lived up to his name, if he gave as good as he got, if he provided people with effective leadership – then he got food in his belly and cider to drink. If he was no good, he would go hungry. He was trusting in the goddess once more. You can therefore measure Arthur's effectiveness by his waistline. The way CJ sees it, it has to be at least 40 inches and growing all the time. That's 40 inches of Arthurian effectiveness.

Eventually, having failed to seek Judicial Review in the High Court over his Poll Tax stance, he was brought up before the magistrates court for refusal to pay.

By now the Poll Tax had been abandoned for another, slightly less controversial mechanism. But they were still pursuing non-payers with all the relentless enthusiasm of predatory birds.

Thus it was that Arthur found himself standing before Viscount Lord Tenby, a Peer of the Realm and the second son of a former Prime Minister, who was so enamoured of our King that he not only allowed Arthur to wear his sword in the dock, but also allowed him to swear his oath upon it, using it as a substitute for the Bible. Another precedence. Nevertheless, Lord Tenby instructed the court to find Arthur guilty. Arthur then proceeded to pay his Poll Tax bill using money he had won in a private action he had brought against Wiltshire police for wrongful arrest and unlawful imprisonment.

So, the police paid his Poll Tax for him and he was still able to claim mendicant status.

And, having registered to vote, but having no one to vote for, there was another obvious next step.

Who else could he have faith in? Who else was worthy of his vote?

There was no one but himself.

He registered himself as a candidate in the forthcoming local elections in Aldershot. He won 160 votes that first time, a figure which has increased steadily in the years he has continued to stand in elections.

Meanwhile, at the instigation of Rollo and Tim, he was introduced to the Council of British Druid Orders. (CoBDO).

This august body had been set up in the late 80s with the specific aim of freeing Stonehenge for public ritual on the quarterly dates which, as a monument, it was built to commemorate: the Solstices and the Equinoxes. Rollo and Tim were two of the founder members, the others being the Order of Bards, Ovates and Druids, and the Ancient Order of Druids. You can imagine Arthur's first introduction to them. Most of them would have looked at him askance. Well, they were sane people, weren't they, despite the eccentricity of wanting to call themselves Druids. And who was this man, this upstart, trying to pretend he was King Arthur? Was he mad? Or just stark, raving bonkers? It's a natural enough response. It's the same response, we imagine, most sane people would have, including many of you holding this book. It's a response that is shared by both of the authors. Both of us think he's a lunatic (meaning, maybe, influenced by the moon) even though one of the authors happens to be King Arthur himself. What do you expect?

It usually takes meeting the man before people are convinced. CJ has long given up the attempt to disentangle the various threads of argument that have led him to this conclusion, which, interestingly enough, is the same as Arthur's. If we have to have an Arthur – a champion, in other words, someone willing to fight for Truth, Honour and Justice (and in these times of crisis, god knows, we need one) – then this is the best Arthur we've got. Arthur himself agrees and adds that if another Arthur turns up who can do the job better than him, then he'd be happy to hand over the reins. Why burden himself with all the unnecessary worry?

So, the Council of British Druid Orders looked at him askance but, being proposed by two of its founder members, reluctantly agreed to allow him entry.

He stayed quiet for the first year. He was proposed and then accepted. He was as quiet and polite as a little dormouse. He minded his Ps and Qs. He may have looked like a ruffian – like a big, bad biker dude in a sackcloth robe – but he wasn't at all offensive. They were nice people at CoBDO and Arthur was nice to them. No one (except, maybe Tim and Rollo) knew what to expect.

It was at this first CoBDO meeting that Arthur met Liz Murray, the author of the *Celtic Tree Oracle*. She was one of the prime movers in the organisation. After the meeting they went to the pub where Liz quizzed Arthur on his views, about the LAW and about what he hoped to achieve. It was the beginning of a lasting friendship.

It was also around this time that Arthur began accumulating the titles of which he is justly proud. He has – to use his own words once more – 'shed loads of titles'.

The first came from Rollo. Arthur was awarded the title 'Honoured Pendragon' of the Glastonbury Order of Druids. Not to be outflanked, Tim Sebastian decided he needed Arthur's continuing support and gave him the title 'Official Swordbearer' of the Secular Order of Druids. This was also, of course, because swords are hard to come by (not to mention, expensive) and Tim hadn't got access to one. Druid rituals usually require that there is at least one sword present and Arthur's sword was definitely the best one going. After that, Arthur decided that he should reward himself with a title too. So he became the 'Titular Head and Chosen Chief' of the Loyal Arthurian Warband.

There were many more titles to come later.

It was 1991, six years now since the banning of the Stonehenge festival and the imposition of the so-called exclusion zone. The exclusion zone was obviously an attack on the British People's human rights, to travel freely about their own country, to assemble freely where they liked and to worship freely at sacred sites of their own choosing.

Every year around the solstice period thousands of police were drafted in from around the country to stop people gaining admission to their temple. The exclusion zone was supposed to cover an area of four miles radius around the monument and to last four days. In effect, it did neither. People drove up and down the A303 within a few hundred yards of the monument and the police left them alone. And tourists were allowed to visit the monument (provided they paid the entrance fee). But on the solstice eve itself, no one – except police and security personnel – were allowed access. Vast amounts of public money was being spent, year in and year out, trying to stop the public from assembling in a public place. It was Arthur's plan to challenge this on every level.

Every year the police would gather, a blue-uniformed tribe, and face the rainbow tribes of hippies and punks and bikers and pagans and wizards and witches and tatty eccentrics in a variety of costumes, with a mixture of colourful and disorientating hairdos, with tribal tattoos and jewellery like Christmas tree decorations, and a variety of differing approaches to the question of personal hygiene.

Every year, marches would set out from London and from Glastonbury to walk across country to the site.

People would turn up from all directions and by every means of transport. Colourful hippie buses, vans, lorries, cars, diesel taxis, public transport, by bike and on foot. They would arrive during the day and throughout the night. The police would stop the obvious ones and warn them. People would be told that if they proceeded any further, they were liable to arrest. Some people would get themselves arrested, while others turned back to try a different route. A number of people would arrive in Amesbury on the evening before and go down to the pub. The favourite pub was the George. They would guzzle down a few drinks until closing time and then make their way by a variety of routes towards the monument. Eventually they would find themselves confronted by the police and then they had to choose whether to allow themselves to be arrested or not.

Arthur always chose to get arrested.

He would walk up to the police cordon – usually within sight of the stones – and hear the warning. He would be told that if he continued towards the stones that it would be considered a possible breach of the peace and that he would be arrested. He would listen in a polite and reasonable manner before informing the police officer of his intention to proceed, and then step over the line, at which point he would be arrested. He would be handcuffed and taken to Salisbury police station, to the cells, where he would remain the night, chatting to whoever else had been arrested, before being thrown out after dawn, when the police considered there was no longer any likelihood of a breach of the peace. Year by year this continued. Every year, solstice on solstice, this was his ritual. It was Arthur's personal religious observance at this sacred time of the year, practiced in the monastic cells of Salisbury police station: his own private sacrifice to the goddess. And he was always in good company. There was always a laugh going on in the cells. The Desk Sergeant got to know him personally and would always laugh when he saw him. 'Oh, it's you again Arthur, surprise, surprise!' And they'd banter about this and that. 'Isn't it about time you gave up on this Arthur? You're never going to win you know.'

'You wait and see whether I'm going to win or not!'

That particular year Arthur and four other members of the Warband set out from Farnborough the night before the solstice. They got as far as a police roadblock in sight of the stones, manned by Hampshire constabulary (who knew Arthur well, of course), where they were told that if they did not leave the exclusion zone immediately they would be liable to arrest. The police considered them a procession, they were told: two or more people constituting a procession under British law. Arthur argued that they weren't, in fact, a procession, but a picnic. He even showed the police officers their sandwiches and flasks of tea to prove the case. He said they merely wanted to wait as near as legally possible to the stones, until the sunrise, when they would eat their sandwiches and leave. The police officers were a little nonplussed by this. What was a procession, and what was a picnic? Did their powers extend to banning picnics? Were there specific provisions in the law allowing them to detain people in possession of cooked meats and sliced bread? And what about mustard? Did mustard constitute a potentially dangerous weapon? It was all very confusing. The Hampshire police called in the Wiltshire police, this being their patch, to help sort out the confusion. When was a procession not a procession? When it was a picnic, of course.

So the Wiltshire police took over. Again, Arthur argued that they were legally entitled to hold a picnic here, and the Wiltshire police scratched their heads and wondered. They called over the Yorkshire police and the Yorkshire police called over the West Mercia police. There was a gaggle of various policemen from various police forces standing round trying to work out whether a picnic constituted a procession or not. Eventually, the Deputy Chief Constable of Wiltshire Constabulary joined in the fray. Again Arthur stood his ground and argued that they were a picnic. 'So tell me,' he said, 'since when was picnicking illegal under British law?'

But the Deputy Chief Constable was having none of it.

He ordered their arrest.

The police had requisitioned a disused army barracks for processing their willing captives. And it was in the echoing confines of the barracks that Arthur made his executive decision that would stand as custom for most future arrests. The other members of the Warband agreed to leave the exclusion zone and were escorted away without charges being brought against them. Arthur, for his part, steadfastly refused and stated his intention of returning to Stonehenge. The Wiltshire police transferred him to the police cells where he was kept over night, before being released after sunrise without charges. This is how it continued, year after year, with occasional variations, Arthur's ritual having to be matched by another ritual by the Wiltshire constabulary. It was a kind of game, or dance, in which each of Arthur's moves would be generously answered by another move by the police. All Arthur was asking for was to have his case brought before the court so that they could test the legality of their position. The police, on the other hand, were studiously avoiding this possibility, British courts being notoriously unpredictable.

It was always Arthur's strategy that he would use the LAW to challenge the Law. He thought, 'Where else should the battle for freedom be fought, except in the English courts of law?'

The following year he set up the Dragon Quest to highlight the cause. While he was busy observing his ritual containment at the hands of the Wiltshire constabulary, several of the knights set out to capture a dragon.

They were Lucan, Dagonet, Guy the Rant and Marcus the Black.

The only question was, where to find the dragon?

Dragons had been somewhat in short supply around these Islands ever since a certain St George, a freelance dragon slayer and all-round good guy, had run through a particularly unpleasant member of the species with his trusty sword, somewhere at the back end of the dark middle ages. After that, the dragons had all retired. They'd said, 'Well, if the human race is going to be so uppity about this, then we're not going to play any more.' And they'd all trooped off to a central-heated Dragon Retirement Home just off the coast of Greenland, where they spent most of their time drinking Cinzano and lemonade out of tall glasses and reminiscing about tasty virgins they had consumed.

There weren't that many dragons available for capture, in other words.

Meanwhile, there was a new fashion in early morning TV weather reporting.

Weather reports are notoriously boring. Some bloke points to a chart with little pictures of glowing suns or grey clouds with drops of rain as icons of the weather and explains what's going to be happening in this, this or this part of the country. Usually people get up to make a cup of tea.

So Granada, makers of the *This Morning!* TV programme, with studios in the Lancashire region, had a good idea. They thought, 'Why not brighten up the weather forecast, and give the forecaster some much needed exercise at the same time?'

Instead of a little map with little pictures all over it, they built a copy of the British Isles, and floated it in the Mersey docks in Liverpool, near the studios. It was covered in green felt (or painted green at least) to show what a green and pleasant land this was. The idea was that the weather reporter would leap about on the floating island, waving his arms about to denote the various kinds of weather. He'd stand in the upper parts of the bobbing model, say, and tell the viewers about the weather in Scotland, being very animated as the embodiment of the weather in those parts. And he would leap from place to place, spinning his arms like windmill sails to make his point. It was all very exciting. He was the domesticated god of his own captive Isle, rousing up storms with his gesticulating hands, condemning the tiny inhabitants to whatever shades of weather his caprice elected.

The high point came when he had to make the leap over to Northern Ireland, risking death by drowning as he did so. The executives at Granada TV were very happy with this. At least, now, he was earning his money, they thought. And, to denote where, exactly on the island he was (just in case the viewer had somehow missed the point) there were these chunky, fibreglass models. So, for London there was a model of the Tower of London, for Scotland a model of Arthur's Seat in Edinburgh. In the middle of the flat patch where Salisbury Plain was supposed to be, there was a model of Stonehenge. And for Wales, of course, there was a dragon. It was about two-foot high and four-feet long, painted red, with three feet on the ground and the fourth foot raised, with a curly tail, all made of sturdy fibreglass.

That was it. The dragon.

So as Arthur was making his way through the wind-blown heights of Salisbury Plain, on his own personal quest to play dungeons and dragons with the Wiltshire constabulary (him being the dragon and Salisbury police station cells being the dungeon), Guy the Rant was driving up the M6 towards Liverpool with Lucan and Dagonet and Marcus the Black as passengers.

It was approaching dawn as they drove into Albert Dock where the Lilliputian version of the Isle of Britain was moored, bobbing about gently on the oil-smeared waves. They had discussed who should take the dragon the night before and the job was given to Marcus, both because he couldn't swim – which would make the quest that much more worthy – and also because he was a Quest Knight, still looking for his heraldic name. Who better for a quest than a Quest Knight?

They parked up and sneaked past the security guards, ducking behind obstacles like medieval SAS men on a mission of National Importance. Eventually, they got to the dockside and the floating Island. There was about a ten-foot gap. Luckily (magically, as Arthur would say) a set of wooden ladders came drifting by. Marcus scrambled along the sinking ladder and rolled heavily onto the Island, soaked up to his waist.

Meanwhile Dagonet was speaking to the local press by telephone, telling them what was going on.

They weren't only doing this in protest at the continuing exclusion zone at Stonehenge, he told them, but also to raise money for the homeless.

Marcus was claiming squatter's rights.

Security had been alerted by now. They were milling about looking ruffled and mean and offering feeble threats. They didn't really know what to do. Guy the Rant was living up to his name and ranting uncontrollably at them. The producer and the director of *This Morning!* turned up and offered more threats. They were due to go on air. They told security to clear the intruder from their precious prop as soon as possible. So the security guards laid down the bridge by which the weather forecaster normally crossed to the Island and were threatening to rush over to evict the unwanted tenant. Marcus, of course, pointed out that he would resist. He was standing at the other end of the bridge. He said, 'There's only room for one at a time over this bridge, and I'll throw each one of you off it.' He was being Little John to their Robin Hood (and mixing up his myths into the bargain).

The security guards looked at each other. None of them fancied a dip in the greasy dock water.

Meanwhile, the press had arrived. The knights were talking to all the local papers. Photographers were snapping the proceedings with a certain glee. Newspaper reporters always like it when their more powerful brethren in TV are made to look foolish. The hacks were asking the producer and the director if they'd like to make a comment and holding out microphones in their direction. The producer and the director just glared at them.

The stand-off lasted for some while and the time to go on air loomed ever nearer. The TV people were panicking. They were having nervous breakdowns. They were dancing about from foot to foot, frantically cleaning their spectacles. They were chewing their nails. They were wiping the sweat from their brows with little dabs of their handkerchiefs. What would the nation think? How could the nation survive without its weather report? People might go mad. They wouldn't know whether to take their umbrellas or not. And then what would happen? (If it rained they would get wet.) This was a crisis in the history of TV production. It was almost as bad as when those feminists had invaded the news, or when the Sex Pistols had sworn on air. It ranked alongside the time when an elephant had done a live whoopsie on *Blue Peter*. The nation would be shocked. A bunch of mad Druid knights had invaded their haven of peace and tranquillity. They had blasphemed the great god of broadcast news and entertainment, bringing their heathen ways into this civilised realm. The nation was in grave danger. Anything might happen.

They agreed on a compromise – if only Marcus would get out of the way and leave their Island. The knights demanded the dragon as Spoils of War.

So, Marcus was escorted off the Island with the dragon under his arm.

Victory!

The captured dragon was then transported to Farnborough town centre where – the local Rushmoor Council having granted a collection permit at short notice – £181 was raised for the locally-based Open Door charity and for the Deptford Centre in London. Open Door fundraiser, Mrs Margaret Taylor said, 'Such outrageous and dastardly deeds by warm hearted characters like Arthur Pendragon and his Warband are needed to draw attention to the plight of homeless youngsters. Our sincere thanks to Arthur and his friends for their magnificent effort.'

The local Liverpool press carried the story that they had done it to highlight the lack of Druid access at Stonehenge and to raise money for a charity for the homeless. The Farnborough press reported that they had captured the Dragon for charity by threatening to disrupt a live TV programme and entitled the story 'When Knights Were Bold.'

The operation had gone off with military precision and the Knights were honoured in the following terms by their King: Lucan, was named Dragon Master; Dagonet, Dragon Herald; Guy, Dragon Rant; and Marcus, Dragon Rider.

Granada, however, lied to the British public and said nothing of where their missing dragon really was, nor who had taken it. The dragon was returned safely to the TV company after it had done its job of raising money for the homeless.

It was at the next CoBDO meeting that Arthur finally allowed the Druids to see just what kind of a creature they had invited into their midst.

CoBDO may have been set up to oppose the continued exclusion of Druids and their congregation from their temple, but they were essentially a pacific group: a lobbying organisation rather than activists. Sedate and orderly, they conducted their proceedings with due ceremony. There was an elected Chair, a Secretary and a Treasurer. They had a bank account. Monies were collected to cover expenses and to use for their campaigns. Members of the council were divided into two groups: associate members and full members – those who had a right to vote and to contribute to their collective magazine, *Druid Lore*, and those merely had a say. There were Minutes of the last meeting, which were read out, and the debate was conducted according to a strict Agenda.

At the meeting in question, the various Druids were ranged about in a circle, sitting on the floor.

The question of subscriptions came up. And Arthur passed around a prepared statement, which he read out.

Until then he had been quiet. Now his voice was erupting volcanically into the room.

And in order to feel the full effect of the following statement, you have to try to imagine Arthur's voice. He has a stentorian voice. He has a voice like a Trojan warrior. A trumpeting voice, like the trumpets that brought down the walls of Jericho. A voice full of depth and resonance, which carries not only a tone of inner confidence, but of authority and proclamation.

It is not a voice that is easy to argue with.

So, having announced this particular item on the agenda, Arthur boomed:

> 'The Golden Rule': he who has the most Gold rules. Or perhaps more accurately, and with the help of a little Alchemy, it should read: 'The Silver Rule'.
>
> Money and legal tender, which, after all, is what the 'Golden Rule' is all about (here in the Isle of the Mighty) is in fact Silver rather than Gold. Pounds sterling. Sterling silver perhaps?
>
> But, more accurately, pound coins made from a percentage of Nickel Silver.
>
> 15 such pounds sterling are required for the 'fee' of the Loyal Arthurian Warband for 1993, and presumably 15 more for '94.
>
> Thus the Golden Rule.
>
> It is not without irony that the Council of British Druid Orders, publishers of The Druids Voice [later to become Druid Lore] should put a price on such a voice.
>
> 5 pieces of silver, 'for a say' or 15 for a voice or vote.
>
> All that remains for a fait accompli is for the Council to accept the proverbial 30 Pieces of Silver, and I feel sure the irony of that will not be lost on those present either.

The Druids were sat around in their circle like naughty schoolboys being berated by a stern headmaster. That's the effect of Arthur's voice. But they weren't naughty schoolboys and he wasn't a headmaster. He was a rebel with an extremely loud voice. And having ended his statement, he followed it up with a dramatic gesture. He threw a felt bag containing his

'30 Pieces of Silver' – 30 pounds in one-pound coins – into the air, so that it landed with a satisfying jangling clunk on the hard floor between them, making them all jump back.

Tim and Rollo, of course, were happy with the dramatics. It was why they had enrolled his support.

The rest of the Druids called for a vote and it was agreed that all subscriptions from now on should be voluntary.

And so it continued, year by year, Arthur, in full battle mode, dragging the poor bemused Druids, kicking and screaming into the fray. Challenging the police. Challenging the law. Challenging the legality of the exclusion zone around Stonehenge – Arthur always called it 'the so-called exclusion zone' to emphasise the point – inventing a variety of strategies along the way.

In 1994, for instance, Arthur actually made it into the stones. He did this by the judicious method of having a Radio 4 documentary crew with him. This was one of only two times that he actually made it through the barricades at the Summer Solstice. Both times involved having the media with him. Which kind of highlights the point, of course. If the police were at all confident about the actual legality of these procedures, they would have been willing to arrest a Radio 4 sound crew as well. As it was, they were not.

Also in 1994, Arthur directed his knights on another Quest, this time to squat Winchester Cathedral. While he and one Radio 4 crew were marching towards the police lines guarding their sacred space, so Guy the Rant and Dagonet, also accompanied by a sound crew, were stepping into another sacred space, calling for squatter's rights.

Well, if they couldn't use their temple – Arthur reasoned – why should they allow the Christians to use theirs?

Or, as Arthur and Rollo had often pointed out: imagine the outcry there would be if the police were to put a four-mile exclusion zone around Canterbury (or any other) Cathedral on the night of Christmas Eve, banning all Christmas services? It was exactly equivalent to what was happening to the Druids.

The knights, resplendent in their colourful robes, entered the Cathedral at dusk, just as it was about to close up for the night, and read out the following statement:

We, Knights and representatives of The Loyal Arthurian Warband, member Order of The Council of British Druid Orders, whose Titular Head is King Arthur Pendragon, Honoured Pendragon of The Glastonbury Order of Druids and Official Swordbearer of the Secular Order of Druids,

1. *Do hereby give notice that being also homeless, we claim Squatters' right to this Cathedral; there being no forced entry, it being our intention to live here.*
2. *Claim also Sanctuary under the rights and acts of both Parliament and Church, this being a place of High Worship.*
3. *And, that we do so to highlight the plight of the Druids and their congregation, who this night are forbidden entry to their Cathedral and chosen place of worship, Stonehenge, on the eve of the Summer Solstice.*

It is NOT our intention to cause any damage whatsoever, nor is it our intention to prevent others from their Worship.

It is, however, our intention to remain PEACEFULLY until, either,

a) *A statement is issued to the national press by The Archbishop of Canterbury, deploring the so-called 'Exclusion Zone' in and around Stonehenge over the Summer Solstice period, thus preventing Sacred Rites and Worship.*
   or
b) *King Arthur's return from Stonehenge, whence he shall break fast, partaking of his meal at his (King Arthur's) round table, herein.*

ALL WE DO, WE DO IN THE ANCIENT VIRTUES OF TRUTH, OF HONOUR AND OF JUSTICE.

Winchester, of course, is also the site of a number of Arthurian connections, not least the fact that Malory places Camelot there. The 'round table' in question is a medieval fake, with a painted Tudor Rose at its centre which adorns a wall in Winchester Cathedral. In other words, Arthur was demanding that the guardians of the Cathedral should remove the table from its privileged position so that Arthur could eat his breakfast from it.

All of this must have come as some surprise to the church authorities. To have a bunch of robed knights claiming squatter's rights was bad enough. To find them demanding the removal of their precious relic – fake or no fake, it is still a spectacular object – so that some mad, hairy biker claiming to be King Arthur could eat his breakfast from it, was simply too much. They were bemused, not to say slightly dumbfounded. Mostly they wanted to get home to eat their dinner, but the knights weren't going to let them. They, meanwhile, weren't going to allow the knights sole charge of their Cathedral. A stand-off occurred, lasting some while. Eventually the Canon was called for and he agreed to write a letter of support from the Church of England for the Druid's plight at Stonehenge. The knights decided that it was enough of a triumph for them to be able to withdraw with dignity.

Another – although perhaps less spectacular – victory for the Loyal Arthurian Warband. They were beginning to 'kick arse' as Arthur always terms it. They were making people sit up and take notice.

And in 1995, Arthur engineered it so that English Heritage (English Heretics) could not gain access to their offices. Excluding them from their offices as they were being excluded from Stonehenge. So – once again – while Arthur was approaching the front line near the monument itself and challenging the exclusion zone directly, Llewch Lleawg, another of the knights, and a young squire were in London, chaining up the entrance doors to Fortress House, English Heritage's head office. They made the papers, *The Independent* running the story under the headline, 'Druid's Stonehenge Revenge'. After, they were taken to Marylebone police station where they were questioned, cautioned and released without charge.

The name 'Llewch Lleawg', by the way, is very easy to pronounce. Imagine a duck's quack. Combine that with the sound of a motor mower running over a pile of damp gravel lying hidden in a clump of grass. Add to this the sound of someone crumpling up a half empty crisp packet (Walker's preferably), while pouring a full can of lager down the sink and belching out the remains of last night's Chicken Jalfrezi all at the same time, and you have it. See? Easy. Anyone can say it.

Later that year, at the Winter Solstice, Arthur and Llewch led a frontal assault on the monument itself, Arthur having first called an extraordinary meeting of CoBDO to gain council approval for his action. The extraordinary meeting consisted entirely of himself, and no one else, he being an office holder in three Druid orders, and three being the required number. And we don't have to imagine all that much procedure taking place. He didn't address himself through himself (being both Chair and speaker at the same time). Nor did he hand himself his own agenda and then read it to himself. Nor did he present a proposal to himself, seconding it himself, speaking for the proposal and then against it before calling for the vote, counting the vote and declaring that it was unanimous. No. He just decided he was going to do it, that's all, in the name of the Council. And having decided, he did it.

Needless to say, the council increased the quorum to five after that.

So, having gained the unanimous consent of himself in the name of the Council of British Druid Orders, he set out to take the Giant's Dance – 'Giant's Dance' being one of the more colourful names for this ancient and mysterious pile of stones.

The following description is in Arthur's own words, written for a magazine article the following year, entitled 'The Liberation of the Giant's Dance'.

> *King Arthur Pendragon led a victorious assault by the Council of British Druid Orders upon the besieged Stonehenge, held by the Black Knights of English Heritage. Having successfully scaled the outer fortifications, King Arthur and the Council Troops marched on the captured Temple from the East. This was with the intention of liberating it from the mercenary hoards therein for the Celtic Nation.*
>
> *Accompanied only by a Fool, a Celtic Minstrel and an unarmed Warrior, King Arthur proceeded to march upon the Temple. The enemy Troops outnumbered our own forces by at least 6 to 1. It is estimated however that they kept 50% of their Army in reserve, whilst the remainder sallied forth towards the advancing druids, it being the enemy's intention to hold a firm line.*
>
> *In the skirmish that followed, they encountered a fully robed Celtic Chieftain, bearing a ceremonial sword and holy lance; a Jester bearing naught save a sacred flame, which all the while he kept alight, before placing on the Altar Stone; a Celtic Minstrel, armed only with his lute and Bardic song (written specially for the occasion and since referred to as a Battle Hymn), who continued to play, despite being temporarily brought down by three marauding Mercenaries. Encountering also, an unarmed Swordbearer, who kept a steady gait throughout, and nev-*

er left his King's side for a moment.

The first line of defence crumbled beneath the Druid onslaught. The enemy withdrew and regrouped, but were no match for the now chanting Druids. After several such skirmishes, it was clear to our own forces that the battle which had been joined would eventually be won, and the Temple liberated. The enemy lines were breached. The Druid forces were victorious and symbolically left their sacred flames ablaze in the inner sanctum.

The aforementioned battle went on through the night of the 21st and 22nd of December 1994 and was joined by Llewch Lleawg, Shield Knight and Chaired Bard to the Court of King Arthur; Steve, Official Swordbearer of the Insular Order of Druids; Chatty, Mabon and Fool (Secular Order of Druids); and led by King Arthur Pendragon LAW.

King Arthur and the Council troops were commended on their victory by the Archdruids of the Glastonbury and Insular Orders on the occasion of the Dawn Ceremony at the Hele Stone some hours later.

And you can imagine this, can't you? You can imagine the torches of the security guards jerking about in the darkness. You can imagine the muffled cries. You can imagine the sound of boot on grass as they run. The creak of Arthur's leather belt, with the sword attached, the rustle of his robes. The shouts of triumph, the cat calls of derision, the minstrel playing his lute and singing throughout. It was all ridiculous, of course. But, the truth is, the police and the security guards welcomed it. Why else were they there? It would have been so boring to have spent uneventful nights at the monument, waiting for nothing to happen. Arthur and his colourful band of mad protesters were a kind of light in their life: something to go home and tell the missus about later. It was all good, clean, idiotic fun.

Two of the characters in this story go on to play a major role later on, by the way. 'Chatty' would later change his name to Bran. He was just a teenager at the time, bright, chatty and optimistic. Hence his name. And the unarmed Swordbearer, Steve, would later become known as the Orc and be made Arthur's second-in-command.

And so it continued, without let, a continuing series of ritualised assaults, not so much upon the monument, which was sacred, but upon the lines of blue serge that were acting as bastions for these dubiously framed pieces of law. It was the LAW against the Law. Higher law versus lower law. The law of the ancient landscape, of the rhythm of the stars, versus the law of John Major and the current Conservative government: well meaning but useless, living in a world of his own.

It's all a kind of blur, now. Arthur has a problem with dates, just as he has a problem with counting. Numbers consist of 'one, two and lots'; dates of 'the other day, the other week, the other year.' 'The other day' could be as close as yesterday or as far off as several months ago.

There was one memorable arrest, when he arrested the arresting officer.

There were a number of them, perhaps a half a dozen. They walked from Bath. When they got to the signs marking the exclusion zone they sat down. After that, Arthur was sending the troops in, one at a time, on opposite sides of the road, at 100-yard intervals. This was so that it couldn't be claimed they constituted a procession. When is a procession not a procession? When it proceeds at 100-yard intervals on alternating sides of the road.

Meanwhile, police surveillance squads were continuously filming them.

As usual, Arthur was intending to get himself arrested, while letting the others back off at the last minute. He was the last to go. Eventually, he came to the lines of police within sight of the stones. The police pulled him over. There was a Superintendent with them.

They asked where he was going. He said, 'It is my intention to proceed to Stonehenge.'

He was informed of the exclusion zone and told that it would constitute an arrestable offence if he continued. The Superintendent said that in his opinion the people walking down the road towards Stonehenge constituted a procession.

Arthur said, 'How can we be a procession? Since when did people walking on opposite sides of the road, 100-yards apart, become a procession?'

The police surveillance crew were filming the whole thing and there were a number of police officers standing around, arms folded, behind the Superintendent.

The Superintendent said, 'If you proceed any further, you will be arrested.'

'What for?' said Arthur.

'For Breach of the Peace.'

'Do you think that I'm likely to cause a Breach of the Peace?' said Arthur.

'No, we don't think that you personally are likely to cause a Breach of the Peace, but if we let you go on, then somebody else might.'

'So, let's get this straight,' said Arthur. 'What you're saying is that you don't believe that I am going to cause a Breach of the Peace, but that my mere presence in this so-called exclusion zone may cause others to do so, and on that assumption, you're going to arrest me?'

'That's right,' said the Superintendent, satisfied that he had made his point.

Arthur was loving every minute of it. So too were the other police officers. Arthur gave a twinkling glance to the surveillance team, indicating that they should keep filming. They replied in a similarly telepathic manner and did as he asked.

We have to be clear now, on an obscure point of British Law. It becomes very pertinent at this point.

An arresting officer is responsible for the arrest. If an arrest turns out to be illegal, it is the arresting officer who bears responsibility for it. A superior officer cannot, therefore, order a lower ranking officer to make an arrest. Whoever makes the arrest does so on his own perception of the merits of the case, which, in theory, he may have to bring before a court of law.

So while the Superintendent was standing back on his heels, satisfied that he had enough grounds to have Arthur arrested, the other officers just stood there.

The Superintendent looked at his sergeant, as if to say, 'Well, go on then. Make the arrest.' The Sergeant just looked away, folded his arms, and started laughing.

'Come on, somebody take this one,' he ventured.

The Superintendent was looking at each of the officers in turn and they would kind of roll their eyes heavenwards and whistle, or look down at their feet, or scratch their heads and glance away. Everyone was ignoring him while trying to suppress spasms of barely concealed laughter.

'This is silly,' said the Superintendent, getting irritable. 'This could go on all day. I suppose I'll have to make the arrest myself.'

And he got out his pocket book and his pencil and read Arthur his rights.

'You do not have to say anything, but it may harm your defence if you do not mention when questioned something which you later rely on in court,' he said.

This was what Arthur had been waiting for. Why he'd wanted to keep the cameras running. And everyone knew it. All of the officers could feel this moment building. It was why hardly any of them could keep a straight face.

'And I must caution *you*,' replied Arthur in that booming voice of his, 'that you're not obliged to say anything, but that anything you do say may be used in Strasbourg against you, because this arrest, this road block, and this so-called exclusion zone is illegal under articles 9, 10, 11 and 14 of the European Convention on Human Rights. As a European citizen I am making a citizen's arrest. In other words,' he added, placing his hand on the Superintendent's shoulder in proper old-fashioned police style, 'you're nicked son!'

At which point, the other police officers finally dissolved into raucous peals of uncontrollable laughter.

Good old Arthur. He'd done it again. He'd entertained them all on another boring solstice night.

The other officers wouldn't even let the Superintendent use their police vehicles and he had to requisition his own car for police use.

The rumour is that copies of that film have been distributed to police canteens around the country and that it is a favourite on stag nights.

Allegedly.

Another year he managed to get into the stones with the help of a TV crew. Once again, the police were showing that special kind of diplomatic reserve in the face of media attention. The film went out on national TV, where it was seen by a certain 15-year-old girl called Shelly. It was Shelly's Mum, Willow, who recognised him. They were just watching the box, when Willow suddenly laughed.

'I don't believe it!' she said.

'What's that Mum?'

'That twerp on the telly, the bloke claiming to be King Arthur ...'

'Yeah?'

'It's your Dad!'

Thus it was that's John's nefarious past caught up with Arthur in the form of a 15-year-old girl claiming to be his daughter. And he couldn't deny it. She was his daughter all right.

And the following year she accompanied him at his arrest. Indeed, she too managed to get herself arrested. That was the kind of father he was. He meets his daughter for the first time in 15 years, and then promptly gets her arrested.

What date is it now?

We have no idea.

One, two and lots.

It was sometime in the 90s.

Shelly had her mother's dog with her, a white whippet called Flash.

The police closed around them as usual. They offered the usual warning. Arthur, as usual, stated his intention of proceeding towards the monument. The police, as usual, stated their intention to arrest him. He stepped forward. They grabbed hold of him. They read him his rights. He listened politely. They handcuffed him and carted him off in the back of a police van, to be processed and then to wait for the dawn in the familiar surroundings of Salisbury police cells.

And then they did it all again, on his daughter, and his daughter's dog.

Arthur said, 'You arrest my Druids, fine. You arrest my Warband, fine. You arrest me, fine. You arrest my daughter, fine. You arrest my daughter's dog, that's over the top.'

Actually, we do know what date this was. It was 1996. It was a memorable year, not least because 19 fully-robed Druids and one deranged journalist were also arrested.

Arthur came out of the cells that morning to the sight of 19 Druid staffs lined up behind the desk sergeant's counter. He recognised them all.

So, he had managed to get the Druids on side at last, to the point where they were (mostly) willing to get arrested.

But he still hadn't got to meet CJ yet.

CHAPTER TEN

FOURTH QUEST:

Lammas

It was becoming a saga, a tale of true epic proportions. CJ was still looking for King Arthur. This was going to be his last effort. He was heading for Avebury once more on the morning of the 3 August, 1996. That's close to Lammas, for all you students of the pagan calendar, the pagan Harvest festival. He picked up a couple of hitchhikers on the way, on an obscure road in Kent. They'd slept in a field, having arrived from Germany the night before. They were on their way to the West Country. One was a hippie musician called Clive. The other was his German girlfriend. Her name was Birghit. They were very much in love. They kept stroking each other and looking into each other's eyes. But Birghit couldn't make head nor tail of CJ's accent. He said, 'D'ya fancy a cuppa?' and she looked at him as if he'd just made an immoral suggestion.

They arrived in Avebury at 1.00pm, about half an hour after the ceremony was due to start, but Clive wanted a pint and so did CJ. They had a pint of Fruggles each. They chose it for the name. It was Clive's first English pint in over a year and you can't get a much more English sounding pint than 'Fruggles'. Clive drank his down in with liquid ease, making appreciative gurgling noises as he did so. CJ said, 'Well, we've not got much else going for us. The worst licensing laws in the Universe. And the most corrupt and dishonest government. But we still make the best beer.' Clive didn't answer. He was too busy making gurgling noises.

They went over to the stones. There was a hand-fasting ceremony taking place. A hand-fasting is a pagan marriage. It lasts for a year and a day. So much more civilised – not to say, realistic – than a lifetime. You re-confirm it every year. Or not, as the case may be.

CJ saw Steve Andrews.

CJ said, 'Is Arthur here then?'

Steve pointed him out, and CJ went over to make his greeting.

'We meet at last,' he said.

'You look different without your beard,' Arthur said. Those were the first words that passed between them. It was a moment of great significance in the history of Western culture. Pretend writer meets pretend king. New Age Livingstone and drink-addled Stanley in the wilds of ancient Wiltshire.

CJ was very much struck by his appearance. He definitely looked like King Arthur, he thought. It wasn't only the robes and the cloak and the beard. It wasn't the shield either, nor the stave wrapped about with copper wire with a crystal on the top. Arthur has a huge brow, like some prehistoric tribesman, on which was perched his kingly circlet, made of iron with a dragon at the forehead. And he has long, dark pointy ears and a strange darkness about him. There is an indefinable blackness under the pale skin, as if the flesh itself is soaked in engine oil, thought CJ. But he couldn't see the sword. 'Where's the sword,' he asked, and Arthur brought it out.

'It's beautiful,' CJ said. And he meant it. It was beautiful.

After that they had the ceremony. They stood in a circle while a Druid in a wolf-skin cloak took to centre stage. It was exactly like that: as if he was performing for everyone on stage. Four Druids stood at the four quarters and made ritualistic gestures and intoned ceremonial phrases. There were obeisances to the guardians of the salamanders of fire – stuff like that. CJ wasn't at all sure. Arthur raised his shield and his sword and intoned to the Guardians of the South. CJ was struck by his accent. Pure Hampshire. A Celtic King from Hampshire: it's a contradiction in terms.

After that, a circle of children were blessed by the Priestess. Steve said that he'd been blessed as a child on one occasion. Someone wanted to know if they'd allow blessings of ferrets. So they did, and Frodo the Ferret was blessed too, along with all the kids. Meanwhile people were singing:

The river is flowing
The river is growing
The river is flowing

Back to the sea.
Mother Earth carry me
A child I will always be
Mother Earth carry me
Back to the sea.

It was a nice song. It went on for about 10 minutes, over and over.

Steve said: 'I arrived here last night. I had to walk from Chippenham. I slept by that stone over there and woke up soaked in dew. But I spotted 14 types of butterfly this morning.' And he brought out a list. 'That one there, Clouded Yellow, it's very rare. People would come from all over the country to see it.'

CJ spotted another name on the list. 'Hmmm, Painted Lady,' he said, 'that sounds nice. I could do with a Painted Lady.'

'Yes, very attractive,' said Steve, thinking that CJ was referring to butterflies.

There was a squabble amongst the Druids. The Druid with the fur stole had apparently forgotten a part of the ceremony. A Druid with a Panama hat (Rollo, again, but CJ didn't know it yet) interrupted him. 'You haven't consecrated the flowers,' he said.

'Oh, all right then,' said the other Druid, tetchily, 'go ahead if you have to.'

So, the Druid with the Panama hat stood over a bunch of flowers and consecrated them.

After that, they were invited to become initiated as Bards of Caer Abiri if they wanted to. Tim Sebastian – who CJ had met before, both at Avebury and Stonehenge – urged him to go. 'Go on CJ,' he said, 'it won't hurt you.'

'Oh all right then,' CJ said, and he did.

They made a much smaller circle inside the larger circle, but facing outwards. They made a vow to honour and justice and peace and love, and to care for the Earth. It was a moving moment. You see, CJ already believed in honour and justice and peace and love, and he wanted to care for the Earth. He'd just never made vows about it before. And then they were sponsored by an existing initiate. CJ was sponsored by Tim Sebastian. Tim Sebastian being an Archdruid, that was an honour. He placed his hand on CJ's shoulder and everyone chanted 'Awen.' It was said as a drone, the way that Buddhists chant OM: 'A-a-a-a-a-a-a-w-w-w-w-w-e-e-e-e-e-n-n-n!' The chant drifted and spiralled, rose and fell, and sparkled like diamonds in the shimmering air, while above sprays of birds arched across the sky.

CJ thanked Tim for that. It had felt genuinely sweet in that circle.

Steve Andrews went into the circle and sang 'Stand By Me.' Only no one did at first. Eventually Arthur joined him and one or two others. Then he changed the lyrics. He sang, 'Dance By Me,' and a few more people did. King Arthur was dancing marionette-like in his robes. It was a moment of startling illumination. King Arthur, the Rock'n'Roll King.

Then the five main Druids went into the circle: that is, the Druids of the four quarters and the one with the fur cloak. They had to vow not to squabble any longer. You see: the Druid movement is split between those who will consecrate trees, but never get up a tree to defend it, and those who will both consecrate and defend the trees. There's also a class division: between the one's who organise Spirit Camps and charge for it, where people gather to increase their spiritual awareness and learn about the ancient Druidic ways, who never drink or smoke or chase women; and those – led by Arthur – who do all of these things and never go to Spirit Camps and whose motivations are fundamentally political and radical.

One of the Druids read from a book. He said, 'There has never been a tradition of holding hand-fastings at those particular stones.'

And Arthur shouted back, 'Then we'll start a tradition.'

CJ turned to Birghit and Clive. 'See, aren't you lucky today? I picked you up in the far East of England, and brought you all the way to the West, where you wanted to go. And on top of that I brought you here to witness a Druid ceremony. There can't be all that many people who get lifts to Druid ceremonies.'

Steve came over to join the group and CJ introduced them. 'This is my mate, Steve. And these are my hitch-hiker friends, Clive and ... er ... I can't remember your name.'

'Birghit,' she said in her heavy German accent.

'That's right, Beergut,' CJ said.

'No Birghit,' said Clive.

'Beergut.'

'Birghit.'

And that was the last time CJ tried to say her name.

Well, there's only a certain amount of standing in circles and chanting and ritual observances a man can take before he starts to get thirsty. The Red Lion was calling. Steve and CJ slipped off to get a couple of drinks. Arthur followed a little later. 'Buy us a drink,' he said. CJ agreed. But people were lined up three deep at the bar. CJ said, 'Wait ten minutes, OK? Or, barring that, here's a tenner, get one yourself.' Arthur looked at the money as if it was poison. 'I'm a renunciate,' he said. 'I don't handle money. Not unless it's for petrol, that is. Then it's not money it's petrol.'

'Well this is for beer. So it's not money either, it's beer.'

But he didn't want to touch it. He drank CJ's beer instead, and smoked several of his cigarettes. He called it tax. They sat in the pool room and made conspiratorial plans.

Arthur said: 'I want to get arrested, only nobody dares do it. The last time, at Stonehenge, all the coppers were standing round wondering what to do. They couldn't arrest me. They had to call a Superintendent to do it. And then I arrested him, in the name of the Law. I told him, "I am the LAW." They won't put me in gaol either. They keep fining me. I tell them, "I'm a Renunciate, I don't have any money." Then I go to the back of the Court, and they um and ah and we make our deals, and they let me go. It's the same every time.'

'I have three personalities,' he added, 'to go with my three names. As a King I have to be concerned with the welfare of my Knights, and as the Pendragon of all Britain I have to be concerned with the state of the country: but as Arthur I can get pissed and smoke and chase women and do what I like. But, obviously, Arthur comes second to the other two.'

'So which are you now?'

'I'm Arthur, of course,' he said, taking another swig on his cider and pinching another cigarette.

CJ asked Arthur to knight him. He went down on his knees in the pub yard and Arthur placed his sword on CJ's head and shoulders in a dramatic fashion, swearing him to truth, honour and justice. Then CJ stood up and Arthur embraced him.

After that things started to get really strange.

Tim Sebastian came out very agitated. 'I've had it with your fucking Warband,' he said to Arthur. 'Orc has just gone off with my tobacco.' He was so angry that he took his staff (which had a crescent moon on the top), laid it on a step and stamped on it. It broke with a healthy-sounding crack. The joke here is that Tim regularly breaks his staff and then bandages it up with a pink scarf in between. So, he wasn't really breaking his staff. He was making a dramatic gesture.

Arthur went and got the Orc, a tall man in a long white robe, with a stud through his lower lip. Arthur made him apologise to Tim and give back his tobacco.

Then they drove to Bath. There was Steve, CJ, Arthur, Tim and a young couple in the car, along with all the Druidic paraphernalia – the shields and swords and robes and staves. It was a Morris Minor. It was very crowded. CJ was drunk and shouldn't have been driving. The car was swerving all over the road. Steve and the young couple were saying, very politely, 'Careful you don't kill us, we don't want to die yet, we're much too young to die,' while Arthur and Tim were shouting, 'Yes, go on, go on, kill us. Kill us now. We want to die!'

CJ didn't care one way or the other.

Arthur said, 'One of the reasons people hate me is that they all think I want to bonk their girlfriends.'

CJ said, 'Well, you can't bonk my girlfriend.'

'Listen to that,' Arthur said. 'Did you hear that everyone? He's questing me. He's offering me a challenge. You know I can't turn down a challenge. I'm really gonna bonk her now.'

CJ omitted to add that the reason that Arthur couldn't have his girlfriend was that he hadn't got one.

They all ended up in a pub drinking scrumpy cider. The young couple were very sweet. CJ kept telling the girl how sexy she was and then telling the man that he was very, very lucky. 'I know,' he said. Later, he found out that the girl was only 16.

CJ doesn't remember much more. They got back to Tim's house somehow, which seemed like a vast stately home. There was a huge hallway and antique furniture on the landing. CJ lay down in someone's bed until Tim came and got him. Then he lay down in the living room and went to sleep overhearing the young couple saying, 'And you know what CJ was saying to us in the pub? …' He was far too gone to listen to any more.

The following day he woke up and his hair was all standing on end. He looked very strange. He was still drunk. He drove Steve down to the bus station and they had some breakfast. After that CJ was going to go back and pick up Arthur so he could drive him to Newbury. Only they got lost in Bath. They were going round and round on the one-way system and CJ's petrol tank was nearly empty. He decided to give up trying to find Arthur again and they went back to wait for Steve's bus.

'What's Arthur's real name?' asked CJ.

'John,' said Steve and laughed. 'My friends are always changing their names. So Arthur was called John, and then he was Mad Dog and Bacardi, and now he's King Arthur. And my friend Pixi is really called Neil, but then he called himself Mordred and then Less Dread. He won't let anyone call him Pixi any more. It's very confusing. And Orc is Steve, and Llewch is Neil. It's such an ordinary name: Neil. Not as interesting as Llewch Lleawg.'

CJ said, 'Arthur is very vain isn't he? I suppose you'd have to be vain to want to call yourself King Arthur.'

'It's his true Aryan nature,' said Steve.

'Pardon?' said CJ, suddenly worried. 'But he's got black hair. I thought Aryans were supposed to be blond.' He didn't like how this conversation seemed to be going. He'd never thought of Steve as a fascist.

'No: I mean Arian. He's an Aries.'

'Thank God for that,' CJ said, 'I thought you were going to start feeding me Nazi propaganda for a minute there.'

Steve lent CJ some money so he could get home. He'd spent most of his money in the pub the previous night. That's the trouble with wanting to write a book about people: they all expect you to buy them drinks. Then Steve caught his bus. CJ drove back along the M4. It was a very boring drive and he was hungover, irritable and with a tongue that tasted like he'd been licking the inside of a dog's bottom all night. He had no money left once he'd bought the petrol, so he couldn't stop anywhere. And then, about 20 miles from his home, he ran out of petrol again. He just managed to make it into a service station. He was going up to people and saying, in his most polite voice: 'Excuse me, I don't normally do this sort of thing, but you see, I'm nearly home. You couldn't let me have a couple of quid to buy petrol to get me the rest of the way, could you?' And it happened every time. They'd look him up and down, their eyes resting on his legs for a moment. He was wearing shorts. It was a glorious summer's day. But it was as if they were measuring his worthiness by the quality of his legs. And then a slight smile would play about their lips. 'Sorry,' they'd say, 'got no money.' It was humiliating.

Eventually he lost his patience. A camper van drew in. CJ marched up to the man and said, 'Give us a quid will you?'

'What for?'

'For petrol.'

'That's a new one,' the man said, laughing, and he reached in his pocket and brought out a pound, which was just about enough to get CJ home.

Well he couldn't help reflecting on this. He couldn't help remembering all those times he'd lent people money without ever expecting it back. In CJ's world, people help each other. Some people blag. Some people beg. Some people would talk the hind legs off an orang-utan for a pint or two. But people always help each other. But now he was beginning to see that in the real world, this world of motorway service stations and soulless Little Chef cafés, the opposite was true. No one blags, no one begs, no one talks and no one helps each other either.

Later, when he got home, he was watching *The Blob* on the TV. He was lying on the settee, exhausted, watching this little, flickering, black-and-white thing in the corner. The film is about a strange amorphous mass which is growing and swallowing everything in sight. A young man (played by Steve McQueen) is trying to warn people about a nameless horror which is about to consume their town. Nobody believes him: until they get eaten by the Blob, that is, by which time it is too late. The young man's name is Steve Andrews. Another little coincidence. CJ thought about his own friend Steve Andrews then. He thought about the Druids, and Arthur, at that point closely involved in the Newbury bypass road protest: how they were all warning us of a strange amorphous mass growing in our midst, threatening to consume our world. But it wasn't only a physical mass. It wasn't just a physical blob. It was a mental thing, a state of mind. An attitude. Something, even now, threatening to destroy our world.

What was it?

Money.

CHAPTER ELEVEN

The Third Battle of Newbury

W e ended the last chapter with a single five-letter word beginning with M. We start this chapter with another.

Magic.

Even writing the word adds colour to the text. The text itself comes alive. Feel it. It is magic.

Magic is the most important ingredient in this book. It is what this book is made of. It is what this book is about.

It is also important in Arthur's life and in the lives of the people around him.

It is not trickery. We're not referring to sleight of hand here – to a Paul Daniel card trick – but to something else. To a deep sense of place, to a deep sense of being. To the sense that there are Divine forces at work in the Universe, playing themselves out amongst us. To a sense of belonging that is older than time. To a sense of the landscape as a living being. To the sense of the breath of the Earth on the dawn of the longest day. To the feeling that history itself is looping, repeating itself in some vast fractal interplay of forces beyond our control.

Sometimes it comes in dreams.

For CJ it came in a dream about Arthur, that told him he would help write this book. CJ was tidying up his house in the dream, when he discovered that he had Excalibur. 'Oh no!' he thought, 'what am I going to do with this?' It was as if he was being landed with the responsibility for it. He was too busy tidying up. So he tried to hide it by burying it under his bedclothes. There were some medieval knights coming out of a church, dressed in robes, with swords strapped to their waists. They had been practising sword fighting. They saw Excalibur and came over to view it. CJ saw that it was damaged and that he was responsible for it. The strap was broken and the blade scuffed and scratched. In fact, it wasn't even a proper blade. It was just a lump of metal that hadn't been worked yet. Then Arthur arrived. He sidled in, floating like a ghost. He started singing this song, while a full orchestra played. It was magnificent music, very powerful, full of surprising shifts in tone and scale. These were the words.

'Some things move by love, some things move by time, but the Earth and the Sun they move by power, by power. Some things move by love and some things move by time, but some things move by power: some by power, some by power.' Something like that. CJ had no idea what it meant.

CJ had wanted to write a book about Arthur since he'd first gone on that quest to find him in 1996, but various things had got in the way. Mainly what had got in the way was that CJ had been indiscrete and had managed to fall out with a number of the Druids. He was a cynic when he started this quest. Meanwhile, Arthur had begun working on a book of his own with Steve Andrews and Liz Murray. Arthur was sitting in Louise McNamara's office at Thorsons sometime in the summer of the year 2000, holding the manuscript from which parts of this present book were formed. Louise was telling him that they needed to get another author in to help with the work.

'Yes, but the Druids tell me, anybody but CJ', he said.

That's when CJ rang. At that exact moment. He called the Thorsons office and was put through to Louise McNamara. He was looking for a book deal. He wanted to write a book about protest.

'That was CJ,' Louise had said, after their conversation. 'He wants to write a book. Um, you know what I'm going to suggest, don't you?'

'You know you said it should be anybody but CJ?' Arthur said later to one of the Druids who had specified his objection to CJ's involvement.

'Hmmmm?'

'Well, you got your wish. It's CJ.'

That's what we mean by magic. Serendipity. Synchronicity. As if the Universe is unfolding of its own volition. As if the Earth contains some presence, some force, larger, deeper, stronger than the human, but like the human. That the human story is part of its story. That we are serving its purpose. That we matter. And that our unfolding stories are the unfoldings of the Universe itself.

That's what Arthur's life has been. An unfolding story of the Universe told to him in magical coincidences.

As children, maybe, we all believed in magic. We believed in presences. We believed in the ghosts that lived in the shadowy places. We believed in stories. Now we don't believe any more. No magic. No presences. No ghosts in shadows. No stories. And then Arthur comes along and he has a story. It's an absurd story, of course. Ludicrous. Crazy. Ridiculous. And all the more appealing for that. He says he has some other name than the one he was christened with. That he's not Johnny Rothwell any more, but King Arthur Uther Pendragon. And why should anyone believe him?

Because there is magic in the name. And by calling upon the magical name, maybe, he has managed to invoke it. He has managed to make it real.

Because names are magic.

Because words are magic.

Because life is magic.

Because there is magic in the air, in the wind, in the storm. Because there is magic in the seas, in the hills, in the vales. Because there is magic in the seasons and in the days of the week. Because the Earth is made of magic and the trees are made of magic and the sun burns by magic and the beating heart opens to its future, to its loves and to its despairs, by magic. Because the Earth is a Goddess and the Sun is a God. Because everything stirs with life. Because intelligence is here, in the Universe. Because the Universe was born of intelligence and human beings are here to learn from it. Because we are its children. Because the gods are waking up. Because they awaken as we awaken to them. Because they are made real by us, by our thoughts. Because our dreams will come true. Because trees whisper an ancient language. Because water remembers. Because the Earth remembers. Because the Earth itself remembers us.

Maybe. Allegedly.

Well, it's either that or we are all already dead.

By the time CJ got to know Arthur, there was something new happening on the British political scene: the road protest. This too was magic.

It seemed to come out of nowhere and to express sentiments and ideas rarely voiced before. It developed an intriguing new rhetoric, a strange mixture of radical politics and magic. It embraced new tactics, even a new language. It set about challenging many of the conventions of political debate. Were these people left wing or right wing? It was hard to know. On the one hand they were challenging the political and economic system that demanded an ever-increasing reliance on cars; but they were also fiercely patriotic, drawing much support from Middle England and the middle classes, while turning to St George for their central metaphor.

The road protesters saw themselves as St George. The dragons were the diggers, come to chew up the land.

There was much talk of the spirit of the land, of its magical rebirth. Of the spirit of place. Of ancient battles being replayed. Of mythical codes written into the very landscape. Of dark conspiracies on a magical level. Of Earth energy and Earth spirit. Of the return of ancient peoples. Of the power of rocks and stones. Of the secret places, of the magical places. Of the magical power of water. Of the ancient tribes and their ceaseless wanderings.

They said they were the spirits of the ancient nomadic peoples, returned to fight for the land.

It's hard to know where such thoughts come from. The people involved in the road protests would say that they came from the land itself. That the land – and all that lives and grows and walks upon it – is a living thing.

The first road protest began on Twyford Down near Winchester. This was sometime in the early 90s. A group of people – latter-day New Age travellers maybe, post-rave drop-outs – were experimenting with sustainable living on the Down. They called themselves the Donga Tribe, after the lines of ancient track ways that crisscross the Down, making towards St Catherine's Hill. They were just quiet people trying to get on. Unfortunately, as they were soon to find out, the Down was about to be desecrated by a road-building project: the M3 motorway extension. Thus, their quiet seclusion was suddenly, rudely and violently interrupted and they were left with a choice. Either move out and find some other place to camp or do something. They decided to do something. They decided to stop the diggers in their tracks.

And that's what they did. They threw themselves in front of the diggers and refused to move until the diggers had stopped. Digger-diving. Using their own vulnerable bodies as their weapons. Later they developed other tactics, often chaining themselves to the diggers, so that it became harder and harder for the contractors to continue work.

They were fighting for their country. Literally.

Well, one of them must have heard of Arthur. He was already making a name for himself, as we know, as early as 1990, getting press coverage for a series of more and more unlikely actions around the campaign to free Stonehenge. They must also have known the literary and mythological threads that linked the name of Arthur to Winchester and to St Catherine's Hill in particular. They'd also had dealings with the pagan calendar. Probably they were pagans too. There was a lot of it about, even then. So, with this in mind, a letter arrived on Wendy's doorstep inviting Arthur to lead a Beltane ceremony in May 1993. Arthur was still using his sister's place as his postal address and his base, as he had in his biker days. He was intrigued by the letter and immediately agreed. Why not? If it was for the preservation of the land, then that too was a cause dear to his heart.

He led the Beltane ceremony at dawn, as prescribed, accompanied by Tim, Rollo and Parsley. So there were representatives from three orders there, calling on spiritual and magical assistance for the protection of St Catherine's Hill. Later, they were watching as a group of protesters started harrying a digger in order to stop it from working. The protesters were running in front of it, being chased by security guards, attempting to clamber aboard. Well, that was intriguing, wasn't it? It was something new. At the same time, it was something that Arthur could identify with. Action. That had always been his creed. Get in there and do something. Don't just waffle on about it.

The four of them were standing on a small rise accompanied by local residents and members of the public. A second JCB arrived and a young warrior quickly shimmied up the arm, locking himself on. The security guards were running round after the protesters, trying to drag them off. It was like a game of tag, or British Bulldog, but with a more serious intent. Once the security had captured a protester, they had to hold on to them and wait for the police to arrive, so that they could be arrested.

All of which was highly enjoyable in Arthur's eyes: to watch these young warriors in full battle mode, women as well as men, in their bright clothing with their dreadlocks streaming, running rings around the police and the authorities. He was chuckling with joy. Where had he seen this sort of thing before? Oh yes! Last year, when he was being arrested on his way to Stonehenge. These were his kind of people.

Then two more diggers came over the hill, belching blue and black diesel smoke, roaring engines, clanking and rumbling towards them. It was obvious that the other protesters were fully engaged already and Arthur found himself striding out towards the diggers, brandishing his Druid's staff, his cloak streaming out behind him. Within a few seconds he found he was surrounded by security guards and, more to his surprise, the two robed Druids, Parsley in his slick leathers and various members of the public just a few feet behind. They had all struck out at the same moment, on the same impulse.

Well Arthur's tactic wasn't quite the same as that of the young protesters. They would skim and shimmy, duck and dodge to get close to the diggers. Arthur just strode. Twelve stone of compact biker energy, with a biker's fist on the end of each arm and a biker's set determination. It was an entirely different situation for the security guards. They grabbed hold of him and he shook them off, growling. They tried again, and he stared at them: that famous Mad Dog expression. They were shouting at him, he was shouting back. The police had also arrived by now and were lined up either side, while the diggers pulled to a halt in front of them. It was a stand-off. Arthur, three Druids and numerous members of the public, in front of the stalled diggers. They weren't actually doing anything illegal as such and the security guards didn't really feel like using violence, not only because they guessed they might get the worst of it, but also, with the police watching, they knew they would be liable to arrest too. So everyone just stood there. A supervisor was called, who consulted with the digger drivers, by now sitting in their cabs with their feet up on the controls, smoking cigarettes. The digger drivers shrugged. This had been going on for weeks and they were used to it. The supervisor spoke to the security guards. The security guards shrugged. They were bored and underpaid. He spoke to the police. The policemen shrugged. They were just doing their job, keeping an eye on things. What could anyone do? 'All right then,' said the supervisor, shrugging, 'we'll pull the diggers out and stop work for the day.' The digger drivers cheered inwardly and started up their motors ready to withdraw, while Arthur and the others went back up the hill for an afternoon of partying, merriment and dance. And a high old time was had by all.

After that, Parsley stayed on to become part of the road protest movement. And we have to add, at this point, that a number of the female

24341883 Pte Rothwell, 1st Royal Hampshire Regiment! ▼

'Mr and Mrs Joe Public.' John, before the name change to Arthur, and his wife Liz. ▼

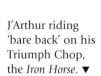

J'Arthur riding 'bare back' on his Triumph Chop, the *Iron Horse*. ▼

1

▼ A Wizard, a Witch and a Warrior (right, left, centre). Barnade, a French Druid who had the expedience to come through on the press bus; Dylan Ap Thuin, who had arrived there moments before; and Arthur, who had been there all night. Summer Solstice 1993.
Photo: Peter Macdiarmid/The Independent

An arresting incident. ▶
King Arthur in one of his many run-ins with the police, Crystal Palace, 1998.
Photo: Mark Chilvers/
The Independent

Llewch Lleawg, a LAW (Loyal Arthurian Warband) knight, who was instrumental(!) in chaining up the entrance doors to English Heritage's head office to highlight the people's exclusion from Stonehenge at the Summer Solstice. Here he is emerging from the now famous staff arch, instigated by Arthur, at Avebury. Vernal Equinox 1999. *Photo: Brock*

Arise Sir Knight, oops sorry you can't. Arthur knighting the author and eco-warrior Greg Sams in his wheelchair, shortly before Arthur's arrest at the Crystal Palace Protest, 1998.

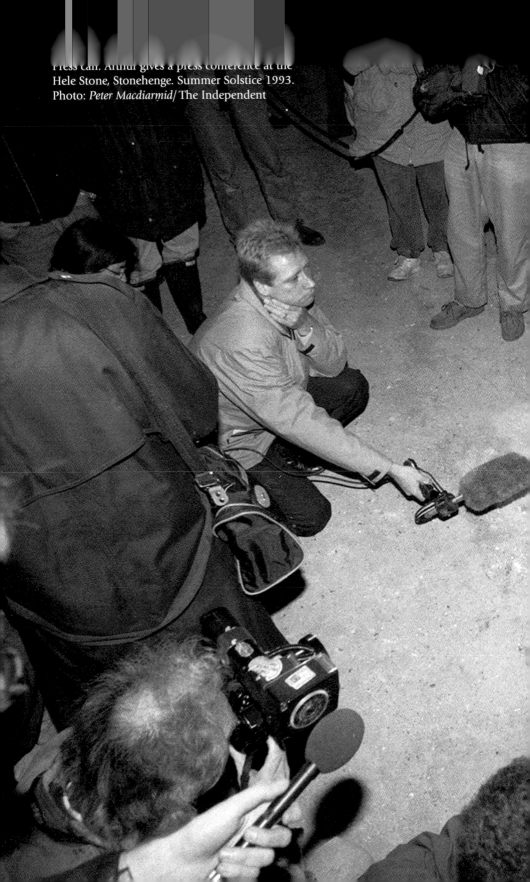

Press call. Arthur gives a press conference at the Hele Stone, Stonehenge. Summer Solstice 1993.
Photo: *Peter Macdiarmid*/ The Independent

▲ The Loyal Arthurian Warband. Over the hill then? Arthur and the Orc (2nd from left) leading the God Party over the bank and ditch at the Avebury Gorsedd to meet the Goddess Party, 1999. *Photo: Brock*

▼ Arthur's charge, or should that be charged? Ten minutes later Arthur was under arrest yet again. The protesters' tree houses are visible in the distance behind the police lines. Third Battle of Newbury, 1996. *Photo: Clive Odinson*

◄ Levitating Druid. Chainsaw Guy and the bailiffs close in on Arthur, whose only escape from the advancing police and security battalions was up into the branches of a tree. Third Battle of Newbury, 1996. *Photo: Clive Odinson*

▼ How many people does it take to arrest a King? Count 'em and see. After two and half hours and a bottle of sherry, Arthur is back on solid ground and under arrest – again. Third Battle of Newbury, 1996. *Photo: Clive Odinson*

....

Overleaf: The sword in the stone. Arthur pulls Excalibur from the 'stonework of London' with the aid of a Crown Court ruling, 5 November 1997. *Photo: PA Photos*

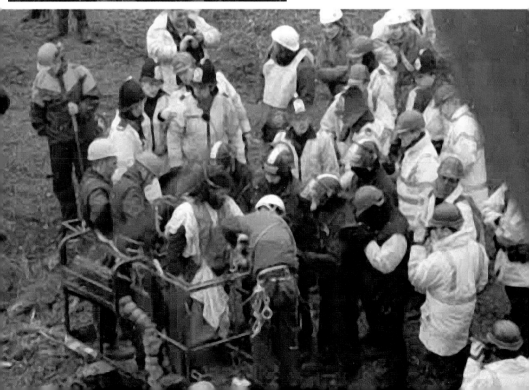

protesters were very, very beautiful, and that Parsley was in his element.

Arthur and the Warband were joining a second front in the magical battle for the soul of Britain.

They were becoming road protesters.

Once more we have to take a pause. We have to ask why? Why were people doing this? Why were people giving up their time and their energy, their homely comforts, their warm beds and their duvets, their TVs and their central heating, to go out on the land, to live in makeshift benders, to suffer the cold and the damp and the alarming proximity of other human beings, to defend a few trees?

This was all rather new.

Traditionally, protest is undertaken out of a sense of injustice. It is the human response to a human situation. People take to the streets to protest against something that is hurting them. They strike for better pay and conditions or to defend their communities. Most often in the last half-century or so, protest has been organised by left-wing groups with a particular agenda. It has had a self-conscious political creed. Not so the road protests. There was no specific political philosophy attached except, maybe, the vaguest notions of being 'green' and having environmental concerns, with a touch of traditional anarchy thrown in. There were the lobby groups, of course, like Friends of the Earth and Greenpeace, but, although these groups were involved to some degree in the road protest movement – usually as office workers and support groups – they didn't organise the protests. The protests were organised by the protesters themselves.

And there were a series of them throughout the 90s – Twyford Down was merely the first – not only protesting against road building, but also against any desecration of the landscape by road or by quarry (quarries and roads being intimately connected, of course). Twyford Down was followed by Solsbury Hill, by the Pollock Free Estate, by Fair Mile, by Whatley Quarry, by the Thanet Way, by Dead Woman's Bottom, by a whole series of increasingly elaborate protests with constantly evolving strategies. At Fair Mile, for instance, an ex-soldier named Kit invented the tunnel system, digging labyrinthine networks of interconnecting tunnels leading to caves leading to holes, with diversionary tunnels, with steel doors and lock-ons and concreted alcoves with hidden stores of food. The idea was that no heavy machinery could be used above ground while anyone was in residence. Once again, it was the protesters putting their own fragile bodies on the line. Other tactics included building aerial walkways between trees, fortified lock-ons, tree houses and the tripod. This last one consisted of three scaffold tubes bolted together at the top from which a protester would dangle precariously, sometimes managing to stay there for days, blocking an entrance gate or whatever, keeping the contractors captive in their own compound. It was this combination of startling innovation and heartfelt commitment that made the road protests so original. It wasn't just a question of marching through the streets and chanting a few well-worn slogans. It was a life-style. A whole culture.

And who were these people?

They not only behaved differently, they looked different too. Wild. Unmanageable. Free. With tattered clothing and body piercings, with tattoos and dreadlocks, with feathers and bells, playing penny whistles and cantering drums, they seemed like something out of story books or legend, like nothing less than the fairy folk of long ago. Coincidentally, like Arthur, they also changed their names.

So it was Lee Tree, Quabollox, Sunflower, Heghist McStone, Swampy, Balin and Galahad, a whole host of names from myth and legend, or made up or discovered, picked up from the forest floor like a feather to be worn in the cap. They were forging identity from the body of the Earth, creating stories for themselves and then living them.

They came from all backgrounds, from all classes: from the public school educated upper-middle class, from the professional middle class, from the aristocracy, from the working class and the underclass, from the drop-out class, the traveller and biker communities. And if they didn't have a unified political philosophy, they had something else. They had a spiritual belief. They believed in the sacredness of the Earth.

So this is what was different about these protests. These were people putting their lives on the line, not only for other human beings, but for the wilderness too, the wildness and beauty of the Earth and its creatures, the plants and animals that live upon it. Putting their humanity on the lines for trees, for birds, for bushes.

If you want to understand the pagan belief system, it's easy. There's no mystery there. There's no invisible God who you can't see or hear or feel, who nevertheless imposes his demands upon you. The pagan goddess isn't at all invisible. You don't need a priesthood to interpret her. Do you want to meet her? Then go out of your front door right now. That's her, out there, in the trees, in the bushes, in the landscape, in the soil, in the wind, in the rain, in the buds, in the shoots, in the clouds, in the air, in the very Earth that gave you birth, that sustains and nourishes you in all her fierce beauty, in her majesty and splendour, in all her moods, from quiet calm to raging, stormy anger, in all her changing aspects, her seasons and her cycles, and her lovely, curving form. And does she have intelligence or feelings, this Earth, this goddess? Of course she does. And who are we to argue in any case? Who are we to say who has intelligence and who does not, with our little, hot, watery brains like soggy walnuts, and without even the wisdom or the foresight to realise that by hurting the Earth we are hurting ourselves? Living lives confined by walls of our own making, in thrall to an abstract philosophy and a god made of paper interpreted by economist-priests telling us that all of this is 'necessary', 'good' and 'progressive', that the survival of whole, complex, delicate ecosystems, a billion years in the making, is less important than saving five minutes on our journey time? Who are we to judge?

And if it's us, as people, who are busy hurting the Earth, then it's up to us, as people, to stop it. It's up to us to do something about it.

We are the Earth.

The road protests can be seen as the revolt of the Earth against the tyranny of abstraction, the revolt of Nature against the tyranny of roads, the revolt of human beings against the tyranny of money. In the end, the argument isn't about whether the Earth will survive or not. Of course the Earth will survive. How can she not survive? It is the vanity of the human to think that we have it in our power to destroy her. The question is whether human beings will survive. It is the question we have to go on asking ourselves, again and again.

Of course, Arthur was only peripherally involved with most of these protests most of the time. He was occupied with other things. But he took a keen interest and watched with amusement as more and more of the knights became caught up in the movement. He would be called to one site or another to take part in a specific action or ritual, or he would use his by now highly-developed media skills to get publicity for the cause. As a 'colourful character' in the 90s protest scene, Arthur was always a hit with media. It made good copy: modern-day Arthur, fighting modern-day battles for the soul of modern-day Britain. He looked good on camera. And Arthur was always ready to oblige, being, as he would admit himself, a media tart, addicted to publicity. There was always some TV crew, some newspaper or magazine, some documentary film-maker hanging about, keeping an eye on his every move.

It was early in 1996 by now. A large protest was taking place around Newbury. It was the largest road protest ever. Nine miles of woodland and wilderness, of silence, of shade, of the delicate interlacing embroidery of living foliage; nine miles of countryside, of laughing streams, of sunlit glade, of woodland walks, of bluebell woods and wild flowers, of the chatter of birds, of memories; nine miles of habitat, of woodland creatures in their abode, of birth and death and rebirth, of foraging through the undergrowth, of snuffling warmth; nine miles of damp and moss and lichen and fern, of leaf mould, of fungus, of fecundity, of abundance, of earth; nine miles of living England, of eternal England, of timeless England, the land of our fathers, the land of our mothers, the land of our birth; nine miles of our past and our future under threat by the A34 bypass, to save five minutes on our journey time, to please the road lobby and the car lobby and the fuel lobby, to serve private enterprise, to bring unnecessary goods and services from around the globe, to pump out fumes.

The protest was being billed as the Third Battle of Newbury. The first two had been fought during the English Civil War, in 1643 and 1644, between the forces of King and Parliament.

Several of the knights were already there. The evictions were starting.

Earlier, one of the other Druids had put out a press statement. He'd said, words to the effect that, 'We're Druids, we're not political, and although we feel for the trees we have no views on whether the Newbury bypass should be built or not.'

Being non-political is always a political stance. It allows those with other agendas to do what they like. Being non-political is to wash your hands of the whole dirty business, to pretend you are above it, to look on with haughty indifference while allowing events to take their course.

This was a challenge, of course. Arthur couldn't remember any such statement having been cleared by previous CoBDO meetings. And it raised a number of ethical points, given that members of several Druid orders were already in residence, it posed a question: one that Arthur immediately set out to answer.

He scrounged a lift to Newbury and arrived late that Sunday night via the pub (so no change there then) and then on to Pixie camp, one of the

30 or so camps that had sprung up along the route. Evictions had begun the week before but the contractors had broken off for the weekend, giving the residents a chance to regroup, to reinforce and to rebuild. There were lock-ons set up at strategic points, tree houses, walkways. A kitchen area and an eating area. Benders for accommodation. A fire pit dug into the living soil and ranged about with planks for seating. A shit pit. All the comforts of home, but in the open air.

Actually, when we say that this was new, that's not quite true. Such innovations of open-air living had already been practiced by the Convoy and free-festival goers at Stonehenge years before, and used as a tactic of protest by the Peace Camps at Greenham and Molesworth. It all goes back to Stonehenge, once again. But here it was so much more evolved, and with trees to defend there were more possibilities for raising the stakes, as it were, to higher levels. Tree houses are just benders in trees. But those who chose to build them and live in them soon found themselves drawn into a sort of psychic relationship with the tree. Trees and human beings meshed in psychic embrace.

Not that Arthur was contemplating such niceties. He was doing night watch. He was sitting by the fire warming his bones. He was having a crack. The Whippet was there, amongst others. The Whippet, the bloody Whippet, Kris Kirkham, the guy who'd named him and set him on his course. He hadn't changed. He was as loud, as wild, as scathing and as funny as ever. Once more fate was intervening in Arthur's life, indicating its approval. He was obviously in exactly the right place, at exactly the right time.

The Whippet had long since gone his own way. After Arthur had left Farnborough to begin his Arthurian quest in Glastonbury, they'd lost contact. The Whippet had become a traveller – though the exact distinction between a traveller and a biker is probably a moot point. It's only down to the choice of transport really. When is a biker not a biker? When he drives a mobile home. And he can always get on a bike again, any time he wants. Indeed, he can carry his bike in the back of his home and be both at the same time.

So it was a long night and a long day and another long night of serious reminiscing before the contractors finally came to continue the evictions.

'Fucking bastard!' said Arthur to the Whippet, indicating his peculiar transformation of dress, his robes and his cloak, his sword and staff: 'Look what you've done to me. Bet you never thought you'd see John the

Hat in a white frock.'

Which once more brought up the question that had been troubling him. Who, exactly, were the real Druids? Were they the guys on the ground wearing the white dresses, consecrating the trees? Consecrating trees that were about to be slaughtered: not so much a consecration as a requiem mass, he thought. Or were the real Druids the ones up the trees actually doing something to defend them?

Both were arguable, of course. He was about to answer the question himself.

It was early Tuesday morning and the alarm sounded a mournful, piercing note, echoing around the quiet woodland like some prehistoric bird cry. Suddenly Pixie camp was shifting from a peaceful open-air campsite to a battlefield. People were scurrying to and fro, shinning up trees to their tree houses, preparing their defences, locking-on to a number of fortified positions in and around the camp. Arthur was just standing there watching, feeling the pump of adrenaline in his blood from the mounting excitement.

And then the troops were moving in: sheriff's officers, bailiffs, security guards, chainsaw operatives, in yellow jackets and hard hats, police in their uniforms, tramping through the hedgerows and the undergrowth, looking and feeling like the Roman battalions marching to battle against the ancient British tribes.

And that was it. Arthur suddenly found himself free-climbing the nearest tree, a beech, fully robed, and with Excalibur at his side, closely pursued by a chainsaw operative. The beech tree already had a tree house in it. It was only on climbing past it that Arthur realised who was in the tree house. It was the Whippet, once more. Of all the trees, in all the world, who else's could he have chosen?

'You all right mate?'

'Yeah, sound. Let's go for it, right? Time to kick arse.'

'Yeah, right.'

So Arthur had the answer to his question: who was the real Druid, the guy in the white frock, on the ground, consecrating the tree, or the guy up the tree defending it? It was neither. It was both. It was the guy up the tree wearing the white frock, consecrating the tree by defending it.

He was high up by now, in the swirling canopy, overlooking the scene below. A cordon of security guards circled the camp, while a 'cherry picker' trundled in. Police were arresting anyone who tried to breach the cordon or as they were cut out from their ground-based lock-ons. Yellow jackets moving around, running this way and that, tree climbers with chainsaws ascending the trees, much noise and confusion, shouts, cat calls, guffaws. People calling across to each other from their different positions. Slogans being chanted. The roar and splutter of the chain saws, like demented mopeds, the creak and crack of branches, the scattering of birds. He was holding on with two hands, his feet wedged between the branches. The chainsaw guy was down below at the tree house. One of the occupants was eventually removed, while the other did a quick shimmy further up the tree.

Looking across, his eyes were greeted by the awesome sight of a Pictish warrior dancing about in some mad aerial ballet, greased up and naked despite the biting January cold, on one of the walkways between the trees. It took several of them at least half an hour before they finally had him in their grasp and he was led away, his Celtic manhood shielded by a policeman's helmet, to the waiting meat wagons.

Only the day before the same warrior, a protester down from Pollock in Scotland, had asked Arthur if the eviction would be tomorrow. He was considering going back up to Scotland for a few days rest and recreation. Arthur told him to wait, that the eviction would be tomorrow. 'I'm a Druid, I know these things,' he'd said.

So it was quite a relief that this prophesy did, in fact, come true. And, oddly perhaps, his predictions mostly do come true. Arthur says he has no idea how this happens since most of what he says is straight off the top of his head.

After this it was Arthur's turn.

Now here's a funny thing. The climber with the chainsaw who had cut away the tree house only minutes before, threw a rope up to him, and he was hoisted a massive bar of chocolate and a full bottle of sherry from the tree house stash. Maybe the chainsaw guy knew what was coming, who knows? Maybe he already admired these people for their dedication and nerve. But it goes to show once more, how easily battle lines can shift, how people on opposing sides can learn to understand and even respect each other.

So Arthur was happy, wasn't he? In full battle mode, with a bottle of sherry to keep him company. He was less interested in the chocolate.

And then the chainsaw operative was ascending, the heavy machine like a two-handed, mechanised sword, whining and wheedling, cutting away the branches as he ascended. Arthur scrambled downwards, thrusting his unprotected arm towards the saw as he did. 'Take my arm off,' he yelled. Well the chainsaw guy was a little bit startled at that. He backed off in surprise. There was a moment of reflection between them. Arthur explained that he would resist any attempt to damage the tree, while the chainsaw guy said that Arthur would be arrested for obstruction.

'Chainsaw Guy.' It was becoming his name. There's a strange intimacy that occurs with one's opponent in battle. It goes beyond right and wrong. Arthur, naturally, felt that he was in the right. Chainsaw Guy probably had no thought of right or wrong, but considered he was doing his job to the best of his abilities. He was well paid for it. But across the ideological gulf that divided them, there was a spark: a spark of blood. They were close enough to smell each other's sweat, to hear the panting of breath, to feel the tension in each other's thoughts.

Let battle commence. It was like this. Chainsaw Guy would raise the saw towards a branch, and Arthur would thrust his arm in the way. Chainsaw Guy would parry and thrust, feint and weave, while Arthur danced, free-standing on the branches, stooping down with his arm held out. Occasionally a branch would fall with a crack and a shiver, but mostly Arthur held on to most of the branches. And on and on and on it went, while they both breathed and sweated, trying to outmanoeuvre each other, trying to guess each other's thoughts. On and on. Thrust, parry, counterthrust, biting machine versus raw flesh. Sinews that screamed. Blood pumping. Hearts swaying. Arms that racked and ached. Bit by bit the branches were falling as Arthur's foothold was beginning to give way. People down below were looking up in stunned awe, as Arthur maintained his delicate stance. People said it looked like he was levitating, so small were the twigs on which he was balancing. But still he held on.

And then something very strange happened. Who knows what goes on in people's heads in the midst of battle? Arthur found himself taking Excalibur from its scabbard, and raising Chainsaw Guy as a brother knight of the Warband. Sir Chainsaw Guy, as he must now be called.

The cherry picker was called up. It loomed up at him like a mutant bird, craning its neck in some mad parody of a mating dance.

Crazier and crazier. Arthur had gone several days without sleep. He'd just drunk a whole bottle of sherry. He was free climbing, unharnessed, between twigs hardly bigger than his fingers. He was swaying about in the wind, drunk but not disorderly.

'Touch me and I fall!' he yelled, as they continued the ascent, trying to cut the tree away from beneath him. Anyone else would have given up hours before. But he was less King Arthur than Mad Dog Arthur by now, still pushing everything to the limits. People who had laughed at him at first, for his pretentious name and ridiculous dress sense, came to see what we all see in the end, that – call it what you will – there's a mad warrior spirit that inhabits the man at times, which is undeniable and, occasionally, awesome. Arthur Uther Pendragon is only another name, after all.

The people were gathered behind the police lines, protesters and well-wishers and other assorted locals, clapping and cheering him on. Centre stage at last. He always was a show-off.

But – well – all good shows must come to an end, and this one had lasted two-and-a-half hours. It was the best two-and-a-half hours free entertainment many of them had had.

Arthur was making another of his flying leaps when Excalibur got caught in a V in the branches, and he was stuck. They managed to get handcuffs onto him, and a line was put around his chest. Only now he'd wrapped his legs around a bough, and was refusing to let go. They were pulling and tugging at him, trying to drag him away, but those old biker legs were staying put. How else had he managed to stay on his bike through all the mad scrapes, but by gripping onto it with fierce determination? No one was going to move him. And you can imagine it, can't you? The gaggle of sheriff's officers and police officers and bailiffs and contractors swaying about on a cherry picker, hands around this one, mad, Druid, biker King, all puffing and panting, trying to drag him away. Crazy.

One of the Sheriff's officers shouted, 'Throw the sword,' but Sir Chainsaw Guy was having none of it. He tied a line around the sword and lowered it to the ground. After that they managed to get another line around Arthur's chest, which was tied and tensioned, and he blacked out. This was illegal, of course, but since when did legality get in the way of 'progress'? He came to in the cradle of the cherry picker, surrounded by boots and arms as it was lowered to the ground, after which he was arrested. And you can see the picture. How many people does it take to arrest a King?

Count 'em and see.

CHAPTER TWELVE

Camelot (of Cabbages and Kings)

Love is rage.

Anyone who tells you that love cannot feel anger at injustice, at the loss of our heritage, at the destruction of our countryside, at the sale of our birthright, is lying to you.

Love is laughter.

Anyone who tells you that love cannot laugh, at its self in particular, and what it sees of itself in the world, at its own absurdity, is lying to you.

Love is intelligence.

Anyone who tells you that love cannot focus, that it cannot concentrate, that it has no capacity to reason and to look into causes, to weigh, to judge, to answer questions, to size up the matter and reach conclusions, is lying to you.

Love is practical.

Anyone who tells you that love cannot build tree houses, that it cannot sew patches, that it cannot cook food, that it cannot learn, and by learning achieve, is lying to you.

Love is surprising.

Anyone who tells you that love will not come, that it has abandoned you, that you will not feel it any more, that it will not renew and revive and refresh you in your daily life like soft spring rain, is lying to you.

Love is down to Earth.

Anyone who tells you that love is out of the ordinary, an exception to the rule, that it cannot be found except in temples with gurus, who does not seek it in the dull and the everyday, in life as it is lived by human beings, is lying to you.

And that's what the Newbury road protest was. A daily dose of love. Love in the bitter mornings, waking with the dawn, falling from your bender, stoking up the fire to put the kettle on. Love in the kitchen making porridge for the crew. Love in the work, as tree houses and lock-ons and fortifications are being prepared. Love in the evening around a communal fire, with songs and jokes and cider for company. Love in the night, with restful sleep and fresh-air dreams and more love tomorrow. A neverending cycle of love and rage and contemplation and wind-stirred trees, and battle and loss and songs and tears and hope and imagination, with inspiration and expiration, and love and love and love.

It is real. Living on the land, so close to the land, between the roots and the branches, looking up to the sky to check the weather, hearing the night birds call in your dreams, to feel the labour of the days, the panting of breath and deep heart-stirrings, where nature never wavers, this is humanity. The raven in flight, wind-ruffled, weaving tales, riding the air, as close as poetry. You absorb it all. You do, you do. It becomes a part of you. It becomes you.

And where would we be without wild Nature, out there somewhere? Where would our dreams be? Somewhere, deep down and far away, we are connected to the land. Somewhere, deep down and far away, the wild creatures stir, even in us, and their lives are lived in us, even as they are lived in the world. This will always be so. It is our nature.

So there were nights and days, evenings and mornings, rains and mists, darkness and light, shifts and dreams. And there was cooking and sewing and knitting and building and planning and conceiving and working and chatting and taking time and time off and making spaces and spaced out laughter and loud laughter and quiet moments and wild moments, out there in the wild, and all the time being human. Because this is the illusion that has been thrust upon us, that nature and the human are apart, separate. We are not separate. We are the same. And there is nothing so lovely, so complete, as when the human world and the wild world intertwine, weaving about each other in the dance, as when the artefacts of humanity grow old and decay, as when the old walls crumble and grow moss and lichen, as when the human symbols, our works of creation, are incorporated into the natural world, not to dominate it, but to be a part. A part, not apart.

Nature loves us. The Earth loves us. We've forgotten our role in the dance, that's all. We've got out of step.

So Arthur decided to stay. This was where he was meant to be.

The next step was to find a site.

Of course, there were many sites ranged up and down the nine-mile stretch, from Mary Hare at one end, to Tot Hill at the other. Gotan, Snelsmore Common, Castle Wood, Middle Oak, Granny Ash, Rickety Bridge, Redding's Copse and more. All of them had their particular geometry, their individual atmosphere, their philosophy, their moods. Partly this was determined by the place, the particular spot on the Earth where the site was located, by the local flora and fauna. Its Genius Loci, in other words, its spirit of place. Partly, too, it was determined by the people.

As we said earlier, there was no unifying political philosophy here. So you had all sorts, from radical anarchist vegans to animal rights activists to drop-out losers to spaced-out mystics to free-party people to yoghurt weavers and tofu welders to reincarnated Arthurian knights. Sometimes, maybe, they didn't always see eye-to-eye. Some sites were run with military precision and stark discipline, while others consisted of no more than a couple of grumpy drunks out of their heads on Special Brew. Some drank beer, some drank cider, some smoked dope. Some were philosophical while others were practical. Some were mystical while others were political. Some were vegetarian, while others were irredeemably carnivorous. Arthur, in particular, didn't want to end up on a site where he wasn't allowed to eat meat. He hated what he called veggie slop, the boiled vegetables in a runny sauce that passed as food on some sites. It's one of the things about him. Despite his raising to high office, he was (and is) uncompromisingly proletarian in his preferences. So, it's meat and two veg, bacon and egg, pie and chips. He even looks at brown bread askance as a peculiar culinary innovation. As for chilli con carné, he'll only eat it if it has baked beans instead of kidney beans.

It was obvious he was going to have to go somewhere else, away from the veg heads and vegan fascists who dominated some of the other sites, self-righteously looking down their noses at anyone with different tastes than theirs.

Not every vegan is a fascist, by the way. Only some of them are. It probably arises out of the fact that, actually, they'd really like to tuck into a nice, juicy steak.

So the knights Bran and Orc were dispatched to find a suitable home. Which they duly did. It was halfway along the route, bordered on two sides by water, surrounded by fragrant meadow, with several reasonably-sized trees and a fallen crack willow at its heart. Now, what to call it?

Camelot, naturally.

Arthur had long since abandoned the idea of building a fixed Camelot from which to hold court. He was an itinerant king, a travelling king. He was never in one spot for long. Camelot was anywhere where he was. It was the travelling court of Camelot. And, indeed, before the fixed court of the medieval imagination, the mythological Arthur had certainly ranged all around these isles, leaving his name like an identity tag on rocks and wells and hills and caves, marking Britain with his presence. Might not the historical Arthur also have travelled this widely, as tradition suggests, fighting battles in all corners of this land? Even the literary Camelot is not always placed in the same spot. Now our current Arthur's Camelot travelled about with him, putting down roots temporarily, only to be lifted again, whenever he moved on.

So Camelot it was, on the proposed route of the Newbury bypass.

The three of them, Arthur, Bran and the Orc, built a fire, and then sat around it keeping vigil on the first night, making plans and contemplating, listening to the crack and whistle of the fire while the red warmth played about their features, keeping the bleak night at bay, until the morning mists arose like dragon's breath, and they set about the work. They built a communal bender of hazel switches, pliable as whips, dug into the ground for solidity, and arched and weaved like spells to give strength – the oldest form of human habitation, of course – which they layered over with tarpaulin and tied up securely with rope. It was as sturdy a structure as you could find. It was about 18-foot high and 18-foot across and slept 12 to 15 people with ease. They called it the Great Hall.

Then Arthur dug the shit pit while the Orc and Bran set about preparing the fortifications. They built aerial walkways and tree houses. They dug a moat, joining the river on one side with the stagnant water on the other. They built a ramparted palisade made of old fence stakes. Arthur tapped in each stake in the palisade with Excalibur, raising it as a rampart of protection. It looked as if he was knighting them. Some of the contractors saw him doing it. Thus it has been passed down in legend that Arthur knights fence posts.

The work went on for days, weeks. Eventually others joined them. First of all Galahad – the guy who CJ had met in Salisbury nick – and then refugees from other sites as they were being cleared. They had a proper little community going.

Do you want to know what life on a protest site is like? It's like this. The heart of any site is the fire, the hearth. Heart, hearth and earth, maybe there's some connection? The hearth is the heart of the earth. The fire is dug into the earth and circled by stones, as guardians. The stones hold the fire in, protecting it. Most of the time there is a kettle boiling on it. So all the elements are there: earth, air, fire and water. Food is cooked upon it and then eaten around it. During the day visitors are welcomed to it, offered tea and conversation. At night they weave their tales around it, drink and carouse, engage in ceremony, sing songs, whisper endearments, smoke, make jokes, laugh, plan, squabble, come and go, feed it, nurture it, poke it with sticks, tap it to see the sparks rise, fall asleep beside it, wake up, blink, look about with wondering eyes, dodge the smoke, before finally deciding it's time to go to bed.

The hearth is the focal point of all human exchange, the centre point for the ancient human economy.

And sometimes magic happens around it.

Spirits are drawn to it. The ancestors gather to be with the living. Ghosts of the night flit amid its fleeting shadows.

Things happen.

And then someone will stand and recite a poem, an epic tale of deeds and adventure, while another will stand beside him miming to the words as they rise and fall, declaiming and gesturing with mannered precision, and it's as if a charm has come over the world, a sparkle, as if the night woods have become a theatre, the backdrop to that most ancient of plays, the human drama. And a feeling of hushed awe descends over the company as they welcome the spirits into their midst.

Because this fire has roots, not in the earth, but in time. And back, back, through the centuries, through the millennia, back through ages past, this fire, these people have been here, back to the beginning of the human story, when the world was new, when the people were shining beings, when the world glowed with its own internal light, this fire has played here in this hearth, the force that made us human. And in its embers we read our own story. In its warmth we feel our own warmth. In its light we see our own light. And the sparks that rise up into the night sky are like angels, and in its dark heart we see the writings of the Old Ones, hoary as the flames, whose language is time. And here we read our future, we read our past, we read our present, we read of all our days and all the things that make us human and alive, that make us want to sing, to love, to laugh, to recite poetry, to give birth, to dance, to grow, to become ever more and more fully human.

And then, maybe, someone will bring out a guitar, and the songs of the heart will be replayed, songs we have known, always, deep-rooted and as ancient as the trees, and the tribe draws in, ever closer, knowing they are one in their diversity, an organism, a life form, knowing that they belong, as we belong, as the Earth belongs to us. Property is a sin. It is a lie. It is a crime. It is the dispossession of humanity. It is our enemy. It takes away what we are. Because we are the Earth, and how can the Earth be owned or sold? It's like selling off our souls.

And then the drums might start, that deep-heart Earth rhythm like a spiralling heartbeat, racing wildly, stirring the night's depths with rhythmic insistence, a battering pulse, running in rivulets of strung-out deep bass Earth-notes and high notes, like the rattled chatter of baboons, all the tension of the stretched skins echoing about the dark woods and through the earth, a stream becomes a torrent, shattering and returning, circling, weaving, running rings around the trees, lighting up the darkness, joining all hearts as one. And don't we all feel it? Can't we all feel it? That pulse that always sways us, that sets our hearts drumming, that sets our hips spinning, that sets our minds swirling, that sets our feet skipping, that sets our legs dancing, that sets our arms waving, that reminds us of who we are: the rhythm of the Earth.

It is round the hearth that the people become a tribe. And it was round the Camelot hearth that the knights found their purpose at last and Arthur was acknowledged as the tribal elder.

And now, do you know Arthur yet? Have you met him? In all of these pages, have you got a feel? Do you know what he is like? You've heard his story. You've seen his photograph – you've seen a number of photographs – but have you experienced him yet? Have you been introduced?

Let's do introductions. Let's imagine we're sitting around that fire, and that you haven't met Arthur yet, and that CJ is about to introduce you.

This is Arthur. An old warhorse. Stubborn as a rock. Tenacious as fire. Gifted with thought. Bright. Hopeful. Funny. An inspiration in battle. A leader you can depend on. Solid. Self-confident. Quick to size up the situation. Quick to make decisions. Alert. Authoritative. Someone who would die for the cause if he knew the cause was just. A warrior. A hero. A patriot of the old country, of heath and hearth and home, keeping the home fires burning, because he knows that Britain is a land, not an identity, is a feeling, not a language, that it welcomes all who arrive on these shores, that its essence is justice and honour and truthfulness and fairness and fair dealings and fair shares for all and that all of these things are worth fighting for.

Just like his dad.

On the other hand, as CJ always says, Arthur's best qualities are also his worst. So the same stubbornness that kept his legs locked around that beech tree, that confronts figures of authority with equal authority, that has him locked up in jail, time and time again, over issues that matter to him, is also, to friends, infuriating. And his quickness makes him impatient at times. And his solidity makes him unable to see another's point of view. And his authority can make him dismissive of another's authority. And he can be self-centred and vain, paying too little heed to another's thoughts and feelings. And his warrior nature, that single-minded self-determination, so useful in the field of battle, makes him emotionally clumsy, unable to sympathise with other people's feelings. He has empathy with the warrior but no empathy for the wounded. He blusters through life's niceties like a bear with bad eyesight, loud and bombastic, and full of his own sense of self-importance, his own sense of being himself. Because that's what he is in the end. He is himself.

And let Arthur introduce CJ.

He has a keen wit and a serious amount of writing skill, but unfortunately his best points are also his worst. His wit can be seen by people who don't know him well enough as scathing, and his writing skill makes him somewhat of a perfectionist, thus throwing any hope of meeting deadlines to the wind, thus aggravating Arthur's impatience as someone who is sworn to honour his spoken word. In short, he is himself.

And – now – who are you? Are you yourself too? Because that's the permission you are getting here. To be yourself, to be truly yourself, to carry yourself with poise and confidence, to assert yourself, to be who you are, to not be afraid, to stand up for yourself, to have your own mind, to be alert to life's adventures, to weave your own tale, to name yourself anew and begin again. To reign as king or queen of your own domain. To be free. To be whoever you want to be.

So that's the communal hearth, with Arthur sitting beside it, as he was wont to do most nights with his friends, drinking cider, making plans and laughing. Because that's all this story is in the end: it's a story about friends.

And the days passed, and the nights, and the people did what humans do. They got up, ate, had a shit, worked, squabbled, had disagreements, lost their tempers, picked on each other, cooked food, ate food, flared up, made tea, drank tea, drank cider, took drugs, whiled away the passing hours, went to bed, fucked – sometimes, if they were lucky – slept and then woke again. The normal round of human activity, but with these two additions. Firstly, that it was all taking place in the open, beneath the sky, and that it rained on them, snowed on them, blew gales, hailed, blustered and stormed. And, secondly, that they never knew in the evening if tomorrow would be their last day. So there was a tension there, a sense of urgency, knowing that all this might soon be gone, all this work, these defences, scattered and ripped apart, as if it had never happened, these trees torn screaming from the ground, this earth churned up in a welter of black mud and derision.

It's strange, knowing your fate. Would any of us do anything if we knew what the outcome would be?

But they carried on regardless, in proper English fashion. Each new day seemed like a victory, each night that passed without incident. Every cup of tea was an act of defiance. Knowing that the longer they held on, the more money it cost the contractors, the less likely it would be that such schemes would be allowed in the future. Accepting the inevitable defeat with equanimity as merely one step towards their final victory. Because they would win, they knew that. They *had* to win. Anything else was impossible to contemplate.

A couple of observations about the economy. Firstly, that the scarcest thing on site was toilet paper, and that toilet paper therefore became a kind of currency. It's an odd parallel with the economy of the outside world, that both of them use paper currency. And Dr Freud said that when you dream of money you are dreaming of shit, and that when you are dreaming of shit you are dreaming of money. And Comrade Lenin said, that, come the revolution, gold will be used to make toilets, because gold and shit are both useless waste products. You can take that anyway you like. On site, they shat in a hole in the ground. But they also learned about value. Value is anything that validates the human, that gives us validity. Value is created by the human, through the valour of our labour. And all the works of love are valuable, to be valued. Every cup of tea is valuable. Every kindly word, every good joke, every slap-up meal, every walk in the woods, every thought that passes, every plan that comes to fruition. Every good thing that a human being does adds value to the world, because we are the only objective measure of worth. And everything that adds to our humanity and our environment adds value, and anything that compromises our humanity and our environment is anti-value: worse than valueless. And in the end we can do without paper currency, whether it's toilet roll or five-pound notes, but we can't do without trees.

Money doesn't grow on trees, you know.

Yes it does. It's paper. It's made of trees.

And a word about the food. They got their food on skip-runs. They would cadge a lift to the nearest supermarket, climb the fence into the backyard, and pick the food out of the skips that the supermarket had thrown away. Supermarkets throw away a lot of food. One day it's for sale on the shelf, the next it's past its sell-by date and they throw it in the skip. They don't give it away, of course, even though it's perfectly edible food. They don't give it away because by doing that they would be compromising their profits. Who would buy food when you knew you could get it for free? We'd all be waiting for the sell-by date. So they throw it in the skip, often spoiling it on purpose: pouring bleach over it, or smashed glass. Such is the world we live in, where food is transported around the globe, from the poorest countries to the richest, and then thrown away.

One day, the Orc and Bran went on a skip run. They found packets and packets of sausages and bacon. So they tied the packages on one of their staffs, like hunters with their quarry, and carrying it between them, marched through the vegetarian's camp, hooting and hollering, whooping with wild glee.

The Orc is a giant of a man, by the way. He needs his meat to feed his bones. After which he becomes a one-man JCB, shifting soil by the ton.

And a word about water. They got their water from the pub, or from the supermarket, or from the service station down the road, lugging it for miles in large plastic containers. They didn't drink the river water. Arthur tried it once and it did him no harm. But having declared it safe, the rest of the tribe tried it and came down with a gut-wrenching illness that had them laid up in their benders for days.

It was while everyone was ill in bed that Arthur did his famous ditchfinder general routine, and got well and truly quogged: that is, bogged down in a quagmire.

He'd been to the pub. He must have been fairly well-done, boiled in booze, because at one time he was seen being pushed home in a supermarket trolley. It's what supermarkets sell these days. Pickled Arthurs. Later still, he was found asleep by the side of the road by the boys in blue, who handed him over to the protesters. And then he must have got lost. He was wandering through the trees in the dead of night, stumbling from tree to tree, till he found the bog, fell into it up to his waist, and promptly fell asleep. It's one of the qualities that marks Arthur out: his ability to sleep in ditches up to his gonads in mud. It's one of the qualities he shares with the legendary Arthur too, the Welsh Arthur, who was himself often swallowed up by the earth by the power of angry saints.

There weren't any saints here, however. When he woke up he couldn't move, and he just had to sit there, bog-drearily quogged in Newbury's own mess of pottage. He wasn't far from Camelot and shouted for help. No one could help him though, being all too ill with the after-effects of drinking the stinking river water. So it was all Arthur's fault for encouraging them to drink it in the first place.

Enter Susanna, and Lee Tree.

Both of them were veterans of the protest sites. Susanna was in her mid-40s at the time; originally from New Zealand, with a clutch of kids from two relationships; she had, she said, been called to these protests by blood. That's what we mean when we say it's hard to know where the protests were coming from at times. 'By blood' has a faintly fascist sound. She meant that she was being called by the spirit, by something deep down and non-verbal, something as fundamental as blood.

Lee Tree is the son of a Yorkshire miner. He'd been brought up during the miner's strike. He had seen his parents strength and resolve. He had known the injustice of their defeat. He had felt the fire of indignation in his blood. Thus it is that our masters make our revolutionaries, down through the generations. Blood doesn't forget.

They were just passing by when they came across Arthur, up to his waist in mud, his cloak laid about him like some kind of a fungal growth.

'You all right, mate? You look a bit stuck.'

'Yeah, yeah, I'm fine. Just get me out of here, will you?'

Which they did, pulling him up by his armpits, and dragging him across the mud. He looked like the Creature from the Black Lagoon, completely smeared in stinking, black mud.

Lee Tree's attitude to Arthur was one shared by most of the protesters on most of the other sites. Well, if he wants to say he's King Arthur, he thought, then let him. We don't care. It's what you do that matters, not who you say you are.

Susanna had witnessed Arthur's performance on the beech tree from behind the security cordon, back at Pixie camp, and had been suitably impressed. She recognised that warrior energy and knew that it was her own. Later, Susanna was one of the refugees from other sites who came to join Arthur at his camp.

Every day the eviction loomed ever closer, Arthur fighting it off through the courts. Until the eviction orders came through it was still officially their home, legally squatted. They had Section 6 notices all around the site, declaring that it was their home.

Two days before the eviction he was at the Royal Courts of Justice in London presenting papers. He was still quogged up from his immersion in the Slough of Alcoholic Ruination. A job's-worth guard at the security desk in the entrance lobby told him that he wasn't to bring the sword in with him.

'I'm King Arthur,' he said. 'I've got an appointment to see a judge.'

'I don't care who you are,' said Job's Worth, 'you're not bringing that thing in here.'

Arthur asked that a judge be brought down to clear this up, but he was told that none were available.

'You've got a whole building full of judges, what do you mean, none are available?'

'They're busy. We can't just go getting judges for everyone who wants to speak to one.'

'Well I know there's at least one judge available. The one I'm supposed to be seeing right now.'

'You're still not coming in here with that sword,' said the guard.

'Well OK, but know this,' said Arthur, in that booming, authoritative voice of his, 'you take a sword off a Druid swordbearer and you make him naked. You want naked? I'll show you naked.' And he threw off his robes. Thus earning himself the title of the tenth most outrageous person in Britain in *Loaded* magazine that year.

Security called the police, who asked what the problem was.

'I've no problem,' said Arthur. 'It's them who don't like to see me without clothes. So it's their problem, not mine.'

'Yeah, you're right Arthur,' said the police, 'see you,' and left them to it.

And so, eventually the judge was called, as Arthur had requested in the first place, who said that of course he could bring his sword in: just get him in here, there's work to be done.

In court he argued that eviction papers had not been properly served, there being no one in residence at the time. His argument was not accepted, and the judge ruled that Camelot could be evicted.

And every day news arrived from other sites of other evictions. Every day the devastation grew, as this once peaceful part of England was turned into a war zone. It began to resemble the Somme.

They had something they called 'The Camelot Pact.' Arthur had conceived it when he had been arrested for the sword at Granny Ash previously. The Newbury police cells were full, so he had to be taken to Basingstoke, in Hampshire. Of course, the Hampshire constabulary were used to Arthur and his sword. They had been the first police force in the country to give him permission to carry it. The desk sergeant knew Arthur well. 'Hello, Arthur, what's up this time?'

'They've arrested me for the sword,' Arthur had said, indicating the embarrassed Thames Valley officers behind.

'They can't do that,' said the desk sergeant, laughing. 'Charge refused.' And they had to take him back to Newbury.

But it was the fact that the Newbury cells were full that gave him the idea for the Camelot Pact. He decided that if they all were arrested and refused bail conditions, that all the cells in the locality would soon become full, and in the end they would have to stop arresting people.

It was this kind of resolve that helped Camelot earn its reputation as 'fluffy but firm.' Hardcore.

They were the first site in the country to use police-issue handcuffs on the lock-ons.

'Fluffy', by the way, is one of the protesters' terms. It means to be

non-violent. It was a tactic employed from the beginning of the movement. The protesters attempted to remain friendly with the contractors
and the security guards, so as not to give them a handle. By being fluffy
they disarmed the opposition of their tribal identity. How do you become
aggressive with a girl who, only minutes before, had been flirting with
you? Later, Class War protesters of the old school had grown weary of this
approach. A more aggressive punk style had developed. 'Spiky'. And so a
debate was initiated: fluffy versus spiky.

Arthur's tactic lay between these two schools of thought. Non-violent,
but we take no shit. Fluffy but firm – although, it has to be said, 'fluffy' is
the least appropriate adjective you could apply to Arthur. He's about as
fluffy as a thorn tree on a craggy bluff in a storm at midnight.

Camelot was the last of the first wave of evictions on the Newbury bypass site. It took place on 1 April 1996, the beginning of the nesting season, and was, therefore, totally illegal. But, as we said before, since when
did they allow the law to stand in the way of so-called economic
progress?

Things had changed dramatically since Arthur's first arrest at Pixie
camp.

For a start, they had hired all security guards to cordon off each site.
There were several thousand of them by now. When an eviction was taking place, they would cordon off the whole area before the contractors
moved in. The security guards would stand around, bored most of the
time. They didn't have much to do barring the odd occasion when a protester would attempt to rush them. They were standing, elbow to elbow,
mile after mile, all in their yellow jackets, with their white hard hats, kicking their heels and having a laugh. They weren't bad people, although
they were badly paid – £3.50 an hour at the beginning of the project,
though the Department of Transport was paying the contractors who
hired them £15 an hour. Mostly they were taken from the army of the
unemployed, stuck on the dole for years, and then forced to take this job
whether they liked it or not. They just stood, hour after hour, waiting for
the tea urn to arrive. Which it would, every three hours or so.

Behind them stood the red hats, the supervisors, on £5.50 an hour,
marching up and down and barking orders.

And then the others would move in, the police, bailiffs, sheriff's
officers, Brays Detective Agency, contractors, specialist tree climbers,

chainsaw operators, digger drivers, cherry picker drivers, all in their different coloured hard hats (and all better paid than the security guards) all of these hundreds and thousands of people to evict a few mad Druids from a tatty bit of land. It does make you question where their priorities lie. The cost, to the DoT, and to the British Taxpayer, was running at £40,000 a day, from January through to April, and this was before they'd even begun working on the road itself.

About the police. Officially the police are not supposed to take sides. There is a lawful right to work, and a lawful right to protest. It is the police's role merely to observe, and to arrest people only when they have broken the law. That should have applied equally to the contractors as to the protesters. In practice, however, the police tended to ignore the contractors breaches of the law – managing to overlook acts of random violence, for example, or the breach of health and safety laws – while enforcing the letter of the law far too rigorously when it came to the protesters.

An example of this is their use of the Breach of the Peace law. Technically, an officer can arrest someone if he thinks that that person is likely to cause a breach of the peace. But he must have good cause to believe that if he wants to bring the case before the courts. In effect, at Newbury, as at other protest sites, police will arrest people for breach of the peace, bail them not to return to within a certain distance of the protest site, and then quietly drop the charges. In other words, the law is being used as a tactic to suppress the protest. In the case of Newbury this resulted in the so-called Newbury Sausage, an area of land either side of the proposed route – long and thin and shaped like a sausage – from which protesters could be effectively banned, without ever being charged with a crime.

Arthur always saw his job as that of bail breaker. In other words, he would allow himself to get arrested – often inviting the arrest – refusing bail conditions, thus ending up on remand, before going back to the court to have the bail conditions lifted, after which the other protesters could go back to court and demand the lifting of their conditions too. Arthur using the law to oppose the law, as was always his intention.

So now we arrive at the morning of the first of April, and the eviction.

You already know what a full scale eviction is like from the description of the Pixie camp eviction in the previous chapter. Camelot was just as mad, just as intense, but with much more media attention. There were TV crews and journalists from around the globe. And you can imagine it, what with the palisade and the ramparts and the moat, with the lock-ons with police handcuffs, and the tree houses and aerial walkways, and the contractors running round, and the police, and all the Druids in their by-now filthy robes, with the addition of spells and curses in the grand magical tradition, with the shouting and the taunting, and the chainsaws going full pelt, as if all hell was being loosed upon the world and nothing could ever be peaceful again. And you can also imagine that Arthur enjoyed himself immensely, relishing the defiance, the blood-boiling intensity, the fervour, the fierce aliveness of it all.

It was battle.

It was struggle.

It was the very breath of life to him.

As he always said, 'I'll fight for peace, but if we ever get it, I'm out of here.'

The notion of a peaceful life is Arthur's idea of purgatory.

And there were one or two funny moments.

One of the favourite pastimes on site had been playing out Monty Python sketches amongst themselves, both from *Monty Python and the Holy Grail* (naturally), but also from *The Life of Brian*.

That's how they saw themselves. More like the Knights Who Say Ni, than the Brotherhood of the Holy Cross.

The job of supervising the evictions and of reclaiming the land for the DoT fell to one Nicholas Blandy, the Under-Sheriff of Berkshire.

Before the evictions began, he would have to address the protesters through a loudhailer telling them that they were about to be evicted. It was a formulaic address, read out from a piece of paper in a bored voice. He always said the same thing.

'I am Nicholas Blandy, Under-Sheriff of Berkshire, you are all trespassing on private property ...' etc, etc.

And on like this, reading them their rights.

Only when it came to the Camelot eviction, he got no further than saying his name.

'I'm Nicholas Blandy ...' he said.

'No you're not, I'm Nicholas Blandy,' someone shouted, from one of the tree houses.

'No, I'm Blandy,' from a lock-on on the ground.

'No – I'm Blandy', 'I'm Blandy', 'I'm Blandy', from all round the site, echoing through the stricken trees, one after the other. And then, 'No, I'm Blandy and so's my wife,' to rapturous applause, as the infuriated Mr Blandy threw down his megaphone and stormed off site.

And then, when the eviction was over, and Arthur was being led off, handcuffed towards the police vehicle, someone spoke to him from behind.

'Arthur, are you sad for the trees?' said the voice, in the worst mock-French accent he'd ever heard.

Arthur thought it was one of the knights playing out the sketch from *Monty Python and the Holy Grail*, where the French Knights hold a castle, and taunt Graham Chapman's Arthur in bad French accents.

So he turned and in a line from the film, in his own worst French accent, said, 'I fart in your general direction.'

Unfortunately, he was saying it on live TV. The man with the bad French accent, was, in fact, French, doing a news report for French TV.

Whoops!

The Camelot Pact worked, and they filled up Newbury, Reading, Andover and Basingstoke police cells before, finally, they gave up arresting people.

In court the following day, Arthur stood as a Mackenzie Friend for all 18 of them, acting as their spokesman.

When asked what they pleaded, he said, 'Guilty as hell, your honour. We have broken your laws and deserve to be punished accordingly. But we are answerable to higher laws, both morally and ethically, and we would do it all again tomorrow.'

The magistrate must have liked them. Maybe he had a soft spot for mad Druid knights in earth-smeared battle frocks. Maybe he admired their dress sense. Or maybe they just didn't want this lot clogging up the cells. He gave them all conditional discharges. Arthur objected. He was already on conditional discharge, he said. His presence here meant that he had broken his conditions. He ought to have a custodial sentence. He was angling to get to prison. So the magistrate tut-tutted and gave him a custodial sentence. He was made to sit at the back of the court until it rose, some 15 minutes later.

Which might well be the shortest custodial sentence in history, who knows?

CHAPTER THIRTEEN

The Ballad of Bullingdon Gaol

And now, do you want to see it? The Newbury bypass site after the evictions, but before the road was built. Can you imagine the devastation?

It was like a war zone: 10,000 trees had died in that three-month period. It is trees that hold the earth together. Heavy machinery plied its way over the sodden ground churning it to mud, caterpillar tracks and treaded tyres gouging deep cuts in the belly of the land, grinding over tree roots like body parts lying discarded in the mire. The smell of death and decay mixed with diesel and the breath of men. Dying trees, ripped screaming from the living soil, now piled up in huge funeral pyres awaiting the release of fire. Dense yellow smoke from the smouldering pyres drifting like a pall over the broken earth. The only sounds the constant droning and revving of the chainsaws as they went about their deadly business. Solitary ravens like bad omens wavering mournfully overhead, surveying the dismal scene.

And what is a tree? It is a life form, a living being. Older than a man, rugged and deep-rooted, clutching the earth with a fierce grip, a tree stands for all that is solitary and unwavering in the soul of man, for all that is ancient and connected. As old as time, trees are the living repositories of memory in the landscape, the holders of time. Some of these trees have seen generations of men come and go, kings and queens and dynasties of men, have stood in silent contemplation while our little, fast, impatient bodies had scurried about their roots, have watched as men pursued their vanities and vendettas, and fought their bitter grievances, adding grief to painful grief.

It is the stupidity of men to think that we are the only form of intelligence on this Earth. It is the arrogance of men to think that we are all that matter. It is the blindness of men to think that the rest of the Earth cannot see us and judge us and weigh our hearts and know what we are.

A tree is all things. It is a living ecosystem, a whole world. From the fungal spores that nestle in its roots, sending sprays of filaments through its fibres, to the birds that ride the air and settle in its branches, from the worms that churn in its dark earth, to the insects that crawl in its bark, from the mammals that snuffle and scurry in its undergrowth, breathing moistness, to the lichens and the mosses and monstrous fungal outgrowths like sculptural diseases, a tree is a universe of diversity, an epic struggle of life for life, a story, an adventure, a witness, a journey.

And don't we already know this? Isn't all of this written into us by our own myths and legends? How many times have we made trees our symbols? It was a tree that gave us the knowledge of good and evil. It was from the World Tree Yggdrasill that Odin hung to learn the secrets of the runes, and it was in a burning bush that Moses met the Ancient of Days, who inscribed the Ten Commandments for him, as a path to lead the blind. The Tree of Knowledge, the Tree of Life, the World Tree, they are our most ancient sacred symbols. And didn't Robin Hood lean against this laughing Oak in Sherwood Forest, waiting for a guest? And maybe Lancelot and Guinevere made love in the hidden recesses of the Yew grove, while Arthur stood distant by a wounded Oak, knowing he had been betrayed.

And Birch and Rowan and Alder and Willow and Ash and Hawthorn and Oak and Holly and Hazel and Apple and Vine and Ivy and Reed and Blackthorn and Elder and Pine and Gorse and Heather and Poplar and Yew, they resonate in us as our hidden language, as Alphabetic symbols taught to us by the wind.

And for how many millennia did we live in these woods, gathering roots and fruits and herbs and leaves, tending them like a garden, roaming from place to place, creating groves and orchards and butterfly meadows, learning forest lore and forest wisdom, before we'd finally cut them down?

All of this gone, gone. All the silence. All the mystery. All the thrusting life force. All the budding. All the sprouting. All the sap rising. All the secret nooks and arbours. Life in its intimate glory, in its flowering and moistness, its snuffling and fumbling, the sanctity of this sexual earth. All of this murdered innocence. How else can you describe what happened at Newbury? It was rape, no less. The rape of our own Mother Earth.

It was this passion, this sense of commitment, this belief, that there had to be a better way, that kept Arthur and the others at Newbury, even after the evictions, staying on an off-route site called Gotan, that had been planted as a garden, harrying the diggers while they waited for their harvest. The Orc was there, and Galahad and Bran. And Balin, a laughing giant of a man, who wore full chain-mail armour, and who had stayed 16 days dangling from an A-frame in front of the security compound gates, keeping them from their work (it had taken six of them to carry him away once he had been, finally, arrested). And Susanna, with her daughter Poppy, aged eight, and her son and her daughter, Sunny and Rainbow, who would visit them all regularly. And one or two that you haven't met yet: Pixi, and Mog Ur Kreb Dragonrider, better known as Kreb.

How to describe Kreb to you?

Thin as a whip, with narrow shoulders and a narrow chest, and a dainty, bird-like stoop, with long, thin fingers and glistening, jet-black black hair, with a whispy, goaty wizard's beard, there is something of the raven in him, something of the magician and something of the saint. It's hard to describe. A kind of holy seriousness, a reverence, an innocence and reserve. Profoundly deaf in one ear, and partially deaf in the other, he has lived his life in a bubble, only breaking free of his protected childhood when he met King Arthur and was given permission to fight for the Earth. He is the only person who refers to King Arthur as King Arthur, using the title as a name. He says he was Arthur's son in a previous life, but not when he was Arthur: when he was someone else. And you can't help loving him. We'd defy anyone to meet him and not love him. Even the police love him. He is so uniquely, so innocently, so seriously himself, pilgrimaging through life's strange by-ways with such reverently serious explanations of what it is, exactly, he is doing, and why, going into such detail, with such a straight face, you start off laughing, thinking it's a joke, and then, seeing that it isn't a joke, that he means it all, you end up smiling at him indulgently as one of life's eternal innocents, a lesson to us all.

Kreb had actually gone to school near the Newbury protest site, at Mary Hare school for the deaf. So it was familiar territory to him, a part of his childhood. He arrived as a well-wisher, still working as a production chemist at the time, properly dressed in a suit and tie, before he met Arthur. Afterwards he put on his white robe and stayed. He's worn that robe ever since.

You have to hear his voice to get a feel for him. Remember, he is practically deaf. Indeed, he was completely deaf until he had an operation that gave some small hearing to one of his ears. So he has that odd nasal cadence in his tone that a lot of deaf people have, pondering each word as if it was the most important word ever spoken, emphasising it with clipped deliberation, each word separate from the word before – As. If. Each. Single. Word. Was. Isolated. By. A. Full. Stop. – with a slight stutter, like Derek Nimmo on scrumpy cider, as he recounts the events of his life in endless dizzying detail, blinking surprised sincerity from behind his glasses, telling his whole life as if it was a comic monologue but without ever reaching the punch line.

One day they were all sitting round the fire at Gotan.

Arthur said: 'I know: what about if we all set light to ourselves? Yeah. Why not? Never mind about immolating Buddhists, what about emulsifying Druids? We could set light to ourselves and then leap onto the bailiffs from the trees. That'd surprise them.'

Kreb said, 'But wouldn't that be dangerous, Sire?'

Kreb always calls Arthur 'Sire'.

'It wouldn't just be dangerous, Kreb. We'd be dead.'

'Oh,' said Kreb, blinking from behind his glasses, weighing up the matter, deliberating upon it, pondering it, turning it over and puzzling about it with almost visible effort. 'Well, all right then. If you say so King Arthur.'

'Kreb, I'm joking. I don't really want you to set light to yourself.'

'Oh,' said Kreb again, his face lighting up with relief. 'Yes. Thank you, Sire. Yes.'

Another day they were sitting by the fire, again, when Kreb announced that in all of his lifetimes he had always been an officer in the army, and this was the first time that he wasn't in the army and he wasn't fighting a war.

Arthur said, 'But you still are an officer, Kreb.'

'Am I Sire?'

'Of course you are. You're an officer in the Loyal Arthurian Warband.'

'Oh. Yes. Yes. I am. Yes. Thank you, Sire. Yes.' And his face lit up like a child's.

That's what we mean when we say he is one of life's innocents. There's no one else like him on the planet.

Pixi, on the other hand, isn't in the slightest bit innocent.

Pixi's story goes right back to the beginning of this story.

He'd ran away from home at the age of 14 and had ended up sleeping on Steve Andrew's sofa for a number of years, a mischievous imp, a scamp, a waif, a rogue, streetwise and sassy, short, wiry and elvin, older than his years. After that he'd become a traveller, living in buses and trucks, learning about engines and how to cope on the road, how to entertain, how to sing with conviction and intensity, how to play the guitar, how to recite poetry, how to compose. He became a bard. Steve lost contact with him. Later, when Steve was becoming interested in the Warband, he'd turned on the radio one day to hear a programme about King Arthur, only to hear Pixi's familiar voice. It had been years since he'd last seen him. Such are the interconnections that make us think we are all related somehow, Steve and Pixi and CJ and King Arthur and Susanna and Rollo and all of us, in a tribal weave of correspondences, as complex and intricate as a tapestry, as delicate as a web.

Pixi was at Twyford Down. One day there was a demonstration in Winchester. Well, three demonstrations, to be exact. Pixi was marching up and down in an orderly procession with the nice Greenpeace people in their colourful anoraks and walking boots, when he saw these mad Druids, led by King Arthur, coming the other way, causing mayhem, making lots of noise and generally having fun. 'I'll 'ave some of that,' he thought, and joined with the Druids, as they went about occupying the college, the MP's surgery and the police station. They had a radio crew with them. And at every place (Arthur having mislaid his herald that day), Pixi would read resonantly from a proclamation in his best bardic voice. That's what Steve Andrews had heard that day. His old mate Pixi, reading from a proclamation, written by King Arthur, in a radio programme about King Arthur. That's when Steve knew he had to join the Warband too.

So it goes on. That's how everyone comes to the Warband. Some mad coincidence, some crazy slice of synchronicity dropping on you like pizza dough, as if the world was making a mockery of our sense of reason, as if – somehow – this was a strange, secret pattern unfolding in our lives. As if it was all meant to be.

It's all right. You don't have to believe any of this nonsense. CJ doesn't

believe it. Neither does Arthur. No one does. It's a load of wanky bollocks. We're all sceptics in the Warband. None of us believes any of the
rubbish we tell ourselves.

Except Kreb that is. Kreb always believes everything.

And life at Gotan went on much as before.

Arthur was always getting himself arrested. He was arrested 39 times at
Newbury, with only one guilty verdict.

In and out of Bullingdon Gaol, like a yo-yo on elasticated string.

In and out. In and out.

It was like a yogic meditation exercise, enforced incarceration. Except
that it wasn't enforced. Arthur did it voluntarily. He would go in refusing
bail conditions as bail breaker, accepting imprisonment as his personal
means to an end. Well, you can call him a twat, if you like – there's not
many men who would choose imprisonment over freedom – but he is
one of Frivolous Bards of Britain, as it says in the *Welsh Triads*, referring to
his predecessor, as well as one of the Very Famous Prisoners.

The only time he was found guilty was when he cut the razor wire
around the security compound. He'd been told by Friends of the Earth in
the office in town ('Friends of the Armchair', as they were affectionately
known) that razor wire was illegal under European law. So for days he'd
been walking around the compound telling the security guards that the
razor wire on top of their fence was illegal, and that if they didn't remove
it, he would. And then he did. He went round the fence with a pair of bolt
cutters and a kitchen chair, fully robed, getting up on the chair, and then
cutting the wire. Susanna witnessed this. She says that it was an awesome
sight. The wire would snap and spring back, lashing at Arthur's arms. His
hands and his forearms were cut to ribbons. Blood pouring everywhere.
But he kept on, deliberately and painfully, picking up the chair, putting it
down, stepping up on it, and then cutting the razor wire with the sharp,
snapping blades of the bolt cutter, moving round the fence with wilful
determination, methodically removing the offending wire. He'd cut 150
yards of it before he was, finally, arrested. He was doing it for 45 minutes.
His fingers were so cut to shreds that they couldn't even take fingerprints.

There's a photograph of this, used as prosecution evidence in the trial,
taken by Brays Detective Agency. It shows Arthur with the bolt cutters cutting the wire. It was taken with a flash, so Arthur's pupils stand out as
eerie, red sparks. But it's like there's something else in his eyes too, some

mad berserker energy, some crazy warrior spirit in the heat of battle, seeing red. He looks uncannily like someone else. He looks like a Dark Ages battle chieftain engaged in fierce hand-to-hand combat with the enemy.

And one day he was walking past the security compound when the security guards started laughing.

'Did you get your sword from Toys R Us?' they taunted.

And Arthur drew Excalibur, and with a roar, brought it down on the fence, sending electric blue sparks spinning ringingly into the air.

The security guards jumped back startled.

'What do you think?' said Arthur.

So it was in and out of Bullingdon Gaol. In and out. In and out. No sooner had he been released, than he would be arrested again. Once he was arrested only 10 minutes after his arrival. He walked towards the line of security guards, a solitary figure facing that vast army, where he was told that if he went any further he would be arrested, the police already having been called. He carried on. He was arrested for Aggravated Trespass, under the Criminal Justice Act. He was doing it on purpose. He wanted to be arrested. It wasn't only the bail-breaking role that appealed to him. He was having fun at the Prison Governor's expense. Arthur and the Prison Governor were at war, you see, and there's nothing that Arthur likes so much as a war.

It was like this. After that first arrest, having refused the usual draconian bail conditions, he was remanded to Bullingdon Gaol. A remand prisoner is someone who has not yet been found guilty of anything, and is therefore allowed to wear his own clothes rather than the drab prison uniform the other prisoners are forced to wear. Arthur's own clothes – pagan priest and Druid swordbearer as he considered himself to be – consisted of his white Druid robe with the red rampant dragon on the front, tied around the waist with rope, with his circlet, and his robe bag, and his swirling green cloak, and all his pagan jewellery.

In the police cells, before he was taken to Bullingdon, the custody sergeant had commented upon his circlet.

'They won't let you wear that,' he said.

'We'll see if they let me wear it or not,' said Arthur, gleefully.

So he arrived at Bullingdon at the reception centre. They must have been a bit startled when he walked in there for the first time. They were used to the protesters now, of course, there having been many arrests. So dreadlocks and tattered clothing didn't surprise them: multi-coloured jumpers and floppy cotton trousers, they'd seen it all. Nor did the special diets some of the protesters insisted upon. They were used to the vegans and the vegetarians too. The protesters were a weird lot, they knew, nothing like the ordinary prisoners – here on a matter of conscience, with all the confidence that brings – but they'd learnt how to handle them. Indeed, even prisoners of conscience can be cowed by the prison rules in the end, by the air of threat and violence that almost clings to the walls, by the routine and orderliness, by the sheer, bloody-minded dreariness of prison life. But they'd never met a Druid King before.

'You can take that off for a start,' said the guard, indicating Arthur's circlet.

'I'm a pagan priest and Druid swordbearer,' said Arthur. 'This is my circlet of office. I demand to see the Chaplain and the Governor.'

And you know what the prison guards were thinking, don't you?

'Oh my gawd, we've got a right one here.'

So – neither the Chaplain nor the Governor being available – the Assistant Governor finally arrived, armed with the official Home Office manual from the Chaplain's office on the rules regarding freedom of religious expression. They were poking through the rule book, looking for get-out clauses. In the end they decided that Arthur might have a point about his jewellery. But as for the circlet and the robe, they were coming off and that was that.

'We can do this the easy way, or we can do this the hard way,' said the Assistant Governor, reading from his internalised script like a cliché from a bad Hollywood movie.

They were looming over him, flexing their muscles, about half a dozen of them, sizing him up in their minds, weighing up his body-size and muscular structure, ready to pounce.

Arthur told them that his co-operation stopped then and there, and he sat down in the corner of the room, bracing himself, with his cloak wrapped tightly around him, elbows in close to his chest, with his hands grasping firmly the circlet on his bowed head, making himself into a ball. The Assistant Governor could see that this could only end up with someone getting hurt. Also, for all his reading of the regulations, he couldn't be entirely sure that he was working on solid ground here. He needed confirmation from the Governor before this went any further.

'Right,' he spat, 'take him to Segregation.'

The Block.

The Segregation Block is the most feared place in prison. It is where the awkward or violent prisoners are taken for punishment. It amounts to solitary confinement, locked up in your cell for most of the day, without recreation, without exercise, without amusement, without association with other prisoners, eating your food by yourself, without privileges, without work, without distraction, without anyone but yourself. Like a monastic cell. Which is how Arthur intended to take it, as a kind of solitary retreat.

So Arthur was being taken into Bullingdon Prison, on remand, having not been found guilty of anything whatsoever, free to leave at any time, if he only agreed to bail conditions, suffering the worst punishment available in the British prison system: segregation on the Block.

That was on the Tuesday.

But there was worse to come.

They left him like this for a couple of days. They were trying to get advice. The prison Chaplain visited him and agreed to look into the matter: neither paganism nor Druidry being recognised religions, at least not in prison, at least until that moment. No one had thought to look into it before. But the Chaplain wasn't able to get the advice he needed and they were left with a stalemate.

That's when the Number One Governor decided to intervene.

It was bad for prison discipline, allowing a prisoner to openly flout his authority like this. The rumours were already circulating. He decided to do something about it.

He sent a trio of prison officers to Arthur's cell on the Thursday evening, with a prison uniform and a direct order for him to give up his robes and change. Arthur refused, which amounts to a criminal offence in prison, the catch-all charge of disobeying a direct order. He was told he was up before the Governor in the morning to answer the charge.

In prison, the Governor has absolute power within the confines of the rule book. He can make any prisoner's life hell.

So Arthur was up before the Governor the following day, answering charges, like a medieval heretic before the Grand Inquisition.

He pleaded Not Guilty to the charge saying that the order was not lawful, and quoting Home Office guidelines on religion and remand prisoners.

His time had been well spent, thumbing through the Home Office regulations, as was his (and every prisoner's) entitlement.

The Number One Governor didn't even bother to deliberate on the matter.

'Guilty,' he pronounced, in a sternly self-satisfied voice. It's good to be the Governor. You can hurt anyone you like.

He added seven days to Arthur's sentence (though he had no sentence), along with other fiscal punishments and loss of privileges, and had him marched out of the door into the waiting arms of the heavy mob. There were a number of burly prison officers outside in the long corridor, along with the doctor, a prison visitor, and what he took to be a social worker, as observers of the coming scene.

And then they were rounding on him: two from behind, locking his arms, one in front with his fingers up his nose, saying, 'Shall I give him some pain, sir?', one or two others standing about, ready to pounce if it got any more violent – the Governor standing behind impassively, looking over the scene like some medieval curate with a penchant for burning witches – holding him in a vice-like grip, intense enough to break his arms if they had wished, while they yanked his clothes over his head, leaving him as naked as Timothy John on the day that he was born. After which they proffered the prison uniform to put on instead. He refused and – still sky-clad naked as the Goddess intended, showing off his numerous tattoos – was marched back to the Block and to his cell.

Slam! Clang! Clink!

Hear the cell door locking behind him, as it echoes down the barewalled corridor, with an awful finality.

Naked, on the Block.

Actually, this wasn't quite as bad as it sounds. He was still in solitary confinement. His only visitors were the screws who would look in on him occasionally. He had his books to read, and occasional correspondence with the outside world, plus there were two people in the adjacent cells he could talk to through the walls.

One was a black bloke up on several murder charges, who shouldn't even have been here, this being a Category C prison, and he being Category A. Which is why he was on the Block, because they didn't have the facilities to deal with him here. It was because they didn't like him, he said. He'd spent 13 years in Category B, C and D prisons, on the Block, in solitary confinement, while other prisoners filled places in Category A prisons. Thus can the rules be bent to punish those considered most dangerous or undesirable.

And on the other side there was Chelsea, a white separatist, who was here because he'd punched a screw on the nose. Allegedly.

Arthur would have political arguments with the guy through the wall. 'I'm against racism,' he said.

'Well, I'm not a racist,' said Chelsea. 'I'm a white separatist. I have black friends. They're all separatists too.'

But they got on because Chelsea had been fitted up for violent disorder: caught on CCTV during a riot, even though he wasn't taking part in the riot.

One day Chelsea told Arthur to go to the window. They all had windows looking out over the courtyard, which opened slightly as far as the bars. Chelsea said, 'Catch this,' and he swung something over on a line. It was a copy of a Chelsea Football Club programme. 'What am I going to do with this?' thought Arthur. He didn't even like Chelsea Football Club. But Chelsea said, 'Have you got it?'

'Ye-ah?' said Arthur, half bemused.

'Right,' said Chelsea. And then there was a sudden tug on the end of the line, and Arthur realised there was something else on the end of it, and he pulled it up, and in through the window. It was a plastic shopping bag, full of all sorts of goodies: food, baccy, papers, matches.

Chelsea was one of the prison's Baccy Barons.

He must have decided that Arthur was an OK geezer.

Meanwhile, Arthur was reading the prison regulation rule book religiously, looking for revelations. He wrote to the Home Office and to Liberty, giving details of his case. He asked for a confidential access envelope addressed to the Area Manager to make an appeal for adjudication. He was going by the book, using their own book against them.

One thing he discovered: he was allowed as many request forms as he wanted, to write to the Governor, and that the Governor was obliged to reply to every one. So he was getting 13 request forms every day and filling them in, asking for the return of his robes, amongst other things – including, on one occasion, an appeal under the sex discrimination act, to be sent to a woman's prison (just being naughty here) – quoting Home Office regulations, and citing examples, arguing that as Islamic Mullahs were allowed to wear their robes and head gear in prison, so should he be. So 13 times a day the Governor was forced to think about this recalcitrant Druid down there on the Block, naked, playing havoc with his authority, knowing he was continuing to flout the rules, and that word was getting round. The Governor sent down with another direct order that he should put on the prison uniform they had provided for him, and again he refused, and again he was up before the Governor the following day on that same catch-all charge.

And now, marching through the corridor to the Governor's office, passed all the cells, passed the little room where they had previously disrobed him, with a white sheet wrapped around him, with a prison officer either side of him, in their blue serge uniforms, with their jangling keys as marks of their office, the Governor calling them in from behind his desk as he looked up from his paperwork in a disinterested manner, shuffling the paperwork, resting upon his dignity and his authority, the absolute ruler of his own, cruel domain: judge, jury, prosecution and executioner all at once. And he stood up, a tall, donnish figure, with a precise military bearing and a straight back, and offered Arthur a seat, which Arthur refused. And then he read out the charge.

'How do you plead?'

'Not guilty, on the grounds that it is an illegal order, me being a remand prisoner, and therefore entitled to wear my own clothes.' Quoting sources and references, making it clear that he was au fait with the rule book, and that he knew what he was talking about.

'In my opinion, your own clothes are not suitable,' said the Governor, in the usual pompous manner, not listening to what Arthur had been saying. Why should he? He was the Governor, and the Governor can do what he likes. So Arthur was found guilty as charged, a forgone conclusion, and the punishment was duly issued. Loss of remission, loss of privileges, loss of a day's pay.

'So, let's get this straight,' said Arthur, his brain suddenly lighting up, 'you're stopping my library privileges, my canteen privileges, my association with other prisoners and you're taking three days remission off a sentence I haven't got yet? Is that right? And then you're fining me a day's pay?'

'That's right.'

'Well I've got news for you. I'm a renunciate. I don't handle money. I don't give a monkey's about your canteen or your library. I'm on the block, remember. I don't get privileges. I don't associate with the other prisoners. And, anyway, I'm up for trespass, and no one goes to gaol for trespass, so bang goes your three days loss of remission.'

And he raised his shoulders and stuck out his chest, doing his growling bear impression, dropping the white sheet as he did so – the Governor visibly fuming, going red in the face – before turning on his heels, and walking out of the door, closely followed by the two screws, barely able to conceal their laughter by now, spluttering visibly as they tried to throw the sheet over his retreating shoulders as he marched determinedly back to his cell.

Had anyone ever spoken to the Governor like that before? Not likely.

Later, he heard that the reason the Governor considered his robes unsuitable was that he thought they looked like a dress, and that it would be a bad example for any transvestite prisoners who might start requesting the right to wear female clothing on the back of Arthur's precedent. Which is a nice picture, at least, and gives a strange insight into the inner-workings of the Number One Governor's own secret mind.

And Arthur had suddenly become very popular with the screws, who started giving him cigarettes and often stopping by for a chat.

One day one of the screws came to his cell.

'Come on Arthur, that's it. You're out of here.'

'Who says I'm out of here?'

'Newbury Magistrates. You're free to go.'

'I'm not leaving,' said Arthur.

'What do you mean, you're not leaving? You're free to go. I've just told you. Get your stuff and you can go.'

'I'm not leaving.'

And the prison guard looked at him like he'd just gone mad. He couldn't believe what he was hearing. It didn't compute. It was not in his field of reckoning. He'd never heard such a thing before. Arthur could see it in his face. When was the last time he'd offered to take a prisoner to the door and had been refused? Well, never, of course. So he was trying to work it out. He didn't even understand what Arthur was saying to him.

Arthur said, 'You said I'm bailed by Newbury Magistrates.'

'That's right. You're bailed. You're free.'

'Well I'm not accepting the bail conditions. I know what the Newbury bail conditions will be,' said Arthur. 'I'm going to wait for Reading Crown

Court to bounce me out on my own conditions.'

Again the screw continued looking at him incredulously. This was normally the high point of a prison officer's day, the moment when he felt most human, most likeable, telling a prisoner that he was free. And now here was this crazy man not only refusing his orders, but refusing to leave the confines of the prison too, making everyone's lives seem stranger and stranger by the minute, sending their heads into lunatic spins, as if the whole world was being turned upside down.

'But you can't stay. We have no legal right to hold you here.'

'Look,' said Arthur, trying to explain it, 'I've got to sign a piece of paper to leave here, is that right? I've got to sign to collect my things. Well, I'm not signing it. So you can't throw me out. I'm staying right here.'

So the screw went off, and sure enough, Arthur had been bailed in his absence not to enter the Newbury Sausage. But the screw didn't know what to do. He was under orders to escort Arthur to collect his property and leave. He went off and got a senior officer, who put his head around Arthur's door, and they repeated pretty much the same conversation.

'I'm not signing anything, and I'm not leaving here,' said Arthur, concluding.

'Are you sure Arthur?'

'Yeah, I'm sure.'

So the senior officer went off and got an even more senior officer – in fact, the Assistant Governor this time – and the Assistant Governor came into Arthur's cell, and they had the conversation yet again.

'Look, are you sure about this, Arthur? You sure you don't want to leave?'

'Of course I'm sure. Now shut that door on your way out.'

And he went back to writing his journal.

A word about the journal. It's what this narrative is based upon. It was written on prison issue toilet paper, like a long linear poem, and is still in existence. He called it *The Ballad of Bullingdon Gaol*, after another, more famous poem, by another, more famous writer. Arthur managed to get it smuggled out in an Archdruidess's knickers, once he was allowed visits again. So, if toilet paper is the currency on protest sites, it's the literary medium in prison.

Thus it continued, Arthur's personal war with the Prison Governor. The Bullying Don of Bullingdon, as Arthur called him.

We have to be clear at this point. All of this was taking place over a succession of visits. He would be up before Reading Crown Court, who would lessen his bail conditions to a level that he could accept. He would go back to Newbury and promptly get arrested again. And then he'd be back in Bullingdon again, carrying on the fight. He'd arrive in the reception centre. They'd say, 'OK Arthur, you know the ropes, you can't wear your robes in here,' and he'd say, 'And you know what I'm going to say, I'm a remand prisoner and I refuse to wear your uniform,' and then they'd allow him to strip – he'd already done the fighting bit and he didn't think it was worth getting beaten up again – and they'd march him back to the Block. At least three times in succession, as Arthur remembers it.

How many times was that? One, two and lots.

Eventually they'd had enough. The Assistant Governor brokered a deal. Arthur would be allowed to wear his robes, but only in his cell. So Arthur was allowed out onto the wing.

And for a while everything was peaceful. He would wear his robes in his cell, and then, to come out of his cell – to eat, to associate, to receive visits – he would put on a tracksuit.

That lasted for about a week. It was during this time that he passed on his journal.

It was approaching the Autumn Equinox, by now. He negotiated with the Assistant Governor to be allowed to hold a ceremony out in the exercise yard. Balin and Kreb were both inside at this time, the laughing giant and the saintly fool. Half of the inmates were either Druids or some other kind of pagan, the cells being full of Newbury protesters. And – surprisingly – the Governor agreed.

But Arthur was up in Court that day. By the time he got back they'd changed their minds. They said they didn't have the staff to supervise them.

That's when Arthur decided that he wasn't going to play anymore. He decided that he would keep his robes on, whatever they said.

The next time he tried to leave his cell – this time in his robes – they said, 'You're not coming out here dressed like that.'

'Fine,' he said. And he went back into his cell.

Unfortunately, this was to go to the canteen to eat.

He got someone to bring his dinner up that first time, but then they banned that too, and he was left, trapped in his cell, refusing to come out unless he was allowed to wear his robes.

CJ went to visit him during this period, when he was on the wing, but not able to leave his cell. He didn't get to see him of course. He was told that Arthur was refusing to leave his cell. Afterwards he went to see a man who had been in the next-door cell before he was released.

He asked CJ, 'What did they tell you when you came for the visit?'

'I was told that Arthur was refusing to come out of his cell.'

'He said they'd say that. It isn't true, you see. They're not allowing him to come out of his cell.'

From the same man, CJ also managed to obtain paperwork showing some of the written exchanges between Arthur and the Prison Governor. One of them was dated September 1996. The form was divided, one half for the prisoner, one half for the Governor. Arthur stated:

> *'I am not refusing visits. Nor am I refusing to comply (in the interests of good order and discipline) with what I deem to be an unlawful order. To remove my robes in order to have a visit would to be to agree that such an order was lawful, which I believe (as a remand prisoner) it is NOT.'*

The Governor's reply was as follows:

> *'If you do not wear prison issue clothes you will not be permitted in the visits room or on the landing. You have already been informed of this.'*

In another application Arthur requested:

> *'To be treated without bias, as any other remand prisoner, and allowed to wear my own clothes. The argument that if you let me do it everyone else will want to falls down, for isn't that the whole point, everyone else already does wear their own clothes. Who are you, fashion police? What comes next, banning loud shirts?'*

One day a female prison officer stopped by his cell.

'I hear you are on hunger strike,' she said: the official policy on hunger strikers being to let them get on with it.

'Nah, I'm not on hunger strike. They won't let me out of my cell unless I remove my robes.'

Later she passed by and kicked a cardboard box through the door.

'Here,' she said, 'it's for you.'

It was a takeaway curry. She'd sent out for a curry for him.

And she wasn't the only one. Arthur was notorious by now. Everyone knew what had been happening. So whenever the other prisoners went down for food, they'd slip something into their pockets and bring it up to him.

When he was finally released, he left a pile of food on a table in his cell. There was a bowl of hardboiled eggs, several packets of biscuits, a plate loaded with toast, and a bowl with bacon rashers in it.

'Here,' he said to the screws, who'd come to collect him, 'help yourselves.'

CHAPTER FOURTEEN

Reclaim The Streets

I t was late September. The Gotan garden was harvested by now, the site evicted and replaced with a security compound like a concentration camp. Miles of linked fence topped with razor wire. Floodlights. Machinery. Gravel. The security guards patrolling the site like camp guards. Except that they were their own prisoners, of course. The fence was there to keep the protesters out.

Arthur, the knights and the other protesters were settled in a shady dell just outside the compound, living in benders and trucks, enjoying the early autumn sunshine as it flickered playfully on the leaves. They were having a much better time of it than the security guards.

But the atmosphere between them was good. They were always bantering through the fence to each other.

And all along the Newbury route there were these little oak saplings. All the acorns in the churned soil were coming alive.

The protesters were potting them and selling them to well-wishers and supporters to pay for the on-going protest.

All over the country, in parks and gardens and open land, in city and in town, the Newbury Oaks were sprouting, bringing the woods alive again, spreading flashes of the Newbury heart all around the British Isles.

Arthur had used his time in Bullingdon well. He had devised all of these new rankings, and was preparing to raise various members of the Warband. Susanna was to be raised as one of the nine Faery Queens of Britain, while Pixi and the Orc were to be raised as Battle Chieftains. Susanna's son Sunny – Sunny by name, and sunny by nature – 13-years old at the time, was to be raised as Arthur's personal squire.

All this was to be done at a belated Autumn Equinox ceremony, a few days hence – Arthur having been thwarted while in gaol – once he had recovered Excalibur from the Newbury police cells, where it had lain in waiting for him during his incarceration. We'll be moving on to that ceremony very soon.

But first, another brief pause for reflection.

We have put forward several thoughts regarding Arthur's supposed identity in the course of this book.

We've offered various explanations, none of them exclusive. You can believe any of them, all of them, or none of them at all. It is entirely up to you.

Was he 'doing' Arthur, or was he 'being' Arthur?

Arthur would say that he was being it by doing it.

Perhaps he was invoking it.

But there's another explanation too. Perhaps all of this was a fantasy. All this Faery Queens, Battle Chieftains, Knights and Squires stuff: wasn't Arthur just making it all up?

Of course he was. That's precisely what he was doing. He was making it up. It was all a complete fantasy.

But then, you have to ask, what's wrong with fantasy? It is fantasy that lends colour to our lives. And by living a fantasy, doesn't that make it real? Arthur wasn't just fantasising his role as Arthur. He was fantasising himself and then being himself. Living his life not only as a fantasy, but as a fantastical adventure story, a tale told to him by his imagination, and then lived out in reality. It was his own story, and he was making it up as he went along.

What is now real was once only imagined.

And isn't that what we all do too? We live our lives as stories we tell ourselves. The difference being that the outlines of our own, sometimes drab, tales are being laid down by someone else.

Who told you you were working class or middle class? Who told you how to behave in any particular circumstance? Who told you what it was to be a man or to be a woman? Who told you you were nothing but a job title, so that when people ask what you do, you say, 'I am an electrician,' or 'I am a housewife'? Who told you you could only be defined in terms of your income and expenditure, or the kind of house you live in, or which part of town, the suburbs or the inner city? Or the kind of car you drive? Or that eating chocolate will make you happy? Who told you you could only be defined in terms of your disability, whatever that is, claiming the disability as your own, so you talk of 'my depression' or 'my deafness', and that you cannot do what you want to do despite it, that you cannot live, that you cannot love, that you cannot dream your dreams and make them real?

It wasn't you, was it?

All of this was someone else's fantasy.

The difference being that Arthur is living his own fantasy. Living his life according to his own rules. Turning symbolism and ritual into reality. Seizing life on the mythological level and making it his own.

When Arthur was in the army he was acting out a fantasy given to him by his dad. As a biker, he was acting out a fantasy given to him by his generation. But as Arthur, the fantasy is all his, and as he lives it, so he becomes it. He is the author of his own fate.

And that is exactly what magic is: making real what previously only existed in your imagination.

Which is what they were all doing, that fateful September evening at the belated Autumn Equinox ceremony: they were performing magic, making real what had previously been a fantasy.

So there were about 13 of them there, some of the protesters from the Gotan site, with the robed Druids, Arthur and Kreb and the Orc and Bran and Pixi, and Susanna with her kids, Poppy and Sunny, on the B4494, Newbury to Wantage road, just outside the security compound gates, with the floodlights (thoughtfully supplied by the Department of Transport) blazing and casting stark shadows, shielding the stars, weighing up to begin their performance, hoping that a little bit of magic might happen.

The reason they were on the B4494 is that Arthur was bailed not to go on DoT land, and there wasn't anywhere else to go. It was also a tactic that Arthur had used before, and would use again, stopping traffic to make a political point. A tactic used, at the same time, by other groups around the protest movement, such as Reclaim The Streets.

We'll talk about Reclaim The Streets later.

It was between eight and nine o'clock in the evening by now, and just starting to turn cold. There was that September nip in the air that told them autumn was on its way, a fresh, clean tang like the smell of distant orchards.

Kreb was on one side, doing traffic duty in that concentrated manner of his, taking his job very seriously, while the Orc was on the other. One car had stopped and turned off its engine.

The security guards were watching from the compound gates, probably wondering what this bunch of nutters were up to this time. And Brays Detective Agency were watching them too, as a trio, one with a video, one with a stills camera and one taking notes.

Pixi had a small single-handed battleaxe with him that he was intending to present to the Orc.

They began by opening the four quarters. Bran was new to this (he was still in his teens) and was given some bantering guidance from the rest of the circle. Arthur had just called the East.

A Jaguar pulled up. A brand new, sleek, purring Jaguar, a shiny beast, with smoked-glass, reinforced windows, with a uniformed chauffeur in the front. No one was paying that much attention at this point.

And then the Jaguar pulled out. It swerved around the other car, and began driving into the circle, breaking through the line of people. Kreb attempted to stop it, but it shoved passed him, knocking him on the hip and pushing him over. He held out his hand as he hit the ground, scratching it. Arthur turned, and raising his staff, stepped in front of it.

The chauffeur put his foot down. Straight at Arthur. Bang! It hit, and Arthur went flying, over the bonnet, and onto the verge.

And then several things happened at once.

Susanna was on one side of the circle, where Arthur had landed. She and Sunny went to see how he was. She says she looked into his eyes and saw that he wasn't there. He was awake, but his mind was dazed and in retreat. He was cut, and blood streamed from his forehead. And then she heard this bellowing roar, like the roar of a wounded animal, before realising it was coming out of her own mouth. How dare they? She had two of her kids in that circle. How dare they? It was something primordial, from the depths, the mother instinct. Fierce and dangerous, like a lioness protecting her cubs, she strode over to the Jaguar and was reaching for the door. She was going to drag the driver out. If she had got to the car, she would have gouged out the driver's eyes. It was that basic. The driver, very sensibly, drove away.

By now Sunny had managed to get a pen from the security guards, and, as the Jaguar sped off, Susanna called out the registration number, which Sunny wrote down on his hand. It was a P reg, no more than three-weeks old.

At the same time the car was nudging past Pixi on the other side, knocking his hip as it revved up to escape. He was holding the battleaxe in his hand. And he didn't think about it. That was his mate, his comrade, over there, lying injured on the verge, and with a warrior's rage he rolled over the boot as he brought the axe down on the reinforced back window. The axe smashed into three pieces and went flying through the air, while the window shattered with a sudden crack, revealing the occupants. He saw two men in the back.

Kreb, meanwhile had picked himself up and turned. Saintly Kreb, with the pure heart of a child. He too saw the two men in the back of the car. He pointed his staff at the speedily receding machine and offered a curse of mutilation.

Yes, you heard it.

A curse of mutilation.

Dear, sweet Kreb.

And now everything was going crazy in the harsh glare of the flood-lights as bleak shadows danced and clashed. More cars had pulled up and were now trying to nuzzle through the circle. One car was pulling onto the verge and trying to pass by the circle on one side. No one knew what was happening. The Orc ended up on the bonnet of one car, holding on to the windscreen wipers. Kreb brought his staff down on the back of another. He was tapping the cars to tell them to stop. Susanna called over to Kreb to let the cars through. The circle was tattered and in disarray. Arthur was trying to stand. He pulled himself up by his staff and hobbled into the circle again. There was a jarring pain in his foot. Once the cars had cleared, he called people into the circle for their raisings. He was in a daze, like a trance.

And from this trance he raised Susanna as Faery Queen and Battle Chieftain, Sunny as a Brother Knight rather than a Squire, and the Orc as Knight of the White Shield, effectively his second-in-command.

He closed the circle quickly with six motions of his staff. Pointing to the four directions in succession, then the sky and the earth, he said, 'By fire, water, earth and air, by all that I deem holy, I do solemnly swear, in the height, in the deep, rite is ended.'

It was another case of him thinking on his feet. He'd never said those lines before, though they have become standard since.

The whole event had lasted no more than 10 minutes.

Pixi had done his shape-shifting bit by now. A quick lickety-split, a swift shim-sham-shimmy, and the white robe was off and over his head, and he was no longer a Druid.

He's from a council estate in Cardiff, remember. He knew what all of this meant. Whoever was in that car wasn't going to like what had just happened. He knew the police would be called. He knew he would be identified by that white robe. He knew that the police, with their in-built prejudices, would prefer to take sides with the owner of that plush, expensive Jag, rather than with a bunch of ne'er-do-wells and crazy pro-testers. As a waif and stray on the Cardiff streets he had often had run-ins with the cops. As a New Age traveller, even more so. His whole life had been a run-around with the police and the authorities. He was watching his back instinctively, cat-like, ready to leap sideways and escape. He took the registration number of the Jag from Sunny, and went off to Newbury to report the incident.

They were all gathered by the side of the road talking to the security guards. No one could believe what they had just witnessed. It was too mad, too surreal.

And then, within 10 minutes, a single policeman arrived in a squad car. He said that there had been complaints, and they told him about the Jaguar, reporting it as a hit-and-run.

Arthur was badly hurt. He had a broken finger, three broken ribs, and several broken bones in his foot. His newly raised Battle Chieftain, Susanna, on one side, and the Orc on the other, leaning on his staff, like the wounded soldier he was, he stumbled back to his bender, and the welcoming taste of cider.

And now they were back in the bender, in the warm flickering candle lit night, dissecting the scene, while Arthur, as the site's first-aid officer, directed them in binding his chest and making a splint for his finger, as he painfully and carefully extracted his wounded foot from his boot.

One thing Susanna was clear of: that was no ordinary chauffeur. It was the way he had driven into Arthur. It was no accident, she thought. He was obeying orders. One of the people in the back had ordered him to drive on. No ordinary person could have overcome their natural instincts like that, and simply driven into another human being, on an order. He had to have had specialist military training. Whoever it was in the back of that very expensive machine, it was clear that at least one of them was a VIP of very high standing, and that the chauffeur was doubling as a bodyguard.

Later, an ambulance arrived – the police must have called it – and a couple of ambulance men looked into the bender. Arthur dismissed them, preferring the company of his friends.

The following day Sunny popped his head through the flap into the bender where Arthur lay, nursing his wounds. The Orc was in there too.

'Arthur?' said Sunny, tentatively.

'Yes, mate?'

'You know you raised me as a Brother Knight last night?'

'I don't know. Did I?'

'Yes you did. And I was only supposed to be a Squire. Only I was thinking …'

'Hmmmmm?'

'I mean … er … is there anyway I can get out of it?'

And both Arthur and the Orc bellowed, laughing: 'No you can't!'

So Sunny was stuck with it: being the youngest Knight in the Loyal Arthurian Warband. It was an honour he couldn't refuse.

Later that day, two policemen arrived to investigate the hit and run. They took statements from a number of people, and then left.

It was the following morning, again, that the police turned up en masse, to arrest them. They came in a long column, 15 of them, tramping through the woods, in their matching fluorescent jackets and helmets, strolling in unison, like the chorus line of a police-based West End musical, in a choreographed dance routine.

You could almost imagine the music to go with it.

'Meet the gang 'cos the boys are here, the boys to entertain you …' High kicking across the stage.

Someone called out, in a sing-song voice: 'Police on site. Loads and loads of 'em …'

They were smiling as they came through, and saying good morning to everyone.

They split up into three separate columns of five. One of these groups went straight to the van where the Orc was sleeping. They knew exactly where to go.

The Orc is a very slow waker. He needs at least three cups of tea before he brightens up enough to think. And then, there they were, all these coppers, standing outside his van, arresting him for suspicion of criminal damage, violent disorder and obstruction of the highway, reading him his rights, 'I caution you that you do not have to say anything but it may harm your defence if you fail to mention something when questioned that you later rely on in court. Anything that you do say may be given in evidence. Do you understand that?'

Orc nodded sleepily. He was still in a daze.

They called him out – still dressed in the t-shirt and boxer shorts he'd slept in – and searched him. Then they searched the van. They were looking for the robes.

They gave him his trousers to put on, having first searched the pockets.

'Is there anything in here that shouldn't be? Any sharps or anything like that?'

'No.'

'Lots of sand.'

'Lots of sand, yeah.'

The Orc had been digging a tunnel the previous day, which had collapsed on him. He had to be dug out. All his clothes were full of sand.

He put on his robes.

Another group went for Arthur, lying injured in his bender, with his chest bound, and two fingers bandaged together with a splint.

He said, 'I really don't know why I get arrested when I got run over, which is strange ...'

He was panting for breath with a fag in his mouth, struggling to load on all of his gear. Arthur always carries a lot of weight, at the best of times: with the sword, the straps, the heavy leather belt, the pouches, the robes, the robes bag, the staff, the voluminous cloak, the iron circlet like a cold weight on his brow. And with Susanna and his staff for support, hobbling on one leg, he was taken off to be charged.

Meanwhile they had already arrested Kreb. They took a photo of him in his robes, and then asked that he give his robes as evidence. He struggled as they forcibly took his robes from him, dragging them over his head before he was put into the back of the meat wagon.

So Pixi had been right. It was the three Druids still in their robes who were being arrested.

Meanwhile the others were standing around: Arthur, the Orc, all the police officers, with Sunny and Poppy and Susanna looking on, exchanging banter.

Arthur said, 'What are the offences?'

The Orc said, 'On suspicion of criminal damage, obstructing the highway, and violent disorder.'

Susanna said, 'You're just a rowdy lot. Can't take you anywhere.'

Arthur said, 'Lying unconscious in the road, 'cos somebody just bowled you over, and we get done for violent disorder.'

Susanna said, addressing the police, 'Yes, we were standing in the road, but who in their right mind drives through a bunch of people who were obviously standing in the road, in a P-reg Jag, at speed, bodies flying everywhere? And the security were lined up against the fence. They couldn't believe their eyes. It's outrageous.'

Arthur said, 'Yeah, that's how it happened, and we just got arrested for it.'

The Orc was told that they would require his robes as evidence. Arthur said, 'I can't see what it's evidence of.'

And the Orc came back, quick as a whip, 'It's evidence of me being me, apparently.'

So he'd woken up at last.

And then they were taken off to Newbury nick to be charged and processed, and then on to Bullingdon Gaol and more confrontation with the Governor. It was almost like coming home.

Question: How do you turn a peaceful Druid Order into a violent disorder?

Answer: Drive a Jaguar straight through it.

A word about some of the characters here. You may have wondered about Poppy's presence on site. After all, she was only eight-years old. It was her own decision. Susanna had brought her to Newbury for the first wave of evictions, after which Poppy had asked to stay. So Susanna had allowed her time off school to continue her education in more interesting and stimulating surroundings. And Poppy is famous on the protest scene. Always bright, always alert, focused and intelligent, confident but polite, there's not many people who, having met her, would ever forget her. She's a unique and beautiful individual.

Susanna had been involved with the protest movement for many years – right back to the 60s, in fact. She was a veteran of that era. Later she'd become involved with some of the groups protesting against the Criminal Justice Bill (as it then was) in 1994. The Criminal Justice Bill was aimed at outlawing the activities of a number of disparate groups: travellers, ravers, road protesters, squatters. In fact, it brought all of these groups together. It was the Criminal Justice Bill which galvanised the protest movement of the 90s, that made it into a concentrated force on the British political scene, uniting anarchists, socialists, communists and environmentalists for the first time, along with travellers, ravers, squatters, road protesters, gay people, straight people, weird people, wild people, witches, warriors and talented non-conformists (or any combination of the above) – the whole of the British alternative scene, in fact – focusing their attention on the source of the problem that confronted them all. It was the beginning of what has since become known as the Anti-Capitalist Movement.

Arthur was at the second Criminal Justice Bill march. It was here that he and Susanna first met. She recognised Arthur and went straight up to him.

She said, 'Is the return of Arthur a sign of the regeneration of the Celts?'

And he said, 'Yes, and I think you'll find that ethnic peoples are rising up throughout the world.' And he gave a list of ethnic tribes prominent in the news at that time.

Those were the first words that passed between them.

But there are many complex threads running through this tale. For Susanna, one of them began in Claremont Road, in Leytonstone in London, in that same year: 1994.

This was another kind of road protest, against the M11 flyover and road-widening scheme: not, this time, in defence of the natural environment, but in defence of a community and a way of life; in defence of the human environment.

Claremont Road, which had stood there for more than a 100 years, a terrace of two-up, two-down workman's cottages, in which lives had been lived and memories forged, a proper old-fashioned neighbourhood, with its own sense of community, its own sense of well-being, where Dolly had chatted to Old Mick and Henry and they had known each other's business, had cared about each other, with a sense of history, a sense of place, a sense of belonging: all of this was to be demolished, once more, to save a few minutes on the commuter's journey time.

The protesters were arguing for alternatives such as improved rail networks to be considered. At the time, money spent on railways was always referred to as 'subsidy' and deplored, while money spent on roads was called 'investment' and lauded. The difference being, of course, that 'subsidy' is what is given to publicly owned and publicly accountable public services meant to serve the public, whereas 'investment' is what the public pays from the public purse to serve the interests of private corporations, for them to make profits from. In other words, there were always two options, and we all know, now, which option was preferred: as rail privatisation has blighted the rail network, and increased traffic continues to blight our lives.

And they call this 'urban planning.' If they'd have let a monkey plan it, it couldn't have come out worse.

But Claremont Road brought a peculiar magic to the urban radical scene.

It was like a work of art, but no longer contained, framed, nailed to a gallery wall. It was art made free, released from its bonds, the walls of the houses all painted, with a rusting car in the middle of the road, filled with earth and planted with flowers, on which was written 'Rust In Peace', with a miniature Stonehenge and a chessboard laid out in the road, with sofas and chairs scattered around, and dancing manikins in a variety of poses, and dolls nailed to telegraph poles, and an Art House where every wall, every item of furniture, every nook and cranny was painted in startling colours with startling scenes, a live-in work of art, art gone mad, gone revolutionary, as if the revolution was a state-of-mind, a presence, a feeling, a mood, a desire, a film-set, a revelation. Walking into Claremont Road was like walking into a weird kind of psychedelic freedom. Freedom of the Imagination. Imagination made real. Urban magic.

It was here that Susanna learned that she was a warrior.

It was the day before the evictions, about 3am, and Susanna had all the kids with her, Rainbow and Star and Sunny and Poppy, holed up behind barricades in one of the houses, in an attic, hidden behind a wardrobe, listening to the subtle interlacing tracery of the reggae beat from a ghetto blaster, when it suddenly crossed her mind.

The kids were all fast asleep.

'What am I doing?' she thought.

There were 300 or more protesters on the street, hidden in hundreds of secret places, behind barricades and in concreted spaces, in tunnels and in attics, in barricaded rooms, with all the paraphernalia of the road protests: lock-ons and A-frames and, most spectacular of all, a huge asymmetric scaffold tower, a hundred feet above one of the roofs, every pole greased, on which a single protester tottered, locked-on, swaying in the wind.

And Susanna knew that the bailiffs and the police and the sheriff's officers and the security contractors would be coming in tomorrow to clear it all, and that it could easily turn out to be confrontational.

She knew that people would consider her the worst kind of irresponsible mother for allowing her kids to volunteer for this, no matter what the cause. It was one of the worst moments of her life, having to question herself on the deepest level.

She asked herself what would happen if anything went wrong. Was she going to regret this for the rest of her life? And she asked herself how she would justify it to the fathers of her children and to the authorities. To her parents, to everyone. She couldn't even begin to imagine.

And she lay there, musing, turning all of this over in her mind, all of it weighing upon her like some awful, dark secret she had to keep. And then it came to her, and she knew.

She was a warrior. She had always been a warrior. She had picked her men because they were warriors. Her children were warriors too. It was in her genes, like an urgent primal calling: the call to battle, the call to arms, the call of honour, of kinship, of blood, like the sound of distant bagpipes in the wind, stirring her to action.

It explained so many things. She had always thought she was strange, never understood why people didn't understand her, never truly understood herself even. And now she was finding herself at last, in this corner of a forgotten England, fighting for something that was worth fighting for, defending something that was worth defending. She was finding something in her own blood, because, of course, it wasn't very English for a woman to be a warrior. It was disdained, frowned upon, scorned, hated even, considered a threat. But it had always been a venerable tradition amongst the Celts. In ancient Celtic society women were warriors too.

And she knew she was there, as a mother with her children, to act as protection, not only for the protesters, but for the eviction teams too. Putting herself there meant that they would have to take care, for their own sake's, as well as theirs, that they would have to pay attention to what they were doing. And she also thought that, by making this stand, and allowing her children to make this stand with her, she was sending a message. These were things that truly mattered, to the next generation as well as to hers. She was there, with her kids, as the representatives of the future.

And then the evictions came, and she was right: they took care.

It took the whole of the first day to evict her and three of the kids. The fourth, Star, was there for another three days. They had generators inside, with TVs, and CNN were showing the evictions 24-hours-a-day. So Star sat inside waiting to be evicted, watching the events unfolding outside, having a view of herself and her surroundings from the cemetery across the road where the TV cameras were stationed.

And it took five days to evict Phil, the man on top of the scaffold tower.

It was out of Claremont Road that a new tactic emerged: one that was to have an effect throughout the world, and to fuel a whole new generation of protesters in the anti-capitalist movement.

Reclaim The Streets.

It was one of those thoughts, brilliantly simple. Why not hold a party on the street? It had been fed by the first Criminal Justice Bill march and rally in May that year, when they had marched from Hyde Park to Trafalgar Square. There was this little bicycle-powered mobile sound system, called Rinky Dink, moving around in the crowd. It was a brilliantly sunny day. And people started to dance. They danced in the square. They danced in the fountains. They danced on the pavements and out onto the road. They danced, they danced. It is the human way. So perhaps the seeds were planted that day. But it was Claremont Road that galvanised it, seeing the whole urban landscape magically transported like that, regenerated, rejuvenated, made sparklingly alive. Looking into the future and seeing the possibilities. Total transformation of the urban environment. Cities built for people instead of for cars; bright, vibrant, colourful places full of hope and joy, with decent public transport – publicly owned, serving the public – free of pollution and congestion, a real community, with parties on the street like the street parties they always call to celebrate the Royal Family or the end of a war. Why not? You are always called a utopian dreamer for having thoughts like this, told that you are unrealistic or naive. But what's the alternative? What we've got now?

You've got to be joking.

Claremont Road was the vision of what might be, of what was yet to come.

The first Reclaim The Streets party happened in Camden High Street on a sunny Saturday afternoon in May 1995. It was organised out of the Rainbow Centre, a squatted church in Kentish Town. They crashed two old cars purposely to create a barricade. And then people were coming from everywhere, bringing stuff with them. They brought carpets and armchairs, and laid them in the road. They brought a sandpit and a climbing frame. They brought flags and banners and painted boards. They brought face paints and colouring books. They brought themselves, all decked out in their finest party clothes. They brought music and laughter and love and romance.

'Let's face the music, and dance.'

Which is what they did. They danced, they romanced, they laughed, they made love (discretely, of course, with their eyes and ears and their fingertips) right there, right then, out on those grim grey streets of old London Town. They brought colour to them. They brought magic. They brought life.

The party lasted from lunchtime till seven o'clock that evening. And then they all went home, taking their stuff with them. And Camden High Street became Camden High Street again.

The police had no idea what to make of it.

What was that? What had just happened?

Was it a protest? A party? An art installation? Some kind of a joke?

It was something new and old at the same time.

After that there were a whole series of actions.

A party in Upper Street, London, in July that year, was followed by actions in Birmingham, Manchester, Bristol, Leeds, Brighton, and Leicester. Everyone was getting the bug. It was the best way to protest: having a party at the same time. What better combination?

Then there was M41 near Shepherds Bush, in 1996. They were getting more and more confident, using more and more elaborate tactics, with more and more people attending. There were up to 7,000 people on the M41, with a huge sound-system playing pumping dance music all day. Banners, streamers, stilt walkers, fire-eaters, jugglers, bagpipes, irony and adventure. They had a conventional traffic sign on the approach to the party. 'Change Of Priorities Ahead', it said. And there was this 24-foot high pantomime dame bobbing about in the middle of it all. And under the skirts of the monstrous dame, keeping rhythm with the pounding Techno, with dancers all around creating a human shield, they had a pneumatic drill banging through the tarmac to plant trees. So when they'd finished, at midnight that night, there were trees growing in the fast lane of the M41.

Reclaim The Streets became famous throughout the world. Everywhere in the developed world, from Australia to the United States, from the European mainland to Canada, wherever there were young people, or people unhappy with the way the world was going, with the prevailing car culture and the continuing destruction of the environment, Reclaim The Streets parties were happening. This wasn't just a bunch of radical individuals in London or Brighton, getting together and causing trouble. It was the focus for a whole culture, a new vision of the future.

And then, on Saturday 28 September 1996, two days before Arthur's hit-and-run incident on the B4494 near Newbury, Reclaim The Streets went up to Liverpool, to meet the sacked Liverpool Dockers.

The meeting with the Liverpool Dockers was one of the most remarkable events of the 90s. It was the new, vibrant, youthful, dance-orientated, environmentalist, anarchic, druggy protest culture, meeting the older, working class, union-based, socialist solidarity, drinking protest culture, who's principle slogan had always been:

NEVER CROSS A PICKET LINE!

Which is why the 329 employees of the Mersey Docks and Harbour Company had been sacked in the first place, because they had refused to cross a picket line manned by representatives of another 80 dock workers who had previously been sacked for refusing to allow further degradation in their pay and conditions.

Some of the workers were second- and third-generation dockers, who had seen the worst of dock labour practices over the years. What they were seeing now was an attempt to return to some of those practices, to the casualisation of labour, where man fought against man for the privilege of work, to the employment of cheap, untrained labour in unsafe working conditions, without holiday pay, or sick pay, working long hours in dangerous conditions. The dockers were making a last stand against the evils of the politics of individuality and greed.

One of them, Jimmy Campbell, 60-years old at the time, 40 years a docker, with only a few years to his retirement, dismissed for showing solidarity with the younger workers, said: 'Our fathers and grandfathers fought and died for jobs that we could be proud of. I did it for the young ones.'

Solidarity is just another name for love. Socialism is just another name for love. Because what is socialism but a recognition that we all live in society, that we are social beings, that we matter, that we are in this together, that we are human, that we are connected, and that, if we are to survive, it will be because we all make that final effort together, to see each other as equals? That we have a duty of care to our old people, to our children, to the sick and the wounded, to the dispossessed, and to all the hurt and hungry of the world? That all human life is sacred, that all life is sacred, that this is a boundless and beautiful world. That we are creatures of love, that's all.

There was a mass picket outside the docks, to stop the scab workers from getting in. Only some of the people in the cars pushing through the picket line weren't scabs. They were activists. They got through the line – unsuspected by the police, who thought that everyone on the docker's side was outside the gates, on the picket – and then promptly occupied the crane gantries and the administration building roof, unfurling banners expressing solidarity with the docker's cause. This must have come as a great surprise to everyone. And you can imagine the roar that went up from the dockers when they saw the banners, and learnt what was happening. The tactics of the direct action environmentalist movement were being employed in the cause of worker's rights.

So maybe there are times when you can cross a picket line. You can cross a picket line when your intention is to stop work from happening on the other side.

The occupation lasted for three days, during which time there were demonstrations and rallies both at the docks and in Liverpool city centre. The Operational Support Division (OBS) were deployed, dressed like Robocops, in black padded rubber suits with blacked-out helmets, displaying no numbers. There were scenes of violence, as is always the way, blamed on the protesters. It was the protesters who were being injured. There were many injuries and many arrests. By the Monday evening, just as Arthur was being run down by the Jag with the smoked-glass windows, activists in Liverpool were being chased down darkened streets by faceless black-clad figures wielding truncheons. It was only the intervention of the dockers that saved many of them from a severe beating. The dockers escorted them to a pub and paid for their drinks, staying with them until their buses arrived, or their trains were due. They spent the evening getting happily drunk and listening to Beatles' songs, which the dockers would join in with, clinking glasses with joyous gusto.

CJ remembers reading about this in the direct action weekly free news sheet, *Schnews*.

'Yes!' he shouted, and jumped up punching his fist into the air.

The direct action movement had come of age.

And now we move on towards the end of our chapter.

Arthur was in Bullingdon Gaol, and Reclaim The Streets had met the Liverpool Dockers.

The Earth was turning, shifting imperceptibly through her heavenly cycle.

Tony Blair had taken over the Labour Party, by now, and was running it like a Stalinist state. The Dear Leader's declarations on future policy were always made without consultation and were always final. He'd changed its name to New Labour, treating the venerable old party like a soap powder, like a brand name, to be repackaged and remarketed, and had had Clause Four removed. This was the clause in the Labour Party constitution that committed it to socialism. John Major's government were deeply divided and unpopular, dogged by sleaze and internal wrangling. An election was on its way. Labour were bound to win. Tony Blair promised not to repeal Thatcher's hated anti-Trade Union laws.

Arthur didn't stay in Bullingdon for long. He had gone before the Royal Courts of Justice where the Newbury bypass contractors, Costain, were attempting to get him injuncted not to go within 100 yards of Costain's goods or chattels anywhere in the world. He argued that, as a Druid, he had immunity on the battlefield. He quoted Caesar at them, and Strabo and Tacitus – all the Classical sources – claiming that it was a custom held from time immemorial, quoting the Statute of Westminster of 1275, which fixed the date of such customs as anything prior to 1189. They were forced to take legal advice. He was facing three of the country's top barristers, and he almost won. They argued that such customs were local, and that there was no evidence of them taking place at Newbury. In the end, he was injuncted not to go back to the Newbury protest site and, given this fact, he decided to accept the bail conditions at last and leave Bullingdon Gaol.

It was a tearful farewell with the Governor.

Not.

So now he moved on to a new protest site, at Stringers Common, near Guildford, in Surrey, where he spent the winter.

Reclaim The Streets, along with the Liverpool Dockers' shop stewards committee, and other sympathetic organisations, had called a March for Social Justice in London in April 1997, just as the election was looming. The country was in the throes of the usual election fever. Which is to say: everyone was mightily bored of it by now.

Arthur went along with a posse of Druids. Which shows just how far Arthur had brought the Druids by now, getting them to march in support of the Liverpool Dockers. He was there because his Dad was from Liverpool, and because he understood the principle of refusing to cross a picket line. It was his proud boast that he never had.

CJ was there. He was standing on the pavement outside the gates at Kennington Park watching as Reclaim The Streets emerged, with their red, green and black flags streaming in the wind, looking like a carnival rather than a political march. The flags took the form of jagged lightning flashes – some dominantly red, some black, some green, but always with flashes of the other colours mixed in – as the party activists danced and swayed to the ecstatic drum beats of a samba band. There was a police inspector nearby, talking urgently into his walkie-talkie. 'Reclaim The Streets have just exited the park.' It was clear that they saw them as a threat.

The newspapers had been talking up a riot for days.

CJ turned to the inspector.

'Those are our people,' he said. 'We agree with what they're doing.'

The inspector turned his back, ignoring him.

One of the RTS banners read, 'They wanna fight, we wanna dance.'

Which said it all.

And the march passed off fairly peacefully, despite the presence of thousands of riot police. There were about 20,000 people on the march.

CJ had met a couple of friends by now, and, once they'd got into Trafalgar Square, they went and found a pub. Arthur did the same, but not because he wanted a drink: because he wanted to use the toilet. It was while they were in the pub that they heard what was happening in the square. RTS had managed to break police lines and had brought an articulated lorry into the square, loaded up with a huge, pumping sound system. They were having a party in there!

The police had blocked off the square, not allowing anyone entry.

And now – but probably at different times and in different locations – both CJ and Arthur were trying to get into the square.

CJ was told that if he stepped any further he would be arrested. So he did and he was. The young policeman was kneeling on his back in the police van, trying to get the handcuffs on.

CJ said, 'You're young enough to be my son. Would you treat your father like this?'

And the officer said, 'But my father wouldn't be acting like you.'

He probably had a point.

Arthur had done pretty much the same. He had gone up to police lines and demanded entry. This was the Queen's highway, he said, and he had a right to pass.

The policeman said, 'There's a riot going on.'

Arthur said, 'No, there's not. Look, it's peaceful.'

And the policeman had pointed to a line of police horses approaching from the other side. 'No,' he said, 'but there soon will be.' Meaning they were about to engineer a riot.

But Arthur had insisted he pass and was arrested. He was charged with possession of a bladed weapon in a public place.

They took Excalibur from him. They were threatening to melt it down.

CHAPTER FIFTEEN

Judgement Days

So now Arthur had two court cases hanging over him. And this was serious, wasn't it? Violent Disorder carries a usual sentence of five years.

Not only that, but some of the Druids were beginning to mutter against him. He was bringing Druidry into disrepute, they said. He'd carried them so far, and over so many obstacles. He'd shown them a new way for Druidry to express itself: Druid activism. He'd tested their patience on many occasions, but had always won them over in the end, by the sheer force of his personality, by his courage and resolve, by his will to win, his optimism and his effervescent good humour. But it was all getting a bit too much. These were serious charges. He couldn't argue, as he had done before, that he had broken the law as a matter of principle. This wasn't trespass any more, his usual offence.

Until the Criminal Justice Act, in fact, trespass had always been a civil offence, a dispute between parties, played out in the civil courts, a recognition, perhaps, that ownership of land is a matter of custom, not of right. Even after the CJA, trespass was only illegal under certain, specific circumstances, and no one was ever gaoled for it. But Violent Disorder: it was a different order of crime altogether. Even if he hadn't committed it, the mere accusation was damaging. It made the Druids look like a bunch of disaffected rioters rather than the dignified, pacific, respectable religious types they wanted to appear to be. More like bad-natured Class War Anarchists trying to overthrow the state than High Spiritual Beings wafting about the planet offering enlightenment.

His position within Druidry was being called into question.

Only the Archdruid of Glastonbury stood beside him.

Rollo said, 'Four words, Arthur: "Can you handle it?"'

And Arthur said, 'I can handle it.'

And then the sword too. It wasn't any old sword, as we've said before. It was more than a sword. It was symbolic, both of his office, and of his will. It was a part of him, an extension of his being. It represented the fulfilment of an ideal. It was Truth, Honour and Justice, beaten and folded into one, hammered on the anvil of time, forged in steel. It was the Sword of Britain, recognised as such by a number of the Druid orders. Without it, he couldn't represent Britain any more and he couldn't be King Arthur. It was as simple and as stark as that.

And even if he wasn't King Arthur, and this wasn't Excalibur – even if this was all just some mad fantasy clogging up his overheated brain – the fact is that he loved it. He loved it to death.

And how many people had knelt down before it, himself included, to swear the oath? How many people had been inspired by it? How many had built their hopes and dreams around it? There were thousands of them, people the rest of society didn't give a damn about. The lost people, the rejected people, the lonely people, the druggies and the drunkards, the homeless people, the dispossessed: Arthur had raised them all with this sword, offered them high office and given them respect, had told them that their contribution mattered, that they mattered, that they were aristocrats too, the true aristocrats of the heart, with something more valuable than gold to share: their own shining humanity.

He would be letting them all down.

Arthur is not a sentimental man. There's not much that would make him cry. But he would certainly have cried if the sword had been melted down. He was even talking of suicide.

It would be the end of everything.

He was bereft without it. Naked. Void. Purposeless. Alone.

So these were testing times. He was being put to trial, as all good heroes must be, with his comrades-at-arms beside him.

The first phase of the magical battle of symbols began on the 12 May 1997, at Reading Crown Court. Proceedings were expected to last from five to seven days. It was being billed in the press as the Trial of the Druid Newbury Three.

So let us step through the elaborate, black wrought-iron gates, up the white marble steps and through the great heaving wooden doors of this Victorian Imperial building, and into the hall echoing like a Gothic cathedral, where the symbols of power and of the British State loom like premonitions over the scene: the famous crest of the Lion and the Unicorn on the walls and above the entrance door. You know the crest of course, the two animals, one mythic, the other symbolic, raised up on two feet either side of a shield topped by a crown, the Lion, full face, looking at you, with a crown upon its head, and the Unicorn, in profile, with a crown around its neck and in chains. And what does this mean, exactly? And who imposed these symbols upon us, and to what end?

Arthur says that the Lion represents warrior energy, and the Unicorn, magical energy. In other words, the British State represents itself as warrior energy unleashed, and magical energy chained.

And then into the court room itself, all dark wooden panelling, with a raised dais for the judge so that he looks down over the court, with the Lion and the Unicorn on the wall behind him and the witness box beside him, with the desks for the court officials below, and the public gallery to one side, with the dock for the accused in front of the tables where the barristers congregate, one for the prosecution, and one for the defence, all facing the judge. And the whole layout of the room is an exercise in control and intimidation, in imposing authority, in asserting the primacy of the Law, with the judge, as the representative of the Law, presiding over it all.

Now the judge walks from chambers, and the court official calls 'all rise', and everyone does, until the judge sits down, when the rest of the court sits with him. And let no one be mistaken: he sits there, deliberating over his paperwork, as the symbol of power, of judgement, of authority, in his red robes edged in ermine, bewigged in the 18th century manner, stern in his demeanour as befits his noble calling, like a lord ruling over his serfs, or a king his subjects.

Or, rather, this is how it is meant to be: the British State imposing its symbols and its authority upon a cowed and respectful defendant, seeking justice.

It was all a little different this day, however, since facing him in the dock were the three Druids, none of them in the slightest bit cowed, one of them claiming to be a king, with all the symbols of his sovereignty – a red, rampant dragon, complete with a visible erection, representing phallic energy, across his chest and an iron circlet about his head, with a raised dragon at his forehead – the two others dressed in white robes, with oak sprigs tucked into their waistbands (Orc wearing a veritable shrubbery in his) reflecting their own symbols and their own sense of autonomy. And in the public gallery, their supporters – protesters, Druids and pagans – many of them in robes and wearing cloaks, with wreaths and headdresses and bright clothing, with beads and bangles and blankets and assorted pagan jewellery about their necks, looking like the performers from some mad heathen theatre just come to town.

It was like a fancy-dress party in there, everyone in fancy dress except the jury, who looked decidedly underdressed in their dowdy off-the-peg street clothes, their Marks & Spencers woolly jumpers and casual slacks. And you can imagine them too, Mr and Mrs Joe Public, as they came in, in a line, and sat down, to then rise and be sworn in one at a time, feeling intimidated and uncertain, as they looked around the room for the first time, blinking, to see the scene as it was unfolded before them: the judge in his red robes and wig, the barristers in their black robes, and then the defendants in their white robes too. Even the people in the public gallery wearing robes: everyone in robes but them. What must they have thought? At the very least they must have understood that this wasn't going to be an ordinary court case. It looked like pure theatre, didn't it? It was bound to be an entertainment.

Before the jury were sworn in, however, the barristers had made submissions to the judge in his chambers. It was the usual legal wrangling. The barristers were concerned with the make up of the jury. They wanted to be sure that they didn't have any prejudices regarding the Newbury bypass. Also there was the question of previous convictions, since they wanted their clients to appear as men of good character, Arthur's old convictions now having been spent, and the newer ones all to do with the protest. There was a little argument over this. And Kreb's deafness was discussed, and a request made for lipspeakers to assist him.

And then one of the barristers, Tony Metzer, representing the Orc, said, as if in passing, 'There's only one other matter, Your Honour, the question of Excalibur, the sword that the defendants would propose to swear on when they give evidence in the case …'

'Hmmmm?'

'Yes, the sword is the most appropriate form the defendants would wish to swear oaths upon. However, it presents a difficulty, as it is presently being held in custody at Charing Cross police station, having been confiscated in another matter. The defendants are anxious that they be given the opportunity to swear by the most appropriate method to ensure that they do justice to the oath. They are quite content not to have personal custody of the sword, but anxious that when the time arises that the sword be brought to court and that they be given the opportunity to swear upon it. In the absence of an order from Your Honour, the police won't release it ...'

And on he went, making his case, being supported by Kreb's barrister (Arthur's being absent at this time), looking at the Oaths Act 1978, section 4, and then discussing the words to be sworn upon the sword, suggesting that they swear by Almighty God, but on the sword, not the book. And on, with a little desperation, perhaps, masked by the professional tone of voice, knowing that this was all highly unlikely, given the circumstances.

This had all been discussed beforehand with the defendants. They all knew that it would not only bring a little more theatre into the court, a little more life and colour to that already colourful scene, but that it would also underline their characters as men of honour, sworn to always speak the truth.

Bringing the sword into court would be an aid to the jury's understanding of them and their belief system.

And on the barrister went, presenting the case as cogently and succinctly as he could, anxious that his arguments be understood and taken into consideration.

The judge paused. It was like he was on a time delay switch. He went completely still. And then it was if the switch went back on and he came alive. He said, 'I consider it desirable that it should be here.' And he issued an order to Charing Cross police station that the sword be given over to the court.

It was the first time in 1,500 years that Druidry had been recognised as a religion within these shores.

And now you have to wonder why. Why did the judge allow this? Because by doing so he was accepting the sword on the symbolic level as being what they said it was: as Excalibur, the Sword of Britain. He was allowing their symbolism into court, giving it weight and substance, allowing them an implicit authority at least comparable to his own.

The British Judiciary are a peculiar bunch, steeped in strange, arcane practices, many of them secretly versed in magic and ritual themselves, in ritual handshakes and mysterious, dressed-up ceremonial, occasionally involving swords. Maybe the judge knew what he was doing. Maybe he didn't. Maybe he understood the symbolism, maybe he didn't. Maybe he just wanted to have some fun, being more familiar and therefore more bored with court procedure than most of them. Maybe he enjoyed a bit of theatre himself.

Whatever the reasons, two Thames Valley police officers were quickly despatched to collect the sword from Charing Cross police station, where it had languished since Arthur's arrest on the Docker's march, with a note from the court ordering its release. The Metropolitan police officers at Charing Cross were not happy with this, as there was a history between the two police forces (Thames Valley having returned the sword to Arthur on a number of occasions) and they refused to release it into their care. So now there was a problem. If the Thames Valley police returned to court without the sword, that would mean that the Metropolitan police were in contempt for disobeying a court order. So the Met loaded the sword into a van, and with two motorcycle outriders out in front – sirens blaring, blue lights flashing – they raced down the M4 at top speed to beat their colleagues and rivals back to Reading to hand the sword over to the court officials.

And then, in the afternoon, the jury were sworn in, and the charges read out, and Mr Daly, the prosecutor, began the case for the crown.

The charges were as follows.

> *First count: all three charged with Violent Disorder.*
> *Second count: Kreb Dragonrider charged with damaging property,*
>   *namely a red Peugeot.*
> *Third count: Kreb Dragonrider charged with damaging a Rover Metro.*
> *Fourth count: all three charged with damaging the Jaguar.*

The defendants pleaded Not Guilty.

And you can imagine Mr Daly now, in his robes and his powdered wig, with the little pigtail hanging down, with his pin-striped trousers underneath and his highly-polished shoes, with his little winged collar and flat,

white tie, addressing the jury, walking up and down in front of them, flapping his robes like wings, holding his notes, peering over his spectacles at
them – occasionally taking his spectacles off to clean them – presenting
the case with a studiously cautious air of informed certainty, reassuring
them of his presence of mind, of his sobriety, of his solidity of person,
going through the case point by point, carefully, deliberately, enunciating
it with poise and precision, like a game-player laying out his pieces,
preparing to make the first move.

'Ladies and gentlemen of the jury,' he said: 'I appear on behalf of the
prosecution. The three defendants are: firstly Arthur Pendragon, secondly
Kreb Dragonrider, and thirdly Steven Warner, known as the Orc. You may
think the names are unusual. You will hear that the three defendants are
Druids, and will have seen that they wear unusual clothing. Please treat
them as people accused of a crime. Any prejudices you might have, leave
them behind. The defendants are accused of quite specific criminal
offences …'

And on, firstly laying out the offences, and then describing the events
as they had unfolded on the evening in question. Except that he was putting them in a different order, starting with the old couple in the red
Peugeot being scared, and then trying to drive around the ceremony, and
then Kreb hitting the car and the Orc climbing onto it, and then other
people kicking the car, and things being thrown at it. And then another
car, the Metro, being surrounded by people and attacked and chased and
objects being thrown. Only then did the Jaguar appear, once again being
attacked without provocation, with Arthur apparently jumping onto the
bonnet and then falling off and injuring himself. There was no mention
of the broken back window, and no reference to the hit-and-run.

The first people to be called were the security guards who had witnessed the scene.

There were three of them, all telling a similar story. They had witnessed
cars being attacked, they said, and they had seen Arthur sprawled across
the bonnet of the Jaguar, as if he had just jumped upon it. Except that one
of them on cross-examination couldn't say for certain whether Arthur had
jumped upon the car or not, and another, without being asked, volun-
teered that he would have done the same, as the Jaguar was driving
straight at him, and he described it as an act of self-protection. He said,
'What I'm saying is, he leapt on the bonnet otherwise he'd have been hit

by the car. There was no other way to go, therefore he leapt on the bonnet.' The defence barristers didn't need to cross-examine him. They all said, 'No questions' and let him stand down.

One of the security guards also stated that he had looked into the back of the Jaguar and seen someone there indicating to the driver to drive on.

After that, the car drivers were examined and cross-examined, and then the police officers who had made the arrests.

You've probably seen enough courtroom dramas on TV to imagine the scene. The careful examination and cross-examination – sometimes three separate cross-examinations as there were three separate barristers, one for each defendant – each witness being sworn in, taking the oath upon the Bible, 'I swear by Almighty God that the evidence I shall give will be the truth, the whole truth, and nothing but the truth'; the slow, ponderous unfolding of court procedure, occasionally the judge intervening, asking for clarification, the barristers all with their little affectations and quirks of character, holding their robes with both hands at the lapel, or flapping their notes, or with their hands behind their backs, elbows crooked, rocking on their heels, with their starched shirts and their starched manners, concise, precise, deliberate, theatrical, exuding confidence and class.

The most damning evidence came from the occupants of the cars.

And you have to have sympathy with three of them at least. They didn't really know what was going on. They hadn't seen the Jaguar. All they saw was a strange gathering in the middle of the road suddenly turn violent, and which they had then attempted to circumvent. They weren't aware that there were children in the circle, or that Kreb and the Orc saw it as their duty to stop them. All they knew was that it seemed as if they were being attacked. And they must have been frightened. It was an old couple in the Peugeot, and a single woman in the Metro. They must have felt very vulnerable and threatened. If the evidence had depended upon these three, the defendants would probably have been convicted.

The driver of the Jaguar, the chauffeur, on the other hand, knew precisely what was going on. He was claiming an unprovoked attack upon his car, him being stationary at the time, with the Druids moving towards him, already angry and violent, banging on the windows and hitting the roof, and then him driving through the crowd only because he was in fear of his life, and that Arthur had jumped onto his bonnet threatening him.

He also stated that he was in the car by himself, 'the Principal', as he referred to his passenger, having been dropped off at Newbury.

The car was one of a fleet owned by Procord Ltd., a subsidiary of Lord Hanson's multinational company, hired out by Sir Anthony Cleaver, the Chairman of the Atomic Energy Commission. Lord Hanson had a home just a few miles further up the Wantage road from where the incident had taken place, and was himself actively profiting from the road building programme.

Arthur later said that you can measure the quality of a man by the quality of his enemies. Well, he would say that, wouldn't he? These were fairly formidable enemies.

The chauffeur reported damage to his car consisting of numerous scratch marks and scuff marks and a bent bumper. There was no mention of the main damage, the shattered rear window.

The cross-examination was fierce. He had three barristers at him, all suggesting that he had driven into the crowd and that there was someone else in the car with him. He held his own defiantly, saying that he stuck by his story, that no action had been taken against him by the police, that there was no one else in the car with him, that he had sworn on the Bible and that everything he was telling them was the truth. He was being questioned over and over again, and repeating his answers over and over, sometimes clearly losing his temper, going very red in the face and blustering. His evidence was in direct contradiction to the evidence of the security guards.

The police denied that there was ever an investigation into the accusation of a hit-and-run.

So that was it: the prosecution case laid out before them. It lasted several days.

In the meantime, the three Druids were being looked after by members of Reading Road Alert, an anti-roads lobby group.

Arthur was staying with a nice middle-class couple, he a teacher, she a lecturer. Every afternoon after proceedings, the Druids and their supporters would congregate in the pub to discuss the day's events. And then Arthur would trudge back the several miles to his nice, comfy billet, to a fine meal and posh wine and interested questioning, and then to a fluffy bed, with clean white sheets, a duvet and soft pillows. It wasn't his normal style of course. But – hey – he could cope, just about.

And then, in the morning, he'd trudge the grey pavement miles back to the court again.

Every day was different.

Every day was the same.

It was half time by now, like a football match.

Arthur's barrister was making his submissions before the judge. He was arguing that the case against Arthur was unsound, and should be thrown out of court. He was only accused of two things: the criminal damage against the Jaguar, and Violent Disorder, both of which were dependent on each other. There could be no criminal damage if there was no Violent Disorder. One witness had already stated that the Jaguar had driven at him, and that he was acting in self-defence, and another witness could not say for certain what had happened, only placing him on the bonnet, while the Jaguar driver had been unable to identify him. No one was accusing him of any of the other charges. The judge paused. It was one of his quirks, the way he would stop completely, as if he'd been suddenly switched off. And then the time delay switch came on and he was there again and agreeing with them. He ordered the jury to find Arthur Not Guilty on all counts, while Kreb and the Orc were to continue with the trial.

So now began the case for the defence.

Arthur elected to act as a Mackenzie's Friend to Kreb and the Orc, that is, he was allowed to sit in the dock with them, and confer.

Their first job was to show that the prosecution case had been stitched together with lies. One of these had involved Brays Detective Agency.

Arthur had been positive that he had seen them there, filming the whole event, as they had been filming most things on the road protest. But when the defence team had summonsed them to present the tape as evidence, they denied that there ever was such a tape or that they were ever there.

So a representative from Brays was called, and questioned.

They asked him about the working procedures. They worked in threes, the court was told. Always in threes. One would film, one would take notes, and one would take stills photographs. And was this always the case? Yes, it was always the case. They always worked in threes. Were there ever any exceptions to this? Were there ever any occasions where one of them would work alone, the stills photographer, say, or the person taking notes? No. There were always three of them.

It just so happened that when Arthur had been injuncted at the Royal Courts of Justice not to return to the Newbury site he had been handed a piece of evidence as part of the case against him. He recognised it straight-away. It was a photograph of him taken just after the hit-and-run, with his face dripping blood, looking startled and slightly mad, taken by Brays Detective Agency. It had served them well in the injunction. Out of con-text is showed a man having just been involved in a scene of violence. It had the time and the date on it. So the photograph was presented to court and shown to the witness, with a request that the rest of the evidence, the notes and the video film, now be presented to the court. And what could he do? He ummed and ah-ed and spluttered, and tried to claim that, yes, well, maybe in this case the photographer had turned up without the others and taken the photograph, even though this was not proper pro-cedure, but that there still was no other evidence.

So that was it: another lie nailed in court.

Their next task was to find the police officer who had led the investiga-tion of the hit-and-run. They knew what he looked like, they just couldn't remember his name. So they called every police officer from Newbury police station to the witness box, one by one. And each one would be called, sworn in, and then be told, 'No questions.' One by one, one at a time, a parade of police officers stepping into the witness box, uniformed and carrying their helmets beneath their arms, only to be sent away again. The whole procedure was beginning to have the air of some grand farce. No one else in court outside of the defence team had any idea what this was for. The barrister would say, 'Call Constable So-and-so.' The court official would repeat the call from the court, opening the doors and call-ing down the echoing corridor outside, the call being taken up a second or a third time – 'Call Constable So-and-so' – and then the man in ques-tion would arrive, huffing, ready to answer questions, only to be told 'No questions' and dismissed. They had every member of Newbury police sta-tion there, ready to answer questions, and everyone was being summarily dismissed.

And then one police officer stepped into the witness box, and three arms shot forward from the dock, with three hands, and three fingers to tap three sets of shoulders in front of them, and that was it, they had their man.

This was Sergeant Chowdry, and he was the only other person in the court, aside from the Druids, not to swear on the Bible. He swore on the Holy Koran.

In fact, he hadn't been a Sergeant at the time of the arrests. He had been promoted since. And he confirmed that, yes, there had been a complaint of a hit-and-run, that statements had been taken, and that he had been the investigating officer.

So now the Detective Constable leading the investigation was recalled to the witness stand.

'Can you confirm what you said in earlier evidence, and in your witness statement, that there was no other enquiry with regard to a hit-and-run allegation?'

Yes, he could confirm.

Did he stand by that statement?

Yes he did. There was no other investigation, and no allegations of a hit-and-run incident.

And Arthur's barrister fired back.

'That's funny,' he said, 'we've just had a Sergeant Chowdry on the stand who stated that there was an investigation and that he was leading it.'

And now it was the Detective Constable's turn to um and ah and look about, flustered and exposed. This was the first time he had heard of this, he said. He had no idea of Chowdry's brief, he said. He had never heard of the investigation before, he said.

And you could see it as you looked about the court, in the eyes of the jury, in the eyes of the judge, in the eyes of the court officials even. A kind of shift in emphasis, a subtle change of light, like a sun ray dancing upon a pond. A shift in their demeanour. This man was being careless with the truth.

It was the turning point of the case.

So, having exposed the prosecution case for what it was, all they had to do now was to tell the truth.

The truth.

The whole truth.

And nothing but the truth.

Which was how Kreb made his oath. To tell the truth, the whole truth, and nothing but the truth. Swearing on the sword, Excalibur, placing his hand upon it, as it was brought to him, reaching out and holding it, with reverence, with care. Only he didn't swear by Almighty God. He swore by the Earth Goddess instead.

'I swear by the Earth Goddess to tell the truth, the whole truth, and nothing but the truth.'

You've already met Kreb. You have to imagine him again now. That air of complete sincerity. That childlike dignity. Blinking and looking round from behind his glasses. Only half in the world. The way he makes you feel as if a saint has just walked into your midst. With that odd snuffling voice of his, as if a badger had just learned to speak. That strange, nasal stutter, enunciating his words with peculiar emphasis. Answering the barrister's questions with a look of thoughtful sincerity. Taking everything so seriously. Weighing up his words carefully and then placing them, one at a time, into the world's hearing.

'My name is Mog Ur Kreb Dragonrider. I live at … At the time of the arrest I was residing at Gotan Camp near Newbury. I am now 39. My date of birth is the twenty-seventh of the first, fifty-eight. I am deaf. I am totally deaf in my right ear and severely deaf in my left ear. I am conversant with sign language. I am able to lip read. I am a single man. I have no children. I am a pagan priest and a shamanic Druid.'

And they couldn't help it. People were smiling. Some people were laughing. Even the judge allowed himself an occasional smile. It wasn't what he said, it was how he said it. He was like Tommy Cooper up there or Stan Laurel. That same air of baffled sincerity. Not knowing why he was funny, but pleased to be so. Glad that everyone was enjoying themselves. Looking around the court while they smiled and laughed, and then laughing with them. Warming to his role as the official court jester.

'I first met King Arthur on the eighteenth of the sixth, ninety-six, before the solstice. I had heard of him nine months before that. I met him at Gotan near Newbury. I saw him at camp. I recognised him from a picture that I had. We became very good friends. I believe him to be the reincarnation of the ancient King Arthur who lived around 600 AD. The day I met him I became a knight.'

And on like this, every simple question requiring an elaborately detailed answer. Telling them how he became involved in the protest, how he was raised as a Shield Knight, how he believed in reincarnation, and that he believed himself to have been King Arthur's son in a previous life; about the oath he took, and what it meant to him; how he engaged

in non-violent direct action in his protest against the road. And on. About
the day he was raised and how it made him feel. How proud he felt.
About the ceremony on the Wantage road. The discussions in the bender
beforehand. How he couldn't quite hear what was going on, but he was
invited to attend if he wanted. How he wanted to attend. How he was
dressed.

'I was dressed in a white Druid robe. The same robe I have on now.'

Telling the whole story, as it happened, in all its exacting detail. About
his role as traffic warden.

'I had a particular function, to control the traffic so that the ceremony
could take place. I did that by holding my staff to my left and putting out
my hand in front to indicate to the driver to stop. This is my staff. I had it
with me on the night.'

And then about the Jaguar, how it had pulled out, how it picked up
speed, how he put out his hand and said 'Stop!' How it didn't stop. How
it accelerated, driving by him and striking him on the hip. How he fell,
grazing his left hand. How he picked up his staff, which had been run
over by the Jaguar. How the Jaguar was pulling away at speed. How he
pointed at it with his staff and said, 'I curse you with the curse of mutilation,' in a loud voice.

And now everyone in the court was laughing. They were falling about
with laughter. 'A curse of mutilation.' It was the best joke anyone had
heard in ages.

He wasn't cursing the driver, he said, he was cursing the car. As for the
driver, 'I reserved my contempt for the driver,' he said.

And now about the other cars, nudging their way through the circle.
How he wanted them to stop. How he was concerned for the safety of the
people in the circle, that no one be injured. How he would tap the cars to
get them to stop, as a warning. How he saw it as his duty.

Then the Orc's barrister asked questions.

Kreb said, 'The Orc is a very hard worker in camp. He could be
described as a gentle giant.'

And now it was time for the cross-examination. This is where Kreb
really came into his own.

Mr Daly was trying to trip him up, firing questions at him. And you
could read it in the jury's faces: how could he? That lovely, lovable Kreb.
How could he be so cruel? But Kreb was poised and in control. If he

needed time to think he feigned deafness. He would say, 'Pardon? Can you repeat that?' And Mr Daly would have to ask the question again. Kreb was running rings around him. And no one can disbelieve Kreb. Even though it was Mr Daly's job to find fault with his argument, even he had to be convinced. Kreb simply doesn't lie. He cannot lie. He's constitution-ally incapable of it. He wouldn't see the point in it even if he could. He was sworn to Truth, Honour and Justice, and Truth, Honour and Justice is his creed.

Mr Daly asked what Kreb had hoped to achieve with his curse of muti-lation.

Kreb said that he hoped that the car would fall to bits.

And so he sailed on through the cross-examination, like a fair-weather craft on a fine day, as light as the breeze. Which is how Kreb is in any case. He's as light as the breeze.

And that was it, really.

Rollo was called as a character witness for Kreb, swearing the Welsh oath in his rounded, loud honeyed voice, holding up Excalibur in a dra-matic fashion, raising it high, lifting it before him with due ceremonial as it lay across his two hands, intoning the words with Shakespearian precision: 'Y gwir erbyn y byd!' It means 'Truth against the World'. It was Boudicca's battle cry against the Romans.

Then the Orc gave his testimony, repeating the story over again. Professor Ronald Hutton of Bristol University was called as a character witness for the Orc.

And then it was the prosecution summing up, then the defence, then the judge's, and the jury were sent out to deliberate. They were told that they must reach a unanimous decision, but that if they could not, at a lat-er point the court would accept a majority decision.

This was at 11.40am, on the morning of the 20 May 1997. They were recalled at 11.55am for a point of law to be made clear to them. At 1.05pm they asked for assistance, on the meaning of the term, 'threatened unlawful violence'. They were told that it must involve the intention to threaten violence, or awareness that their conduct was threatening. Words are not enough, they were told. At 2.15pm the jury came back in. They had been unable to reach a unanimous decision. They were told that a majority decision of 10–2 would do. They went out again, and returned at 2.40pm. They had reached a majority decision of 11–1.

And then the court rose, and the verdict was given.

Count one, Kreb Dragonrider, Violent Disorder: Not Guilty.

Count one, Steven John Warner, Violent Disorder: Not Guilty.

Count two, Kreb Dragonrider, Criminal Damage: Not Guilty.

Count three, Kreb Dragonrider, Criminal Damage: Not Guilty.

Count four, Kreb Dragonrider, Criminal Damage: Not Guilty.

Count four, Steven John Warner, Criminal Damage: Not Guilty.

Yes!

Everyone cheered and clapped, and the three defendant's embraced each other in the dock. Costs of £50 were awarded to each of them and they were discharged. Time to go down the pub!

So that was it. Excalibur was returned to Charing Cross police station, ready for the next court case.

Now was the hardest time for Arthur. Not having Excalibur. It was like a bit of him was missing. Outwardly he was confident. If anyone said they were sorry that he'd lost the sword, he'd say, 'Don't worry, I'll get it back.' But he wasn't really all that certain. And he felt guilty too, for having put it at risk. He was supposed to be the swordbearer. He was supposed to look after it. And if he'd have thought about it, would he have taken it on that march? He knew the Met had it in for him. They'd declared several times that they would nab him if they found him with the sword on their patch. They weren't like the other police forces, with a soft spot for his eccentricity. They were more hardcore, with an ingrained hatred of the protest movement, and therefore of Arthur, who they would have seen as one of the ringleaders. The fact that the protest movement didn't actually have any leaders was a point that they were always unable to grasp.

He couldn't knight anyone. He tried knighting somebody with a bread knife once, but it didn't have the same effect.

He was in and out of Bow Street Magistrates' Court, trying to get the sword back. He was charged with possession of a bladed implement in a public place, on two counts: one for the sword, and one for his Athame, his witch's dagger. He was remanded, but refused to leave without the sword. He wouldn't accept bail. He said he would rather go to prison than leave without the sword. The magistrate found him in contempt of court, and he was sent down to cells, while they bailed him against his wishes, and then kicked him out. There were a number of visits to Bow

Street – one, two, lots – before he finally had a date set for a jury trial.

It was to be November the fifth, at Southwark Crown Court.

November the fifth! Either there was a joker in the Crown Prosecution Service, or they really didn't know what they were doing. It was certainly an auspicious date.

Arthur was going round saying that when he got the sword back the British people would celebrate with fireworks.

He was referring to it as the Sword in the Stone. He was going to pull the sword from the stonework of London, he said.

He decided that he would organise a march on London for the date. He would walk from Stonehenge to London, gathering troops along the way. The British people were going to rise up in defence of his sword. He was declaring a revolution. But first he had to know how long the walk would take. So he marched by himself from London to Stonehenge for Halloween. CJ was there, along with Rollo, and Susanna, Kreb, the Orc, Bran and about 20 others. He had wrecked his shoes on the way, and had to bind them with silver insulating tape. And then, the following morning, they all set off. All of them but CJ, that is, who had his mind on other things.

Trudge, trudge, trudge. Tramp, tramp, tramp, the long miles to London Town, in a pair of shoes stuck together with insulating tape.

It took about four days.

And then it was November the fifth, and here he was again, up before a judge again, taking on the might of the British legal system again, in a magical battle of symbols.

It was the usual theatrical event, with the public gallery full of Druidy types.

Professor Ronald Hutton had written a defence statement. (You can read it in the appendix.) So the judge went away to his chambers to read the statement and to see the video evidence from the day. And then he came back. He looked about the courtroom. He looked back at the statement. Then he looked at Arthur.

He said: 'Having seen the evidence I have come to the conclusion that it is not in the public interest to try this case.'

And that was it. As easy as that. Arthur turned round and hugged the nearest person to him, who just happened to be a female security guard, standing by him in the dock. She was blonde.

The judge wrote Arthur a note, and then the raggle-taggle brigand band set off to Charing Cross police station to recover the sword.

The police were reluctant to hand it over. They couldn't quite believe what was going on. They had all these mad pagans in their reception area, playing music and drumming, and a scrappy note from the judge ordering the return of the sword, and Arthur standing there expectantly, looking at them. And, in the end, they couldn't delay it any longer.

They handed it over, and Arthur and the sword were reunited.

He went out to be greeted by the mass hordes of the press.

He had tears in his eyes. Tears of joy.

Raven Quest and Coronation

B ritain. The Dark Isle. Wind-lashed, rain-seared. Land of damp
and mist, of moss and fern; of dark woods, dripping dew; of
wild heaths and wild moors, of the Wild Hunt, where goblins
keep their fairy moots and the changeling baby is exchanged in the night;
of dark dreams and dark myths, where the old dark gods roam, with the
spirit of a raven at its heart.

And now, do you see it: that old grim bird, black as the night, riding
the wild skies, its hollow croak like an omen, scaling bluff and crag and
mountain fastness in the hollow hills of Wales, circling above the lonely
places where the wind blows cold and fresh like a purification and the
clouds' shroud over the looming sky? What is it doing? What is it waiting
for? It is waiting to die.

Let us follow it down now, down, down, on wavering wing, along the
mountain gorges and into the opening valley's greenery, wide and slop-
ing, spacious, where men dwell, bent-backed in their labour. Let us watch
as it sails on, riding the air's currents like a wave, feeling the air's movements through its rippled feathers, sensing the air's swift passage over the
land, reading the air like a rhyme.

The raven is old, old. As old as time. As old as the mountains. As old as
the trees. It has seen many things. It has observed the works of nature and
of men. It has watched with an indifferent eye as dynasties have come and
gone, as buildings were raised and then crumbled, as the works of men
shone and then decayed. It has seen the new motorways cutting swathes
through the landscape like thin grey ribbons, and it has known that these

things too would fall into disrepair and ruin. All things come from nature. All things return to nature. This the raven knows.

And so it sails, resting on the swift wind with outstretched wing, over hills and woods and farms and factories, over cottages, over streams, over the green patchwork fields like torn-up playing cards, over roads, over cars, over out-of-town shopping complexes and housing developments, over Swansea Town and Port Talbot, over the M4, winging its way from Cader Idris to the Gower Peninsular, like the spirit of the ancient Cymri, as it wrestles with the wind, waiting for the old gods to return.

And then, just as the bleak night begins its slow descent, in the enclosing evening, shady like a storm, the gods demand their sacrifice, and the raven gives up its life to the wind, and falls, whirling to the earth.

There was never such a raven, of course.

It's a metaphorical raven. A mythological raven. A raven only dreamed of in dreams.

But there was a dead raven in the undergrowth, in the woods where Bran found it, somewhere on the borderlands between England and Wales.

He saw it there and then left it, not thinking very much about it.

You'll remember Bran. He was originally called Chatty, a young lad with a bright and lively disposition, a little older now. He was with Arthur at the Liberation of the Giant's Dance, and then at Camelot, where he took the name change. Bran Bendegeit Whitedog MacGregor, to give you the full name. Later, he had accompanied Arthur on the Stonehenge march, to collect Excalibur from the stonework of London. And it was on the march that he told Arthur about the raven.

He said he'd seen this raven in the woods, 'fairy-shot', as he said, meaning there was no visible sign of how it died. He said he wanted the head for a particular purpose and that he was going back to collect it sometime.

And Arthur said, 'No, no, you go and find it and then give it to me. I'll take it. As it happens I know exactly what it's for.'

And he told Bran this story.

It goes right back. Right back to his early days as Arthur. Before any of the protests. Before the Stonehenge campaign had got properly underway. Not long after the meeting with Rollo and before he became a Druid. Way back when he was still living in that apple orchard, just after the publication of the *Latterday Book of Arthurian Bards*. When he was still a biker really, still fantasising about the future. Before he knew what being Arthur would actually entail.

He got a letter from someone named Chris Turner, calling himself the Dragon Bard.

This is the letter.

We print it in full because it is the work of a true poet, and because no one else could tell this story with the same depth and poignancy.

How Arthur Pendragon, King, came to know of the Dragon Bard and his son, the Young Treespeaker.

The Builder of Circles, The Singer of Songs

Behold I was conceived in the days of peril and born in days of darkness. As I grew in the womb, winged knights fought and killed and died in the skies of Albion and fiery death fell upon the children of the Island of the Mighty.

I claim the Dragon of the East and the Dragon of the West as my birthright for both are my guardians and talismans in great and little, broad and fine. The year of my birth is set under the seal of the Dragon in the traditions of the East and the day of my birth is the Day of Days, the Dragon Day in the Western mysteries, known to our ancient Fathers as Yule. This, is the time of my coming into the world; 25-12-40 and the place was the Isle of Wight, Vectis Insula, an Island of an Island, a place apart.

In my twenty-fifth year I came to the city of Bristol and met the late and sorely missed Jess Foster, founder and inspiration of the Pendragon Society. With her and her colleagues, I first heard the High Histories of the Grail and Table Round and with them I journeyed down to Gwlad Yr Haf, the Land of Summer and fired a beacon on the summit of Cadbury Castle that is Camelot. For the next three summers I spent such time as I had, working on the excavations which were the first ever to honour the names of Arthur and Camelot and I stood in the place where the Great Hall of Arthur stood before ever the Saxon came to Somerset and looked far across the Land of Summer to the Isle of Avalon.

I took myself before the dawn through the ice and fog of the Winter

Solstice down into Wiltshire to Stonehenge, the Giant's Dance. Alone I entered the Sanctuary and saw the Sun strike the Stones on the Midwinter alignments, kept the vigil and honoured those who built and those who worshipped in ages past.

I worked a May morning magic and passed for seven years through the Faery Gate of the Beacons. I saw the Old Gods walk the hills and heard the Stones talk one to another as they have since time out of mind. The trees bled me until I learned their ways and the darkness blinded me until I learned to see with my soul. I nurtured the art of the Dowser so that secrets beneath the Earth were no longer hidden from me and I spoke muzzle to muzzle with the horses of the Hills.

In time, I came to see the white and the black and made my choice with no hesitation and no regret and set a seal thereto.

And then they came to me and asked me to set a circle of Stones in the mountains. So I rose before the dawning throughout the Novena of St John and took me to the appointed place in the Mountains of Ceredigion and marked the rising of the Midsummer Sun and scribed and laid out a Sacred Enclosure in the ways of the Holy Men of the Elder Days. At my call came all manner of people from the land roundabout and they carried Stones and set them in a ring to my instruction and dug a ditch round about them and raised a bank of Earth outside. Then as now, sits the circle in the wind-scoured height and shines in the rays of the Midsummer Sun. A place of comfort.

In the fullness and rightness of time, children were born. Three there were in name and attribute thus:

- *Alison the Fair who tends the Fire and commands it to her will.*

- *Richard Treespeaker, beloved and mourned, born 18-5-71 of whom more anon.*

- *Benjamin of the Nimble Fingers who understands the Turning of Wheels and the Meshing of Gears.*

We lived in a cot in the Cambrian Mountains and watched Moonrises and Starfall. We counted the Sun's slow swing from season to season and saw the making of the weather across the Irish sea. At this time was the Building of the Circle and we all with our hands shaped and fashioned a Ring of Stones and set them to greet the Midsummer Sun.

In the Mountains and Mysteries we lived and grew and found each our own Way until at the dictates of the Real and Present world we removed once again to Bristol, but this time we brought with us the Magic of the Hills in our hearts. Richard's gift was knowledge of the wild animals and the trees, and in due course he started training in the craft of horticulture. He knew the names of the plants and trees, and the ways of tending them. As I had taught him my lore in the mountains of his childhood, so he now taught me the craft and lore of his calling.

Where others cut the ancient trees, Richard planted healthy new saplings and nurtured them with love.

Where others covered the green land with concrete and tarmac, Richard planted the flowers of Spring and Summer that ease the Heart and soothe the Eye.

Where others broke and tore in bitter vandalism, Richard healed and repaired and tended back to health.

Where others sulked in mindless apathy, Richard took joy in the green, growing things.

Richard and I stood and honoured the Ancient Circle Builders in Carn Meini whence came the Bluestones of Stonehenge.

Richard and I stood and honoured the Old Ones before the altars of Knossos.

Richard and I stood and honoured the Old Ones before the Sphinx at Giza.

Richard and I stood and honoured the Old Ones before the Temple of Apollo at Delphi.

Richard and I stood and honoured the Old Ones before the Sanctuary of Artemis at Ephesus.

Richard and I stood and honoured the Old Ones before the Temple of the Virgin, the Parthenon.

Richard and I stood and honoured the Old Ones before the Pharos and the Colossus.

Richard and I stood and honoured the Traditions of the Book of the Wailing Wall.

Richard and I stood and honoured the Traditions of the Book at

Bethlehem.

Richard and I stood and honoured the Traditions of the Book on Olivet. I have and tend an Olive tree, a gift from my beloved son in memory whereof.

Richard and I stood and honoured the lore of Arthur of Albion on Cadbury which is Camelot where we made a likeness of Excalibur in stones upon the ramparts.

Richard and I stood and honoured the Lore of Arthur of Albion on the height of Glastonbury and looked out across the misty plain of the Vale of Avalon that lies in the heart of Gwlad Yr Haf, the Land of Summer.

As is the way with joyful young men of this and all Ages past, Richard delighted in the company of his peers and tested his strength and wit and quickness on them as they did on him. He matched them laugh for laugh and dance for dance and effort for effort. He bought him a motorcycle and played loud music and exulted in his youth. He was quick in the defence of the weak and kind to the aged and infirm. He had an abiding respect for the traditions and lore of his Land and his People. Life was sweet for him and he was a sweetness in the lives of others.

In the icy early hours of Wednesday, 28 November 1990, Richard lost control of his bike on a long right-hander. He and his companion were killed outright. His age was nineteen and a half.

I saw him then in a plain room with tall windows, lying on a bier and clad in the Cloth of Glory, in purple and gold. And my heart broke.

We committed his body to the flames with just a simple circle of Holly and Ivy for the plants and the Land he loved so dear.

We scattered his ashes in the Circle of Stones that he had helped fashion with his own hands and where he sleeps now and forever in the Dreaming Hills with his face set towards the Sun at its rising.

Among the sad little bundle of trinkets left behind, I found a copy of The Latterday Book of Arthurian Bards *dated MCMXC. On page 7 I read 'The Circle. That which has neither beginning nor end, life after death, death after life, that which must come full circle, that which is continuance.' I was much comforted thereby.*

And so I move into the time of the unknown with the knowledge that time itself is a circle I am travelling. What has gone before is necessary for what is to come after, but just as valid as cause-and-effect. This tale, this history, this song of patches starts with Arthur Pendragon, King and likewise ends. But which end of the circle are you, Arthur Reborn?

I do not know if Richard was known to the Warband. However, I do know that he had an interest and may have offered his hand in knightly fellowship had he been spared long enough so to do. He would certainly have been a worthy Brother Knight (for such I suppose him to be, but who may now tell?) and the Warband has suffered a loss no less than the rest by his passing.

If this true tale has found approval in the Fellowship of the Table Round, I ask a boon of Arthur Pendragon and the Warband. Pause for just a moment and drink a drink for a Brother you lost before you found, and a tale that started after its own end. Then turn down the empty glass and press on once more to your several destinies. You will not be the weaker.

As for me, who shall know himself and knowing, tell the secret to another? And yet, and yet. Know you this, however, that I carry no sword for this I have forsworn, but when I saw the true nature of the sword and the shield and chose therefrom as was my right and duty, then I took to myself the shield and have borne it these many years.

So ends the tale of Richard, the young Treespeaker, maybe Fellow of the Table Round and Son and Companion to the Dragon Bard, Teller of Tales, Shieldbearer and Dreamer this feast of Samhain in the year of Common Reckoning 1991.

The odd thing about all of this is that Arthur had never met Richard. He was not a member of the Warband.

What was even odder is that *The Latterday Book* was never given to anyone outside of the Warband. It was written by the Warband, for the Warband only.

In other words, Richard should never have had a copy.

Where he got it from is the greatest mystery of all.

But he did have a copy and his bereaved father found it, and wrote to Arthur as a consequence.

This was the same year as the Dragon Quest.

You will have noticed something about Chris Turner's letter. You will have realised that he was a learned man, not only a member of the Pendragon Society, and an accomplished poet, but an archaeologist too, skilled in many things. He knew all the historical material relating to the Arthurian legend. In particular, he knew of one of the historical Arthur's misdeeds.

At the time he was living in Newcastle, and Arthur, having replied to his letter, went up to see him. Chris was raised as a Shield Knight and Dragon Scribe. And then he gave Arthur a quest.

He told him that this was something only Arthur could do. Because the historical Arthur was guilty of a terrible crime, he said. He had dug up a magical talisman from the White Hill in London, meant to protect these Islands from invasion.

His source of information was the *Welsh Triads*. These are a collection of medieval mnemonics designed to aid the ancient Celtic Bards by giving them the broad outlines of various stories, always in threes. Many of them refer to Arthur, and are a tantalising glimpse into how the ancient Welsh people regarded their hero.

We've referred to two of them already. Arthur is said to have been one of the Three Frivolous Bards, and one of the Very Famous Prisoners. He was also one of the Three Red Ravagers. And there were three Guineveres too. But he was also responsible for one of the Three Unfortunate Disclosures, as follows:

> *And Arthur disclosed the head of Bran the Blessed from the White Hill, because it did not seem right to him that this Island should be defended by the strength of anyone but by his own.*

This was the quest that Chris Turner had put upon our Arthur all those years back. To replace the head of Bran in the White Hill in London.

Bran the Blessed was one of the ancient British Gods. He was so large that no house could contain him. He fought the Irish because they had dishonoured his sister Branwen. The royal swineherds of Ireland had seen a marvel in the Irish Sea. They had seen a forest in the sea, and nearby a mountain with a ridge, either side of which was a lake. This was Bran. The forest was the British fleet. The mountain was Bran's head, as he waded out into the sea, the ridge was his nose and the two lakes were his eyes. A battle was fought and eventually the Irish were defeated. But Bran was wounded, and there were only seven other survivors on the British side. Bran ordered that they should cut off his head, and then predicted what would happen next. They would go to Harlech and feast there for seven years, conversing with Bran's dismembered head, as if it were still attached to his body. After that they would journey to Gwales – that is, Gresholm, off the coast of Pembrokeshire – and spend another eighty years there. And still the uncorrupted head would be talking to them agreeably, as if Bran was still alive. But then someone would open a door which looked towards Cornwall, and after that the head would be taken to 'the White Eminence of London, a place of splendid fame.'

And so it was. They chopped off Bran's head, and everything that he had told them came true.

Thus the magical head of Bran was hidden on the White Hill, as a protection for these precious Islands, until the vanity of Arthur had disclosed it.

It was after this that the Saxons had completed their invasion, finally taking over the majority of the country.

Which is all very strange. Not an easy wrong for a modern day Arthur to correct.

It was through his conversations with Liz Murray that Arthur was finally able to disentangle all the mysteries.

The White Hill was Tower Hill, the site of the Tower of London. And 'Bran', the name, also means raven.

Thus when Bran the knight told Arthur that he had found a dead raven in the woods on the borders between England and Wales, and said that he intended to take its head, Arthur knew precisely what it was for.

And Bran went off to find his head, and returned with it just after Christmas 1997, to where Arthur was staying, at Liz Murray's house. It was a skull, clean of flesh. He had it in a jam jar.

And on New Year's Eve, the three of them, Bran, Arthur and Liz, went off to complete their quest.

They were broke, and it costs money to go into the Tower. But there is an outer ring, before you get to the turnstiles, where you don't have to pay. And they walked around this for a bit, trying to locate the spot. Arthur asked to look at the head. And then he did his disappearing bit.

One minute he was there, holding the jar, and the next he was not. Bran and Liz were looking for him, wondering where he'd got to. And then he was there again, suddenly, out of nowhere, with the jam jar, now empty of the raven's skull, and full of earth from the White Hill.

And that was that. Arthur had corrected his predecessor's historical misdeed.

We won't tell you where it is. It is our little secret.

It was only later that the full significance of all of this dawned upon them, and people began to realise that Arthur really was who he said he was: if not the actual reincarnation of the historical Arthur, then of the same spirit at least. Come back to heal the land. To heal the wounds of the old times. To make Britain whole again.

On the question of reincarnation: you will notice that we have avoided making that claim in this book. We have suggested it, but then we have suggested a number of other possible mechanisms too. It's not easy to explain the peculiar set of coincidences that have conspired to transform this man's life. Reincarnation is too easy a claim to make: impossible to disprove, impossible to prove. And if reincarnation actually exists, then – obviously – the world is full of it. All of us must be reincarnated beings.

And the world is indeed full of people making all sorts of claims about who they might have been in some past life or another.

There's a reincarnated Guinevere, for instance, who has stated that they ate potatoes in the court of Camelot. And if she believes that she must have a very short memory.

If you ask Arthur, then he will tell you that he sincerely believes that he is who he says he is, that he is the reincarnation of the historical Arthur. But he's not out to prove it to you. You can take it any way you like. The only certainty is that he believes it himself.

Or as one Druid once put it: 'I sincerely believe that he sincerely believes that he is Arthur.'

As for CJ: he finds the reincarnation explanation too pat – and in a strange way, too mundane – and has offered you a variety of other ways of looking at the matter. But it doesn't matter in the end how you view it. In CJ's terms, it's a good story, that's all, a rollicking, lively adventure tale. And it is instructive of how we may choose to relate to the world we live in, and to our specific relationship to the State.

Because that is precisely what Arthur has managed to do, reincarnated being or not. By adopting the persona – by taking the name, and claiming it as his own – he is making claims on a legitimacy that precedes that of the current British State. He has empowered himself in relation to the State. He has become – to use an old expression – a law unto himself. And if this is the only lesson we draw from this book, it is still a worthwhile lesson to have learned. It is from this legitimacy that he draws the confidence to challenge the State.

As the State disempowers us, so we re-empower ourselves. As it dispossesses us, so we repossess ourselves. We repossess ourselves of our historical identity. We become who we were meant to be.

We do this on all levels at once: magical, spiritual, political.

The only true politics are the politics of the heart. The only true spirituality is the spirituality of engagement. The only true magic is the magic of friends. We will never find our heaven by excluding anyone else. The world is a much better place than we have yet imagined.

We all claim a legitimacy that precedes that of the British State. We claim the legitimacy of ourselves, as free human beings.

And it's not as if the British State itself is or was ever unaware of all of this.

The Tower of London was built on that sacred spot precisely so that the new Norman elite could make claims on a British legitimacy that preceded the Saxon rule they had just overthrown.

They adopted the identity of Arthur too, likening their own courts to Camelot. And they practiced Bran's magic, bringing the ravens to Tower Hill, and making them the magical talismans of protection in place of the head.

It was also the custom for new Monarchs to process from the Tower to Westminster Cathedral for their Coronation, on the Stone of Scone, the Stone of Destiny, the last remaining symbol of the ancient British State, said by some to be one of the Four Hallows of the Holy Grail. It was stolen by the Norman's from its original resting place in Scotland.

Arthur, Bran and Liz, meanwhile, had got themselves back to Liz's house. There was a phone call. It was from a group of protesters in Kingston-upon-Thames in Surrey. Developers were building luxury flats and had managed to persuade the local council to remove a row of poplar trees, so that the residents of the new flats would have an unimpeded view of the river. A protest site had been hastily constructed to try to defend the trees. The protesters were asking for Arthur's help.

Arthur had never been to Kingston, though he liked the sound of the name. He asked Liz how far it was: whether it was within walking distance or not.

Well it was. It was within Arthur's walking distance, which is to say, probably not within what anyone would commonly call 'walking distance'. Walkable, but distant.

It was also, he was reliably informed, the site of the King's Stone – from where it gets its name – the place of crowning of a number of the pre-Norman English Kings. One of the places of the historical enemy, in other words: the dreaded Saxon invaders whom the historical Arthur had so valiantly – and, finally, vainly – fought.

'In that case,' he said, 'the King should definitely go to Kingston!'

And the following day, New Year's Day, 1998, Arthur and Bran set off, saying their goodbyes to Liz at Kew Bridge, which is as far as she was willing to accompany them for the time being.

They arrived in the evening. And if they'd been on some strange protest sites in their time, this one was one of the strangest.

The setting was Canbury Gardens in Kingston. It was a neat little suburban recreation ground. A patch of well-kept turf, with a gravel footpath cutting across it, surrounded by substantial suburban terraces, an ornamental garden nearby, and a line of Lombardy poplars ranged against a fence. These were the offending trees, tall and lanky like guardsmen standing to attention, whipping about in the wind. The protest was established around the trees, amongst the roots and up the trunks. There was a large communal bender and a number of tents, and clinging desperately to the inhospitable trees – poplars not being ideal for such construction work – were the tree houses, spanning the gaps between the trees, rather than around individual trees as is normally the case. They had named each of the trees individually, with the names of all the British Kings. And the fires were not in fire pits but in braziers, oil drums on legs with holes punched through: the sort of fires that workmen use, or strikers on picket lines. And there was no shit pit either, this being far too public a place for open-air toiletry. They had to walk about 15 minutes to the nearest public toilet. The main advantage, however, was that there was water available on site. The protesters had built a huge scaffold tower over the tapped water mains, several stories high, boarded with chipboard, painted grey with black lines like brickwork, and crenellated on top as a pastiche of a medieval stronghold. A suburban Tower of London.

They were preparing for the worst.

Arthur and Bran were made right royally welcome, being honoured guests.

It was that evening, in the communal bender, sitting around the dusky light of the brazier, that one of the protesters asked Arthur if he had ever been crowned. Well, no, he hadn't.

'You know about the King's Stone, don't you?'

'Ye-ah?'

'So why don't we crown you then?'

It was a thought. In fact, it was a funny thought. They were all laughing about it. Yeah, why not? Why not crown him? The joke was made even more pointed by the fact that the King's Stone is Saxon and not Celtic. So, if the historical Arthur had fought the Saxons, the contemporary Arthur was now considering getting himself crowned on their turf. It was a nice irony.

It had to be done properly though. It was no good just having a bunch of scruffy protesters crowning him. Not that anyone had anything against being scruffy or a protester. But there had to be some formality to the proceedings, some authority. So Arthur handed one of the organisers – Martin – his address book, and quested him to get representatives from at least five Druid orders there.

The coronation was planned for Saturday: the day after tomorrow.

Why five orders? Because he bore five symbols of office: his sword, his staff, his horn, shield and circlet.

The plan was that the five Druids would each hand him an item, and thereby acknowledge him as the Druid King of all Britain.

It was mad, of course: gloriously insane. But he had, after all, just processed from the Tower of London, to this site of coronation, in the correct manner, according to ancient traditions (even if he didn't know why he was doing it at the time) having righted an historical wrong, having just performed his own brand of secret magic in the appointed place. So, if it was a crazy plan, it was also peculiarly appropriate.

The following day Martin did as he was asked, and began ringing round, using Arthur's address book. And you can imagine this too, a strange phone call, from a strange person (that is, unknown to everyone) making a strange suggestion about a strange rite, that no one had ever heard of before. Bells were going off all over the British Isles, and not only the electronic bells of their telephones, but in people's heads too. What was this all about? And Martin didn't know any of the people in the address book, so he couldn't tell a Druid from a non-Druid. He was ringing everyone up and anyone (anyone with a name) breathlessly telling them to get their arses down to Kingston-upon-Thames by a certain time on Saturday, because King Arthur was going to be crowned. And it's typical Arthur too, leaving it up to someone else – leaving it up to fate, as it were – just letting it happen, as if it was the most natural thing in the world for strangers to be ringing up his friends telling them he was about to be crowned. So there was a mass of frantic cross-checking to see if others had just had the same call.

'Um, did I hear it right? I mean, did someone just ring me up to tell me that Arthur was going to be crowned? Am I going loopy or what? Oh, so you heard it too. Maybe we're both going loopy.'

And on like this. Telephones firing off all over the country, like neurons in the brain of the nation, having just succumbed to a mad mystical hallucination.

And so it had. The nation was hallucinating Arthurian legend. It was a hallucinating nation. It was like Arthurian legend coming to life. And it's hard to say, when there's a mass hallucination on this scale, whether it is a hallucination or not. If enough people believe in something, then doesn't it become a reality?

Who cares?

It depends on the nature of the hallucination, of course: and this was a funny one as hallucinations go. Mad Biker Druid Eco-Warrior Cider-Belly King of all Britain. With Brass Knobs On.

So that was it: they were all to be at the appointed place at the appointed time, just off the High Street in Kingston, where the ancient English Kings were crowned.

And you can see them now, processing from their strange suburban campsite, to the High Street, in all their regalia, on this damp Saturday morning, with their robes and cloaks and feathers and bells, their staffs, their circlets, with wreaths in their hair, in all their peculiar finery, looking like the forgotten rejects from a mad Medieval Mummer's Play, traipsing down the comfortable High Street, in this comfortable suburban setting (it was enough to make you want to wear slippers) past the Guildhall and the Cop Shop, to where the King's Stone brooded in a patch of forgotten ground, behind a wrought-iron fence, a relic of a bye-gone age. Martin, the road protester, turned out to be a secret Druid too, and appeared splendidly robed.

It was typically busy for a Saturday morning. People were just going about their ordinary Saturday business, visiting the bakers and the butchers and the greengrocers, trying to work out what to do for tea tonight, when this procession jollied on passed them, tinkling with peculiar good humour. And did they give them a second glance, wondering what on earth was going on? Hardly. People didn't even seem to notice them. And then, there they were, at the King's Stone itself, this grey, rough-cut piece of stone, with patches of lichen, hardly distinguished, a large group of mutually hallucinating Arthurian legends trying to pass themselves off as sane.

And, one by one, the five Druids handed Arthur his symbolic marks of office, consecrating them with their thoughts, making appropriate mutterings in the grand manner, with a circle of people looking on, I-A-O-ing at this, and I-A-O-ing at that, doing their Druid-type thing, raising their King, who stood upon the King's Stone, where seven ancient English monarchs had stood, calling them back as witnesses, maybe, to this historic occasion, exactly 1,020 years since it had last been called into use. And still no one outside seemed to notice. It was as if coronations happened all the time here, or as if they had entered some loop in time, and they were not really there at all; not in the 20th century, that is, but in the 10th, when the Saxons had ruled the land and made oppressive marks upon the lives of the Celtic peoples. And it was as if Arthur was forgiving them all this by this act (hadn't they too been oppressed by the Normans?) as if he was truly healing a historic wound, and making the British nation whole again, raising the whole nation by his unifying presence, giving it back its blood.

And Edward the Elder had stood upon this stone in the year 901. And Athelstone had stood upon this stone in the year 925. And Edmond and Edred, and Edwy and Edward the Martyr, in the years 940, 946, 955 and 975. And then Ethelred the Unready in 978. And now Arthur Uther Pendragon, in the Year of Our Lord 1998. Arthur the Unsteady, once he'd had a drink or two. Arthur the Ever-Ready when it came to bedding damsels. Arthur the Frivolous Bard, when it came to composing ditties. Arthur the Undiscloser, having performed secret magic and hidden Bran's head in the White Eminence of Old London Town once more.

Meanwhile, the police were eyeing them through the windows of the police station. They did nothing. They let them get on with it. Maybe they too thought that coronations were an everyday occurrence in Kingston.

And that was it. Done. Rollo anointed him with oil, and placed the circlet back on his head as a last act of consecration. And now he really was who he said he was. The nutter who calls himself King Arthur.

Three cheers for Arthur.

Hip-hip, Hooray! Hip-hip, Hooray! Hip-hip, Hooray!

Time to go to the pub. The nearest pub being, appropriately enough, the Druid's Head, they looked in there first. And who should be sat there but Tim Sebastian of the Secular Order, having got mixed up by the time (so he claimed), with his Archdruidess, Denny Price, beside him, already pleasantly merry, with the obligatory Pet Yank in tow. Tim. The most useless Druid on the planet!

Well, the thirstiest one at least.

After that it was a couple more pubs for a jolly afternoon of post-coronation merriment in the good old English manner (there being no disagreement between the English and the Celt over the need for liquid celebration), when some of the women suddenly realised that the ceremony had only involved the men.

They called Arthur out to the Thames, to anoint him in their own way, with showers of sullen river water. And then several things happened at once, and it all depended on your point of view how you understood the next event.

The Archdruidess of the Secular Order saw what was going on outside, and, along with her sidekick, Alan – both of them a little torn down by drink – went out to join them. She was objecting to what was going on. She wanted to say that, no, the women should not be holding another ceremony, that it was right, as King, that he should have been crowned by his male peers. And she rushed out and down towards the riverbank, sliding as she did so. And her and Alan were just approaching the circle when …

Meanwhile the women were rounding on him, getting ready to anoint him in their own chosen way when …

And Arthur was standing by the riverbank, surrounded by his posse of women suddenly looming towards him when …

Fully robed, seeing Alan and Denny running towards him, a playful thought slipping suddenly into his head, and a mischievous glint sparkling in his eye, as he looked towards the approaching Alan, when ...

When he did a kind of tick-tack backspin, like a backward cartwheel, spinning lick-splickety into the air and straight into the River Thames.

Alan was there immediately, and had hold of his arm, while Liz Murray and another of the Druidesses nabbed another arm soon after, and he was whisked quickly out of the murky waters, only sodden to his waist.

Did he do it on purpose, or was he merely overwhelmed?

Well, Arthur says he did it on purpose.

He says he was only testing Alan, who he had newly raised a knight.

And you should have learned by now – at least according to his own testimony – that Arthur is always right.

CHAPTER SEVENTEEN

After-Weird

W here are we now?

Oh yes, we're circling towards the end.

There's not much left to say. Or rather: there's plenty we could say, but very little room to say it in. We have to draw a line somewhere.

There's one more court case to mention, and two more stories to complete before we round off.

We touched upon the court case earlier, when we told you the story of Arthur arresting the arresting officer. It was brought before the European Court of Human Rights in Strasbourg under articles 9, 10 and 11 of the European Convention of Human Rights: the right to freedom of thought, conscience and religion, the right of freedom of expression, and the right of freedom of assembly and association. It was Arthur's contention that the so-called Exclusion Zone around Stonehenge during the solstice and other periods violated all of these rights. The application was introduced on 21 November 1995 and registered on 7 May 1996. On 27 May 1997 the Commission communicated the application to the UK Government. The Government's written observations were submitted on 5 November 1997 (the same day that Arthur got the sword back). Arthur's Counsel (Liberty) replied on 6 March 1998. On 12 December 1997 Arthur was granted legal aid. The case was finally heard in private by the President of the Commission and 28 other members on 19 October 1998. Application number 31416/96, by A.U. Pendragon against the United Kingdom.

On 21 June 1995, at 00.11 hrs. the applicant was arrested outside the Stonehenge perimeter fence in the proximity of the Hele stone, which was within the four-mile exclusion zone. There was in excess of 20 people at the service being held by the applicant, who was in full ceremonial dress. The police approached the gathering and using a loud hailer made a broadcast that the assembly was contrary to section 14A of the Public Order Act 1986 (as amended) ('The Act') and the participants should leave immediately or be arrested. The applicant was in addition served with a written notice explaining the four-mile exclusion zone. The police requested the applicant to leave the site; however, he refused and was consequently arrested. The applicant was taken to Salisbury police station, where he arrived at 00.53 hrs. He was charged at 5.37 hrs. on 21 June 1995 with taking part in a prohibited assembly contrary to section 14A (5) of the Act (the charge was subsequently amended to refer to section 14B (2) of the Act). He was detained for approximately 11½ hrs. in total and was then taken before the Magistrates and released on unconditional bail at 11.45 hrs. on 21 June 1995 (several hours after the Summer Solstice Sunrise had taken place). The applicant was tried before the Salisbury Magistrates' Court and acquitted on 13 September 1995.

Such is the background to the case, as recorded in the judgement. The case was heard in private. It's a fair bet that most members of the Commission would have spoken English, but that the English members, probably, would have spoken very little of the others' languages. We can only guess what strange debates went on behind those venerable closed doors. The English members, no doubt, briefed by Her Majesty's Government, would have been arguing for the dignity of English Law. Some of the other members, on the other hand, may well have allowed themselves a titter or two at the position the UK government found itself in: being made to stand before the European Court of Human Rights, in these, the final years of the 20th century, by none other than an historical figure posing as a legend. King Arthur Pendragon himself. We will have to imagine the kind of comments that were being passed around, but some references to particular historical personages and events, as well-known on the Continent as they are in the British Isles, would almost certainly have been made. Remember: the Matter of Britain – as Arthur's stories were historically known – were even more popular in France and Germany than they were in Britain itself. Most educated Europeans, especially of the sort who might find themselves sitting on the European Commission of Human Rights, would have heard of the great, the fabulous King Arthur. And even though our own Arthur was not standing before them this day, it must have amused at least some of them to find out who this case was being brought by.

Of course, these were serious legal issues before them now. When is a human right not a human right?

In the words of the Convention: 'No restrictions shall be placed on the exercise of these rights other than such as are prescribed by law and are necessary in a democratic society in the interests of national security, for the prevention of disorder or crime, for the protection of health or morals, or for the protection of the rights and freedoms of others.'

In other words: you may have rights, but governments have the right to take them away from you. Or – to put it another way – in a democratic society, democratic governments can suspend democracy in order to preserve democracy. As to what national security, crime, disorder, health, morals and the protection of other people's rights might be: well, that's obviously up to the government of the day to decide. As long as laws are passed by due process, it can be argued, then a suspension of human rights by legal means is not necessarily against the Convention on Human Rights.

So, regardless of what arguments had passed between the Commissioners, in the end they decided in favour of the UK government, though by a majority, not a unanimous decision.

On the other hand, you could say that Arthur won the case, as the Exclusion Zone has not been implemented since.

That's how Arthur likes to tell the story anyway. And after ten years of exclusion during which the Druids had been forced to hold their ceremonies by the roadside, perhaps he has the right.

Of the remaining stories: the first belongs to Kris Kirkham, the Whippet.

He died on the 3 March 2001, during the writing of this book.

We won't say what, exactly, he died from. He was still a relatively young man. You can take a guess if you like and – depending on what kind of life you have lived and the experiences that have come within your orbit – you may well be right. Neither Arthur nor CJ will deny it: but we won't confirm it either. Death is a part of the round of life: and the Whippet had always scorned it anyway. But the years had taken their toll. He'd never quite found his place after the bike club had broken up. Arthur had transformed himself and become Arthur. Chesh and Wendy had got married and settled down. Everyone had gone their own separate ways. For some people that's just a matter of growing up. But the Whippet was a warrior, who, unlike Arthur, had never found his life's battle. What's life without the buzz of friendship: the camaraderie, the wildness and joy of pushing it to the limits? And what's the point of pushing it to the limits if you're not, at the same time, scaring the shit out of everybody else? That was always Kris' great talent: making sure that no one else ever got complacent around him. Giving everyone a run for their money. But – well – it had all become a little wearisome of late. There was something missing. What was missing was himself. Because he was never himself unless he was giving everyone else a hard time.

Arthur's sister Wendy said: 'Let's face it, he was a little shit. But he was *our* little shit.'

Actually, we can tell you what the Whippet died of. He died of meanness and isolation. He died of lack of contact with the Earth. He died of frustrated hopes and misplaced dreams. He died of lack of adventure. He died of trivia and advertising slogans. He died of toys, trinkets and tittle-tattle. He died of soap operas and sitcoms, of McDonald's and Starbucks, of car parks and leisure complexes, of Toys R Us and DIY, of out-of-town retail parks and shopping on a Sunday. Of polishing the car. Of washing the curtains. Of never wanting to own a washing up machine. He died of boredom. He died of tiredness. He died of witless irritation.

He died of the 20th century, in other words. As yet there is still no known cure.

And what is life but a turning, an endless turning? Who are we to say what it's for? Or whether, when someone dies, there's any loss at all? Whether it's cause for celebration or commiseration. His death was a loss for those who remembered him maybe: but to the Earth, it meant nothing at all. Not a whisper. Perhaps, in the end, the Whippet was better off out of it. Perhaps it doesn't matter either way.

The Whippet died, that's all.

The particular significance for Arthur – aside from the fact that here was another old friend popping off before his time – lay in the date of his demise. March the 3rd. That was also his Dad's birthday. Just another of those little coincidences that seem to punctuate Arthur's life: the two people who had named him accidentally choosing the same date, one to be born on and the other to die. But it left Arthur doubly bereft because, although the Whippet was much younger than him, it was as if his father was dying for the second time. Because that's what a father does. He names you. He names you then leaves you, then dies on you, leaving you alone in the world once more, having to make your own way.

The Whippet was buried in early April, around noon, on a woodland burial site. It was chilly for the time of year, and a grey mist clung to the trees. The mourners were all bikers. There were about 20 of them. No ex-bikers, even if some of them had other modes of transport these days and declined to wear back patches. There's no such thing as an ex-biker. Once a biker, always a biker. Arthur was wearing a cut-off denim jacket, especially ripped and sewed, with his colours stitched to the back. He'd given up the pagan priest identity for the day, in deference to his past. He arrived on the back of a motorcycle.

This was the year of foot-and-mouth disease. Much of the British landscape was out of bounds. They'd originally planned to have the Whippet enter the site on a horse and cart, but that wasn't allowed. Instead, they dragged him on site themselves on the back of the cart. In order to enter the woods they had to wipe their shoes on disinfected straw. He was housed in a bamboo coffin, and they trudged through thick mud to get to the burial site. There was a stark hole, with the mud piled up beside it, with a shovel resting at a slight angle.

Various people said various things.

Arthur said: 'I'm reminded of something Kris always used to say. "Life's a shit and then you die."'

He paused.

'Yeah,' he added, almost under his breath: 'but didn't we have a lot of good shit on the way.'

The coffin was lowered into the ground, and they all threw handfuls of earth down onto it, which splattered with a sodden echo. The hole was filled in unceremoniously, and a tree planted on the grave. That was the only marker.

Afterwards they went to the pub, and in a break from normal practice, no one punched anyone else. In fact, many ancient feuds were buried that day, along with the Whippet's body. Peace was breaking out all over.

Of course, that tree is still there, even as you read this book. It feeds off the Whippet's bones. Its roots curl down, mingling with his ribs, where the heart used to be, stirring the bones into piles. What kind of tree is it? It is a bad-natured tree. It spends its time turning with the Earth, giving all the other trees in the quiet woodland as hard a time as possible.

The final story is the story of Stonehenge.

Of course, that's far too big a story to try to tell here. It's been around on this Earth for at least 5,000 years. No one knows what it was built for, or why. No one even knows who built it or for what purpose. It's a mystery, that's all. And it has seen endless generations of humans come and go. It has seen tribes and it has seen tribes. Peace and war. Love and betrayal. Life, life and more life.

In Arthur's life it has played a central role, of course. That has been the story of this book. He has dedicated his life to it: to another interpretation of its meaning than the one offered by the Heritage establishment. For Arthur its meaning is as a place of celebration, as a place of commemoration. A place where memories linger. A gathering place, where the humans seek to remember what we are and how we got here. A place that marks us off in the cosmos. Because that is its secret, that its knowledge is deeper than scholarship allows: that it knows that we come from the stars.

Because, to us, that's what it's here for. It marks the turning of the Earth around its axis, once every 24 hours: round and round, round and round. It marks the turning of the Earth around the Sun, once every 365¼ days. Round and round. Round and round. Maybe – who knows? – it marks the turning of the solar system around the galaxy we know as the Milky Way. Round and round. Round and round. Or the movement of the galaxy around some other, unknown source. Round. Round. Round.

The restless movement of our globe around the constantly moving Universe. Shifting through time, careering through space. On and on and on.

So, if anyone ever tells you, on reaching a particular spot on the Earth, 'I've been here before,' you can say: 'No, you haven't. Not one of us has ever been to this place before. No one has been here before.'

But whatever its purpose, its recent history was moving towards some sort of a climax.

In May 1997 a Labour Government was elected, for the first time in 18 years. In October 1998 Arthur took his case before the European Court of Human Rights. Also in 1998, English Heritage set up talks to discuss the future of the monument. Round Table talks: the title tells you who was responsible for instigating them. Members of English Heritage, the National Trust, the Wiltshire Constabulary, local landowners and farmers, representatives of the local and district councils, various Druid organisations (including CoBDO and the LAW, of course) assorted witches and warlocks and astrologers and other members of pagan and mystical groups, ramblers and horse riders and all-round healthy folk, who just loved to see the monument in the distance, all gathered together in a variety of venues, with tea and biscuits laid on by English Heritage (no smoking except in the garden), to decide on the possibility of some kind of access. There were numerous heated exchanges, plus the occasional walk out for dramatic effect.

In 1999 there was an attempt to hold a restricted ceremony at the Stones, with access given to particular chosen groups. 100 people were allowed tickets, plus the media.

Arthur was offered a ticket but declined. As he said, what's the point of a church service without a congregation. He simply walked through the trampled fence instead, along with all the others who had not been allowed entry: meaning the vast majority of pilgrims, several thousand of them. He kept returning, and he kept being ejected. It was like a game of tag: except that the police had riot shields and batons. Arthur had his ribs broken before he was, finally, arrested.

It was just like old times.

Eventually English Heritage relented. They realised that it was impossible to give restricted access, given the sheer weight of numbers. And in the year 2000, they finally opened up the monument for full public access for the first time since 1984.

It rained. 8,000 people attended. It was a sodden, soggy affair. No one saw the sunrise.

Arthur was being filmed.

He was called into the crowded Henge at dawn to great applause. He said, bawling above the noise of the crowd: 'This is your Henge. This is your Temple. Do not ever let anyone tell you otherwise. You have as much right to be here as anyone else.'

And then he intoned the Druid's oath, three times, as is the custom:

We swear by peace and love to stand,
Heart to heart and hand in hand.
Mark, oh Spirit, and hear us now,
Confirming this, our most sacred vow.

After which he took a drink from his drinking horn, shouting: 'I wish you a happy Solstice, and many more of them to come.'

Later he was being interviewed by the person holding the camera.

'This is what it's all about,' he was saying: 'The only thing that I believe in is that this is our Henge and that it's open to every fucker – not just Druids, not just pagans, but to everyone who wants to come here – and that's what I've been fighting for, that's what we've got and that's what's happening. It's the culmination of 14 years' work.'

'I don't know what it means to me spiritually, but what it means physically is: I'm wet. Normally I'm dry cos I'm in Salisbury Police Cells. This year I'm wet. You can take that as it comes.'

Two days later he received the following email from Wiltshire Constabulary:

> *Dear Arthur,*
> *Sorry I missed your call yesterday and thanks for phoning.*
> *An excellent evening all round and many thanks to you and your Warband for all the help during the night. It was a brilliant evening, just sorry about the weather.*
> *The only person disappointed was my custody sergeant as he'd got you a really good breakfast lined up!*
> *Yours in the peace of the Solstice.*

It was signed by Chief Superintendent Andy Hollingshead of Wiltshire Constabulary.

So that's it. The first of many solstice nights at the Stonehenge monument. And many more to come.

Our story's ended, our tale is told.

If you can't be rich, then at least be bold.

Good morning Planet Earth.

It's much earlier than you think.

Appendices

1 King Arthur Pendragon – Titles
'Shed Loads of Titles'

Honoured Pendragon, Glastonbury Order of Druids
Official Swordbearer, Secular Order of Druids
Titular Head and Chosen Chief, Loyal Arthurian Warband
Battle Chieftain of the Council of British Druid Orders
Bard of the Free Gorsedd of Caer Abiri
Former Swordbearer to and of the Cotswold Order of Druids
Honorary Member of the Berengaria Order of Druids
Honoured Member of the Druid Grade, South Downs Dragon
   Order of Druids
Champion of the Free and Open Gorsedd of Caer Badon
Member of the Ancient and Modern Order of Druids
Honoured Member of Whitestone
Priest of Merlin and the Horned God, Fellowship of Isis
Grand Knight Commander, Noble Order of Tara
Elder of the British Council of Traditional Witchcraft

Raised Druid King of Britain, on the Coronation Stone at Kingston-upon-Thames, January 1998

2 The Royal Tour

King Arthur Pendragon, appearing at a Courthouse near you.

1994

Odiham	Hampshire County Court
London	High Court
Aldershot	Magistrates' Court

1995

London	High Court
Salisbury	Magistrates' Court
Frome	Magistrates' Court

1996

Frome	Magistrates' Court
Bristol	Crown Court
Aldershot	Magistrates' Court
Newbury	Magistrates' Court
London	Royal Courts of Justice
Reading	Crown Court

1997

Salisbury	Magistrates' Court
Western	Magistrates' Court
London	Bow Magistrates' Court
London	Royal Courts of Justice
Reading	Crown Court
London	Southwalk Crown Court

1998

Frome	Magistrates' Court
Bristol	Crown Court
Frome	Magistrates' Court
Strasbourg	European Court of Human Rights
Aldershot	Magistrates' Court

1999

London	Bromley Magistrates' Court
London	Royal Courts of Justice
London	Marlborough Street Magistrates' Court

Note:

At many of these venues, due to popular demand, King Arthur gave repeat appearances.

To be continued ...

3   **Witness statement prepared by Professor Ronald E Hutton for the trial of Arthur Pendragon at Southwark Crown Court, November 1997, regarding Arthur's right to carry the sword Excalibur.**

Virtually everybody in the Western world has heard of the Druids; they are part of the common cultural inheritance of our civilisation. This familiarity is increased, rather than diminished, by the fact that the 'original' Druids, of the Celtic Iron Age, remain such shadowy figures.

We can say with confidence that they were the public magicians, soothsayers, religious experts and political and judicial arbitrators of the tribes of north-western Europe at the time when history begins in this region; about two thousand years ago. It is also fairly certain that Britain was recognised as their original homeland, in which the system of thought and action which they represented was first developed. Beyond these facts, however, we run up against the problem that since their own teachings were never committed to writing, we possess no sources produced by Druids themselves.

Instead, we depend on views of them developed by outsiders, either contemporary Greek or Roman writers, or those of the later Christian Middle Ages; and these varied wildly according to the prejudices and propaganda needs of the authors concerned. There is thus no 'authentic' original Druidry against which later Druids can be judged; rather, Druids are powerful symbolic figures, which have been appropriated and re-imagined in different ways by successive generations ever since ancient times, That is their true power to move the imagination.

In the 18th century Age of Reason they were most commonly seen as rational, pacific and patriotic thinkers who combined rigorous training and close observation of nature to produce a reasonable and benevolent religion which reconciled God, humanity and the other parts of creation in a harmonious system.

From this time sprang a succession of modern Druid orders, some of which survive to the present day, dedicated to the task of putting together the wisdom of all the worlds' great religions, within a single framework with a distinctively British character. Since the mid-1980s a set of new Druid groups have appeared, which are devoted to the work of developing a new spirituality based upon the traditions, monuments and landscapes of the British Isles.

I have been studying these intensively since 1991 as part of a research project into such new 'native' religious movements. Arthur Pendragon is one of the most prominent and significant figures within them.

The groups concerned have a membership of just over 6,000 [Ed: over 15,000 with recent affiliations] individuals between them and are growing fast; furthermore, the ideas and images they represent are rapidly spreading among British youth and among specific sub-cultures such as New Age travellers. They all have in common a powerful reverence for the land of Britain as something sacred in itself, with this sanctity especially concentrated in certain places such as Stonehenge.

All are also dedicated to improving the spiritual quality of life of the British, by assisting people to greater self-knowledge, to a still more positive set of relationships with each other and with the natural environment and to a greater personal freedom, within a framework of social responsibility.

All, therefore, feel compelled by their beliefs to oppose specific projects which damage places of natural beauty and historic significance, such as particular road-building schemes and quarries, and to safeguard or extend civil liberties. All are committed to a pacifist ethic which condemns violence and prefers to campaign by employing moral pressure and drawing public attention to the issues at stake.

From that point onward, however, practice between both groups and individuals diverge considerably. Some adopt a quietest stance, preferring to advance their ideals through meditation and personal example. Others prefer to take part in direct and public political action, including demonstrations and protest camps built on the route of controversial developments. Arthur Pendragon is one of the most important of the latter.

Before concentrating on him, it may be helpful to emphasise that Druids of his kind are contributing to debates which involve a much larger cross-section of the national community and are commonly recognised to possess a great deal of validity.

Their religious ideals represent only one part of a constellation of movements, some within established traditions such as Christianity and some outside them, which are striving to develop a spirituality which is more feminist, more sensitive to environmental issues and more dedicated to individual freedom and personal growth, than those which have prevailed in recent centuries.

The specific issue of access to Stonehenge has divided the community of professional archaeologists in the past few years, with some of the most respected figures joining the Druids in arguing for reopening the monument at the key solar festivals with which it is associated.

The controversy over national transport policy and the road-building schemes which are the main feature of the current one, has involved a very large number of people and range of ideologies and interests. The question of who owns the land and who may have access to it or should be concerned in its preservation, has generated another major debate in the past two decades.

The new Druids and especially those involved in direct action such as Arthur, are therefore not fringe figures with ideals and preoccupations detached from those of a wider national community, but some of the more colourful contributors to a set of arguments and activities which involves a large part of that community.

Now to Arthur Pendragon himself. I first saw him in person in May 1993, and have been observing him at regular and frequent intervals ever since. It would be impossible for me to conduct my present study without doing so, because he is such a major and respected figure among the new Druid groups. Indeed, he holds formal office in no less than three, being the Pendragon of the Glastonbury Order of Druids and the Swordbearer of the Secular Order of Druids, as well as leading his own order, the Loyal Arthurian Warband, as Chief. These represent between them, the three groups most heavily involved in direct political campaigning.

Although a strong mutual respect has developed between us, it would be stretching this too far to term us as friends. My opinion of him therefore reflects my own viewpoint as an onlooker and an academic scholar.

He is clearly a sincere natural mystic, whose very strong libertarian political convictions are bound up with a sense of guidance by supernatural forces. His belief in reincarnation was stimulated by the experience of vivid dreams and reveries, known since childhood, which seemed to him to be memories of previous lifetimes. His assumption of the identity of King Arthur, in 1987, was precipitated by a series of apparent signs and omens. His love of the land is charged by his belief (shared by hundreds of thousands of modern Pagans in Europe and North America) that it is sacred in itself and represents a living entity, most often called Gaia, Mother Earth or, (to Arthur as for many others) The Goddess.

In taking up this identity, he has identified with a well-known legend that Arthur and his knights are not dead but sleeping in a cavern, from which they awake when the land is in danger. Hitherto, that has usually been interpreted as signifying an external danger (from foreign invaders), needing a military response.

To Arthur and his comrades, it is an internal danger, from pollution, destruction by needless building or digging programmes and the erosion of civil rights and it demands a non-violent response of demonstration and the building of public opinion. It is to that they have dedicated themselves.

The Loyal Arthurian Warband, over which he presides, is now one of the largest modern Druid orders and is divided into three levels or circles according to the degree of commitment desired of its members.

Its members define themselves by swearing to three things: to tell the truth, to uphold honour and to fight for justice. The first is fundamental, as it is believed that insincerity and dishonesty would corrode the bonds of the Warband and destroy any hopes it has of winning and retaining the public esteem.

It also carries the connotation that only displaying the highest personal probity (as 'knights') can the Warband's people prove themselves worthy of the causes for which they campaign. Honour and justice are combined in those causes, by the perceived need to defend the land against damage or destruction and civil liberties and human rights – a category extended upon occasion to include workers' rights against encroachment.

The language is chivalric and military, but the ethics of the Warband remain pacifist and its members are expected to engage in only non-violent direct action. In its passive form, this consists of putting their bodies in the way of developers until dragged aside. In its active one, it takes the form of digging tunnels or building tree-walks in the path of proposed development and trying to evade capture and joining protest meetings and marches. These activities are, of course, common to many other groups concerned with the same causes.

The central emblem of the Loyal Arthurian Warband is the ceremonial sword, which Arthur himself has carried from 1987 until its confiscation by the Police upon 12 April 1997. He identifies it with the original Excalibur of the Arthurian legends. It has been used to dub Knights of the Band, which is the formal rite of admission to the group, and oaths are taken upon it in other ritual contexts.

The latter include marriage ceremonies of members of the group and of their friends, solemn undertakings to carry out particular tasks and (on one occasion) the formal affirmation to tell the truth in a Crown Court. I have myself witnessed examples of all these different kinds of proceeding.

The use of swords in such contexts is, of course, itself a mediaeval tradition, but the symbolism has been reinforced in modern times by the

related tradition of high ceremonial magic, as developed in the 19th century by the French occultist Eliphas Levi and the British Order of the
Golden Dawn.

Within this, a sword represents the human will, which is expected for
solemn purposes to be as strong and straight as the blade and pure as the
steel of which it is made. A related aspect of this tradition is that a sword
used in a sacred and ritual context is polluted by being used for violence
and, indeed, on none of the scores of occasions on which I have closely
watched or interviewed Arthur Pendragon have I noted any suggestion
that he does not hold to this rule.

The legendary Excalibur was a fighting weapon, employed in battle;
this one functions in virtually the opposite role, as a purely symbolic
object, comparable to the four swords carried in the coronation ceremony of British monarchs, or to the maces of town councils, universities and
of the House of Commons.

Precisely the same considerations apply to the ceremonial dagger carried by Arthur Pendragon until its confiscation by the Police upon the
same date.

In the Western tradition of ritual magic, described above, the dagger
functions as a miniature equivalent to the sword and likewise represents
the human will. It is often deployed in a magical context for which a
sword would be unwieldy, such as drawing sacred signs upon the air, but
it also functions in a more practical role, of cutting herbs, plants and
flowers used for medicines or as ritual decorations and symbols. The
most celebrated example of this in Druid tradition is the ritual gathering
of mistletoe. I have seen Arthur employ his own ceremonial dagger in this
latter capacity and for no other purpose.

It may be helpful in the context to note that a black-handled ritual
knife, known as an Athame, has become the prime symbol and ceremonial object of the modern Pagan religion of Wicca, drawing upon the same
body of tradition, no Wiccan can practice his or her religion without the
possession of one.

A curious and paradoxical aspect of Arthur Pendragon's role is that he
has adopted the trappings and persona of mediaeval monarch and his
companions the identity of mediaeval knights, as part of a cultural movement which in general dislikes authority figures and hierarchies and
prefers an ethic of communal work and comradeship.

The paradox is resolved by Arthur's consistent refusal to be treated as a
guru or cult leader by the Warband and its allies. I have repeatedly seen

him use his considerable sense of humour to divert or deflate attempts to give him this sort of stature and this behaviour is the best illustration of an important feature of the Loyal Arthurian Warband which has contributed considerably to the success with which it has functioned.

On the one hand, as indicated above, Arthur and its other members are genuine mystics and visionaries, who take the causes to which they have dedicated themselves very seriously indeed. On the other, they go to some lengths to avoid taking themselves too seriously and so acquiring the disposition of fanatics; there is a great element of playfulness and parody in their self-image.

Their identity as Arthurian knights lends to their activities something of the atmosphere of carnival and street theatre and it has the undoubted practical advantage of attracting and holding the attention of the mass media and therefore of the public, in which more conventional and less colourful protesters do not have.

In this respect they stand firmly in another tradition of British popular political movements associated with a fancy dress which gives drama and adds meaning to protest, examples between 1600 and 1900 include Captain Pouch, Lady Skimmington, the Waltham Blacks, the Scotch Cattle, and the Hosts of Rebecca. This is a distinguished company and the Loyal Arthurian Warband very clearly represents a modern continuation of it.

A contemporary historian has therefore, to take Arthur Pendragon seriously. Upon the one hand he is a major figure in modern Druidry, leading one of the largest orders and representing a distinctive form of spirituality. On the other, he has an equally important place in the history of groups concerned with environmental issues and civil rights. It is an impressive duel achievement.

RONALD E HUTTON
PROFESSOR OF HISTORY
BRISTOL UNIVERSITY

4 Section 6, Criminal Law Act

Legal Warning
(Section 6, Criminal Law Act 1977) as amended under the Criminal
Justice Act (1994)

Take Notice That
We live here in this wood, it is our home and we intend to stay here.

That
All times there is at least one person in this wood.

That
Any entry into this wood without our permission is a CRIMINAL
OFFENCE as any one of us who is in physical possession is opposed to
any entry without their permission.

That
If you attempt to enter by violence or by threatening violence, we WILL
PROSECUTE YOU. You may receive a sentence of up to SIX MONTHS
IMPRISONMENT and/or a Fine of up to £2000.

That
If you want to get us out you will have to take out a summons for possession in the County Court or in the High Court, or produce us a valid certificate in terms of Section 7, Criminal Law Act 1977.

That
It is an offence under Section 74 (8), Criminal Justice and Public Order
Act (1994), to knowingly make a false statement: when signing the said
certificate. A person guilty of such an offence may receive a sentence of up
to SIX MONTHS IMPRISONMENT and/or and Fine of up to £2000.

Signed
The Occupiers

[NB. Signing this legal warning is optional, it is equally valid whether or
not it is signed.]

5 **Presentation to the Council of British Druid Orders by King Arthur Pendragon, 3 September 2000.**

I have been requested to prepare a short paper and to define the role and responsibility of Battle Chieftain for the Council of British Druid Orders.

I was 'charged' by the Council (Stargrove) at a ceremony on Primrose Hill to lead the 'fight' through the courts for the Free and Open Access for ALL at Stonehenge.

After various 'arrests' and initiatives on my part through Magistrates, the Royal Courts of Justice, County and European Courts, the rest, as they say, is history.

Since my appointment as Battle Chieftain to the Council, I have been called in to lead a Pagan protest against the imposition of a Christian cross on a Pagan Site.

But better I let my adversaries speak for me. The following email was received 23rd June from Wiltshire Constabulary:

> *Sorry I missed your call yesterday and thanks for phoning.*
>
> *An excellent evening all round and many thanks to you and your Warband for all the help during the night. It was a brilliant evening just sorry about the weather.*
>
> *The only person who was disappointed was my Custody Sergeant as he'd got you a brilliant breakfast lined up.*
>
> *Yours in the peace of the Solstice*
> *Andy*

[The Andy in question being the Chief Superintendent Andrew Hollingshead, A division, Wiltshire Constabulary.]

and this appeared in the local paper in the Weekly 'Christian Comments' column by Canon Wood.

> *In the end, it was a dignified affair. The debate had been raging for 12 months and there were powerful arguments on both sides. But the Christians were finally allowed to mark the millennium with their monolith on a grassy bank on the other side of the lane that runs beside Mayburgh Henge. The service may have been overlong, and perhaps it was a mistake to interrupt it halfway through with a 45-*

minute picnic, but it was Holy and it was fun.

Ranged along the lip of the henge, a long way from the action, the Pagans held their silent protest. Some of them were dressed in Druidical costume and there were black and silver banners with ancient and earthy symbols. But the protest, though very visible, was without rancour: it was silent and good-natured. When Canon Markham acknowledged 'Our friends on the hill' and wondered if they could hear him, they waved their affirmative.

They taught us a valuable lesson that day. You can make your views known without being offensive. Fervent opinions don't have to be expressed in violent language or conduct.

Contrast the recent scenes at Drumcree. There should be no enmities between different religious or political traditions.

It took a group of non-Christians at Mayburgh Henge to show how differences of opinion really ought to be expressed.

On another note, Canon Markham wrote to the local paper last week asking for donations. It appears the festival didn't make a profit, and he is personally down £18,000 on the cost of the stone.

The role of the 'Battle Chieftain' is to lead the 'troops' in Battle, by non-violent direct action, to motivate and lead by example and, just as importantly, to control any elements of overzealous Warrior energy. Only a strong commander and tactician can do this, and only then with common assent.

Whilst consultation and negotiation are of paramount importance and such lines of communication should always be kept open, there are times however when by necessity we must take to the 'field' under the direction of such a strong commander. And I respectfully submit I have shown myself to be such.

Blessed Be.

Yours in the Heat of Battle, the Peace of the Grove and the Sacred Space Between.

KING ARTHUR PENDRAGON

Glossary

A-Frame Usually made from scaffolding poles, a device from which a protester hangs 'locked' therein to delay the contractors, often used as the first line of defence.

Allegedly Yes, but you try proving it!

Arch Pharaoh Irreverent term for an Archdruid wearing a wimple.

Army Barmy Army term, meaning to love Army life. An overwhelming tendency to want to shout and march up and down pointlessly. (*See* Khaki-Brained.)

Arthur-Proof Very little is 'Arthur-proof'. Something that doesn't break or fall apart when it comes in contact with the King.

A-Team As Arthur says, 'We are the A-Team (Arthurian), and only the A-Team could get away with having a deaf dyslexic running the office, not to mention all the other improbable officers in our Warband.'

Away With The Faeries Most Druids have their heads in the clouds and their feet on the earth, so it is very hard to know where they are coming from. Term used to denote their own ability to forget, and in particular to denote the disposition of a certain Witch from Farnborough.

Awen

(i)   The spirit many Druids believe moves through them.

(ii) A publication: *Arthurian Warband Environmental News*.

(iii) A chant sometimes used in Druid rituals.

Backpatch Biker term for club insignia of Outlaw MC worn on cut-offs.

Bail Breaker Arthur's self-appointed role of refusing draconian bail conditions, choosing to be held in custody to argue for better ones before a crown court. When achieved, others return to magistrates to ask for 'variance' thus gaining more liberal conditions for all.

Battlefield Protest site.

Battle Frock Druid robe slightly the worse for wear after an eviction.

Bender Temporary shelter, often found at festivals and protest sites, usually made from hazel poles and tarpaulins. A communal bender is used to accommodate visitors and guests. Also used to denote several days of alcohol abuse with a bad hangover at the end.

Biker Modern term for a motorcyclist as opposed to an enthusiast. Formerly known as Grebo/Greaser/Rocker.

Black Frock Barrister's robes, often as tatty as the Druid's white ones, as they, the barristers, traditionally believe in keeping the same one throughout their career.

Blag Charm offensive for desired object, usually cigarettes and alcohol.

Bonk Media-invented diminutive for the much more robust Anglo-Saxon. (*See* **Fuck/ed.**)

Bread Sword Misspelling of broadsword by a London court. However, while Excalibur and Carnwennan were in police custody, Arthur 'raised' (with the help of a bread knife) a Knight of the Bread Sword.

Brew Crew Habitual drunks (useful but not in an emergency). Troops usually kept in reserves and cannon fodder in an eviction.

Brickwalled Biker term for hitting an immovable object.

Camelot A series of protest camps/sites and temporary dwellings therein, occupied by Arthur and/or the Warband.

Care In The Community With regards to the protest movement: 'We're the only community who care for them', i.e. the dispossessed and disenfranchised hangers on.

Cherry Picker Mobile hydraulic crane used, as the name suggests, to pick cherries, and for the removal of protesters from trees.

Chop Biker abbreviation for a chopped motorcycle. Where the front end of the frame is effectively chopped off and replaced at a different angle.

Clock Adopted mispronunciation of the word cloak. So named after a French Priestess's inability to pronounce correctly.

CoBDO Council of British Druid Orders. Now comprising 17 Druid Orders and representing over 15,000 people. Set up in the late '80s with the specific aim of freeing Stonehenge for public ceremony and celebration on the quarterly dates – the Solstices and Equinoxes – which, as a monument, it was built to commemorate.

Colours

    Blue is the colour often associated with the Bards (musicians, storytellers and poets).

    Green is most often associated with the environmental movement and also in the magical and intuitive sense.

    White is traditionally associated with the Druids.

Regal Red, Imperial Purple, and many more go to make up the Rainbow
Warriors and the Rainbow Tribes, self explanatory terms often used to denote
large groups or gatherings, not of the norm.
Also refers to the backpatch traditionally worn by Outlaw Bikers.

Congregation Members of the public at Druid/Pagan ritual. Used in similar way
to Pilgrim, at Sacred Sites.

Cut-off Sleeveless denim jacket worn by bikers.

Cyclops The one-eyed god on the altar table, TV.

Decked Where the motorcycle is intentionally thrown over to the ground to
avoid an even worse danger.

Digger Diving Risking life and limb to put oneself in the path of large
machinery in order to stop work.

Ditchfinder General Arthur, so named for his ability to get drunk, fall over and
sleep where e'er he lands, preferably in a ditch.

Dragon's Breath Early morning mist or Arthur after eating garlic.

Druid Fluid Arthur's name for cider.

Dungeon Master Police custody sergeant.

Dungeons And Dragons An annual 'game' played with Wiltshire Constabulary.
Arthur the dragon and Salisbury police cells the dungeon.

Eisteddfod Used by some Orders to open up the Ritual or Ceremony for more
open and informal Celebration, often with poetry and song.

Electrickery Electronic wizardry.

English Heretics Arthur's term for English Heritage pre-Solstice 2000, now
reverted to Heritage or simply EH.

Equipment Carried by Arthur when robed and sworded.
  1. **Holy Lance** Arthur's Druid staff, crystal tipped (as wand) and copper
     bound (as rod) named Rhongomyiad.
  2. **Holy Grail** Arthur's drinking horn. Also (possibly, and under certain
     circumstances) a cup of tea.
  3. **Ceremonial Sword** Excalibur.
  4. **Ritual Dagger** Named Carnulennan (used in the preparation and
     cutting of herbs, etc).
  5. **Vampire Stake** A sharp pointed stick carried by Arthur on the occasion
     of his arrest at Kingston.
  6. **Robe Bag** Usually also contains reading material for whiling away time

on remand in HM Prisons.

7. **Pouches** Including, Healing, Alchemy, Divination, and Shamanic (containing tobacco or cigarettes – Superkings, of course).

Exclusion Zone Media hype, there is actually no such thing. Processions are merely excluded within a set radius over a set period of time.

Fluffy Non-violent. (*See* **Spiky**.)

Fluffy But Firm Take no shit.

Freegan Vegan usually but will eat meat from skip runs.

Fuck/ed Anglo-Saxon term used by CJ (now living in Kent) to mean make love or bonk.

Glastos or Glasters Slang for Glastonbury. Transitory inhabitants are called Glastofarians, whilst locals are generally referred to as Glastonians.

Good God! It's Sod's Law Playful term for Glastonbury Outer Order of Druids, Glastonbury Order of Druids, Secular Order of Druids and Loyal Arthurian Warband when they descend upon you en masse.

Gorsedd A meeting or gathering of Druids and Bards.

Ground Zodiac A phenomenon, (first identified at Glastonbury earlier this century by Katherine Maltwood) whereby the figures of the Zodiac circle appear through the landscape outlined by contours, rivers, roads, etc. Place names are also crucial indicators. Mary Caine continued Maltwood's work. She and others have since identified several further Zodiacs, such as Kingston.

Handfasting A Pagan wedding, the vows made between couples in front of others. Can be for a year and a day (trial marriage), a lifetime or longer.

Hard Hats (Sheriffs officers).

Red hats – lead yellow hats.

Yellow hats – security and bailiffs.

Blue hats – police evidence gatherers.

Green hats – Brays Detective Agency.

White hats – specialists, climbers, etc.

Healthy Shit Veggy slop and brown bread, etc. 'I need my toxins', as Arthur claims when forced to eat said food.

Hearth Moot Pagan meeting at home.

Highsided Biker term for failing to negotiate a bend, usually due to too high speed.

Iron Steed Motorcycle.

J'Arthur An ancient miss-term for Arthur.

Khaki-Brained (*See* **Army Barmy**.)
King 'What idiot put me in charge of the King', as Arthur says, usually under ciderance.
Kingnapped When Arthur is taken off (voluntarily) usually by Women and/or Warriors.

Lid Biker term for crash helmet. Sometimes referred to as Piss Pot, reference from the First World War, when the British Tommy's helmet was often used for just that!
Lock-On Usually on the ground, a way by which a protestor locks and thereby in the way of the contractor. Invariably involves handcuffs and pipes set in concrete.

Mackenzie Friend A legal term for a lay (unqualified) adviser.
Magic Carpet Car pet. Driver whilst hitch-hiking.
Master Plan 'To put the Knights on horseback, the Druids on donkeys and the Brew Crew on ostriches.' Arthur's fancy scenario for an eviction.
Media Tart King Arthur when involved in his many TV appearances.

Namby-Pamby, Wishy-Washy, New-Age Fuckwit Arthur's derogatory term for a Dippy-Hippy or an all-round goody-goody. Person with tendency to Yoghurt Weaving or Tofu Welding. CJ on drugs.
Nutter 'The Nutter who thinks he's King Arthur'. Arthur's irreverent term for himself, sometimes replaced with 'The Tithead in the White Frock', as in Titular Head.

One Percenter Biker term for outlaw motorcyclist. With reference to a remark made by American motorcyclists federation that 99% of motorcyclists are law-abiding citizens.

Pagan Festivals
Agricultural
Imbolg/Candlemas   1/2 February

Beltane/May Day Eve	30 April/1 May
Lugnassadh/Lammas	1 August
Samhain/Halloween	31 October/1 November

Astronomical

Vernal Equinox	21/22 March
Summer Solstice	21 June
Autumn Equinox	21/22 September
Winter Solstice	21 December

Penguin Arthur, black tabard on white robes or white tabard on black robes.

Pet Yank Every British Druid Order usually has – nay, must have – at least one American in its number.

Phrases

'Trust me, I know what I'm doing' – Arthur when he does.

'Trust me, I'm a Druid, I know these things' – Arthur when he does but doesn't know why.

'Trust me, I'm a devious bastard' – Arthur when talking about his ability to read the enemies' tactics.

'Are we going to bonk or not' – Arthur chat up line.

'I just do me shit' – Arthur when asked what he does.

'I'm the best Arthur we've got because I'm the only Arthur we've got.'

'If there is another King Arthur, I'm getting his mail' – Arthur after receiving unaddressed letters.

'Don't quest me' – Arthur when told something is impossible.

'We're Druids, we rise above it' – Arthur, hopefully.

'Lead, follow or get out the way' – Arthur's Druid rant.

'I'll fight for peace, but if we ever get it I'm out of here' – Arthur's last words.

Pilgrims A word used by the Druid community to describe others. Not necessarily members of any organised group and therefore difficult to identify, consult or quantify.

Pixi Mission When some protesters clandestinely go out into the night to knobble machinery, etc. Allegedly.

Pratpatch Biker term used by backpatch-wearing MC for frontpatch-wearing MCC insignia.

Pub Moot More social Pagan gathering in a hostelry, usually ending with someone having to carry Arthur home.

Quest A magical test, a journey of significance.

Quogged A Newbury protest euphemism, a cross between bog and quagmire, meaning covered in mud.

Rant Can be a person, a speech or a document, in the case of a person you wind them up and point them at the enemy; otherwise it's a case of friendly fire or a home goal.

Red Lining Biker term for speed with reference to high engine revs.

Repetitive Loop Arthur talking when under ciderance. Endless repetition of the same phrases, over and over again. Time to go to bed.

Santa Suit A Judge's robe (often red – edged with ermine).

Sausage The Newbury Sausage, the name given to the so-named area around the proposed by-pass from which bail conditions banned protesters.

Section Six A legal document required to claim squatters rights on land.

Shed Loads Of Titles Arthur's lighthearted term for his various Pagan and Druid titles.

Skip Run Protesters scavenger hunt through supermarket waste skips which usually means, in Arthur's words 'We live like tramps but eat like Kings'.

SSSI Site of Special Scientific Interest, usually totally ignored by Local Authorities in the granting of planning applications.

Staff Training Arthur's playful habit of 'tapping' his colleagues on the head with his staff. Variations include 'Squeal the Bard', 'Burn the Journalist' and 'Burn the King'.

Sworded A fully-robed King in possession of Excalibur.

Tart 'The King's a Tart.' It's official, Arthur says so.

Tax Cigarettes and cider provided for Arthur by anyone who happens to be around. (*See* **Blag**).

Technophobe Most Druids, Pagans and Protestors have a natural disability to deal with even the most basic electrical and/or mechanical equipment.

Them And Us Or, as Arthur says, 'They are only us who don't know it yet.'

Time Arthur's concept of time is fairly nonexistent, or as he says:

'I don't do linear.'

'Catch you later' – it could be anytime, he once nipped out for a packet of cigarettes and returned six years later.

'The other day' – could be sometime last week/month.

How long ago? 'One, two, lots', Arthur's maths.

Tofu Welding Advanced yoghurt weaving, as spouted by many Druids and protesters alike. (*See* **Yoghurt Weaving**.)

Torture Chamber Threatened car journey with a certain Druid at the wheel, a certain Witch navigating and two rants in the back seat chatting to you.

Tree People Eco-warriors who prefer being up the trees, rather than down the tunnels or on the ground (one more than two people).

Triad Truth, Honour and Justice. This could of course just as easily be Maiden, Mother and Crone, or Father, Son and Holy Ghost.

Typling Error A typing error.

Two's-Up As in the phrase, 'two's up on your fag', meaning, 'give us a smoke'. A good way to avoid paying for tobacco.

Under Ciderance Arthur's play on the Druid term 'Under Guidance'. Usually referring to when he weaves homespun philosophy, the worse for drink.

Vegan Fascist Or vegan police, evangelical vegheads: as Arthur says: 'I eat vegans, it's the only way I take my vegetables'.

Veggie Slop Most communal food on a protest site, also found lurking in and around Glastonbury.

Veg-Heads Vegetarians.

Walkway An aerial ropeway usually made from polypropylene connecting two or more trees, used during eviction.

Wanky Bollocks First coined by a certain Faery Queen of the Glastonbury persuasion. In no sense. What everyone does to avoid the main issue. Diversionary tactics. Denial. Bluster, bullying and bullshit.

Weekend Warrior Biker term for motorcycling enthusiasts.

White Frock Arthur's slightly irreverent name for his or anyone else's Druid robe.

White Lining Biker term for sitting in the middle of the road (on the white line) and constant overtaking.

Wicca Modern Witchcraft as revised by Gerald Gardner in the mid-20th century.

Wiccan A practitioner of Wicca.

Wierd/Wyrd Anglo-Saxon term meaning Fate. A sense of the inevitable. Magic. Co-incidence. Synchronicity. In modern times adopted to mean peculiar.

Wizards' Duel

(i)   Argument (often political) between two Archdruids.

(ii) Psychic or magical battle, real or imaginary, between two parties.

(iii) Arthur, when he plays chess with HMG, wielding Knights (nobody knows where they'll turn up), Faery Queens, Bishops in the form of Archdruids and even the occasional castle, such as Odiham.

Wizards, Witches And Warriors Arthur's phrase for Druids, Priest/esses and Activists. Some of whom are occasionally referred to as Whingers, Bitches and Worryers.

Yagwar Mispronunciation of Jaguar used by Mog-Ur-Kreb Dragonrider and adopted by the Warband.

Yoghurt Weaving Harmless term for endless circular philosophy, often found around the fire on a protest site.

Zulu Warrior No meaning other than its own. Just fancied putting it to bed, and giving you a zzzzzzzzzzz …